The One Year® Book of Bible Promises

THE ONE YEAR® BOOK OF
BIBLE
PROMISES

365 MEDITATIONS ON THE WONDERFUL PROMISES OF GOD

JAMES STUART BELL

Tyndale House Publishers, Inc.
Carol Stream, Illinois

Visit Tyndale online at www.tyndale.com.

TYNDALE, Tyndale's quill logo, *The One Year*, and *One Year* are registered trademarks of Tyndale House Publishers, Inc. The One Year logo is a trademark of Tyndale House Publishers, Inc.

The One Year Book of Bible Promises: 365 Meditations on the Wonderful Promises of God

ISBN 978-1-4143-1608-6

Printed in the United States of America

20   19   18   17   16   15   14
7   6   5   4   3   2   1

To Brendan, my son, my hero.

JANUARY

PERSEVERANCE

I focus on this one thing: Forgetting the past and looking forward to what lies ahead, I press on to reach the end of the race and receive the heavenly prize for which God, through Christ Jesus, is calling us.

PHILIPPIANS 3:13-14

TODAY MARKS A new beginning. We celebrated it with fireworks, parties, and lots of fun and revelry. But now we need to get down to some real work. Perhaps this statement from Paul is a great one to make your year's verse, or at least a motivation for your purpose in the new year. What does Paul say?

First, forget what's past. Look forward. Like Abigail did as she thought about all the problems she had had during the past year. A stillborn child. A husband who lost his job. Some mistakes she never wants to talk about again.

She told God, "Okay, I'm committing this year to you. I look forward to your guidance and to good things from you. Thanks for giving me this promise of your blessing."

Second, press on in your race. Don't give up, even when trouble comes. Keep running with God. Abigail faced each new circumstance in her life with new faith and verve. She refused to be overwhelmed by discouragement or to lose her trust in God. And she pressed on. In return, God blessed her greatly.

He will do the same for you. When we persevere in the path God gives us, he promises not only to lead us to our destination but also to reward us along the way.

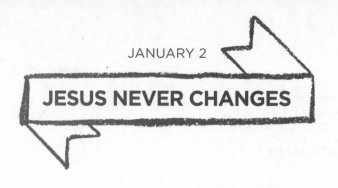

JESUS NEVER CHANGES

Jesus Christ is the same yesterday, today, and forever.
HEBREWS 13:8

ONE OF THE great doctrines of the Bible is the immutability of Christ. This simply means that he will never change. Like WYSIWYG ("What you see is what you get") in computer terminology, what you saw of Jesus in the past is who he is now and will be forever.

What does that mean in our lives? For one thing, we can trust that Jesus' words and character are as trustworthy now as when he was on the earth. We can trust his promises. We can rely on the fact that he is always wise, loving, compassionate, and righteous. He will never exclaim, "I've had it with the lot of you. Sin once more and you're out. I'm taking your names out of the Book of Life."

No, Jesus' promise was, is, and will be forever that he is consistent. And he is consistently loving. No matter what we do, he will never give up on us, desert us, or turn against us.

Think about the grandeur of it. How many people have you known who say one thing and do another? Or have reneged on their promises?

Such things can never happen with Jesus. His promise is, "I will always be the person you find on the pages of the Bible. Trust those realities, and live in the confidence that I will always be with you."

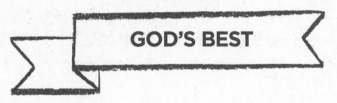

GOD'S BEST

It was by faith that Moses, when he grew up, refused to be called the son of Pharaoh's daughter. He chose to share the oppression of God's people instead of enjoying the fleeting pleasures of sin. He thought it was better to suffer for the sake of Christ than to own the treasures of Egypt, for he was looking ahead to his great reward.

HEBREWS 11:24-26

TAKE A LOOK at all you have in this world: a home? a nice car? a fulfilling job? What do you think you could never live without?

Now consider Moses. He lived in the palace of those ruling one of history's greatest empires. Servants supplied his every need. Wealth? He shared the pharaoh's treasures. Fame? Everyone knew he was the adopted son of the pharaoh's daughter, the boy she'd made her own.

Although he seemed to have everything, something was missing for Moses. He longed to be part of something greater, something that went deeper than the earthly life he knew. He longed to visit the Israelite slaves, his true people, and associate with them. All the other sons of Abraham worked themselves bone weary every day serving the pharaoh Moses loved. But Moses was not a slave. Finally Moses faced a choice: remain in the spiritually empty life of wealth or find his true spiritual calling among the Hebrews.

These verses tell us that anytime we have to give up something for God, he offers a great reward, far beyond anything we could gain on our own in the best of the world's circumstances. Hold this promise close.

FELLOWSHIP

I want them to be encouraged and knit together by strong ties of love.

COLOSSIANS 2:2

DARLA WALKED INTO the church with a heavy heart. She and her husband, Ken, had exchanged harsh words that afternoon. Plus, her work wasn't going well. The boss repeatedly criticized her about her performance, even though she felt she did her best every time. And then one of their kids ended up in detention at school—something about talking back to the teacher.

She sat in the prayer meeting, not even sure she wanted to be there. One of her friends, Wanda, whooshed in, all smiles.

"How're things going, Darla?" she chirped.

Darla shrugged. Wanda sat down. "You look like you just got run over by a Mack truck."

For some reason, Darla began spilling it. Other members arrived and joined the discussion and prayed about Darla's problems. She left that night feeling bolstered—encouraged that she was not alone in her struggles, but supported by friends and feeling a fresh sense of God's presence and love. Their counsel had even given her some practical ideas on how to deal with her situations.

That's the power and promise of fellowship. Whenever we face tough times, we can rest assured that we are not alone. As we look to other believers, they can give us the boost and the reminder of God's power that we need.

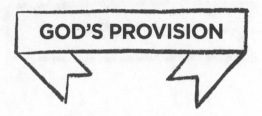

GOD'S PROVISION

*Even though the fig trees have no blossoms, and there are
no grapes on the vines; even though the olive crop fails, and
the fields lie empty and barren; even though the flocks die in
the fields, and the cattle barns are empty, yet I will rejoice in
the LORD! I will be joyful in the God of my salvation!*

HABAKKUK 3:17-18

IF YOU WANT to see an excitement junkie, look at someone who's been in
ministry for a long time. Look especially at the lives of people who work
full time with a Christian organization in which they raise their own salary, or support, from donors.

Talk to these folks for a while, and they'll tell you about times when
people stopped giving because of the economy—and God provided anyway. Or perhaps their best donor died, and God still provided. You'll
hear stories about God not just sending money but also miraculously
supplying food, clothing, and other necessities. What a rush to see God
show that he is indeed in charge and truly does take care of his people.

This also happens in the lives of those who aren't in full-time ministry. Our sources of income may be drying up, our food supplies getting
low, our bills pouring in. Yet we can still be glad and praise God, for
the greater our need, the more obvious it is when God provides for it.

Do you have needs? Then get ready to watch how God will provide!

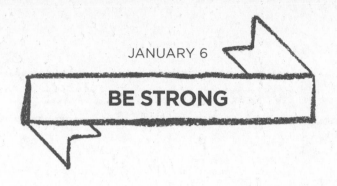

BE STRONG

This is my command—be strong and courageous! Do not be afraid or discouraged. For the LORD your God is with you wherever you go.

JOSHUA 1:9

JOSHUA HAD JUST lost his finest friend and mentor, Moses. God was entrusting Joshua with the mission of taking the Israelites into the Promised Land. Moses had lost that right when he sinned against God by striking the rock with his staff after he had been ordered only to speak to it (see Numbers 20).

Understandably, Joshua probably felt frightened and worried. How could he lead this group of people into the land when Moses had not been able to control them so many times in the past?

At that point, God came to Joshua and spoke the words in today's verse. Imagine the relief on Joshua's face when he realized God was promising to be with *him* just as he had been with Moses, through good times and bad.

God gives the same promise to you. So what are you waiting for? God has given you work to do. Get to it!

WHERE WE REALLY ARE

You have come to Mount Zion, to the city of the living God, the heavenly Jerusalem, and to countless thousands of angels in a joyful gathering. You have come to the assembly of God's firstborn children, whose names are written in heaven. You have come to God himself, who is the judge over all things. You have come to the spirits of the righteous ones in heaven who have now been made perfect. You have come to Jesus, the one who mediates the new covenant between God and people, and to the sprinkled blood, which speaks of forgiveness instead of crying out for vengeance like the blood of Abel.

HEBREWS 12:22-24

DR. LEWIS SPERRY CHAFER, founder of Dallas Theological Seminary, once researched everything that happens to us when we become Christians. He determined that more than thirty specific things happen the moment we ask Jesus to be our Savior, including the realities listed in the promise above.

When you ask Jesus to be part of your life, you come into the "city of the living God." But instead of your needing to go somewhere to get to this city, it actually comes to you and is with you all the time. Angels surround you. An assembly of believers surrounds you. God the Father is there, welcoming you into his family. Righteous people who have been made perfect greet you. Jesus stands there too, ready to intercede for you about anything and everything. Above all, you enter this place clean, whole, righteous, and perfect.

You are probably not even conscious of most of this, but God says it happens. His promise is that you are not alone in this world, and you will never be alone again. Trust him, and trust that the realities he speaks of surround you every second.

PURPOSE

I pray that from his glorious, unlimited resources he will empower you with inner strength through his Spirit. Then Christ will make his home in your hearts as you trust in him. Your roots will grow down into God's love and keep you strong. And may you have the power to understand, as all God's people should, how wide, how long, how high, and how deep his love is. May you experience the love of Christ, though it is too great to understand fully. Then you will be made complete with all the fullness of life and power that comes from God.

EPHESIANS 3:16-19

WHAT IS YOUR purpose in life? After his conversion, one young man said his greatest purpose was to experience God as fully as he can be known in this world.

That's not an unrealistic goal. This Scripture passage guarantees that we humans can experience and know God. Even though these verses were Paul's prayer for the Ephesians, it's really a prayer inspired by the Holy Spirit for all of us.

The goal of our lives should be that God grows us into the areas Paul mentioned in this portion of Scripture. First, we can grow in our faith to know the true depth and height of God's love for us. Next, we can grow to be strong spiritually. The Holy Spirit wants to guide us to dig deep into God's love. Above all, as we mature and experience Christ's love, we are "made complete" in all the good things God has for us.

Make the prayer in today's verses your own, and relish its great promises. Let God fill your mind with every good thing you can know about him and his love. Experience the promise and privilege of being able to have a relationship with him.

THE SOURCE OF OUR STRENGTH

*My health may fail, and my spirit may grow weak, but God
remains the strength of my heart; he is mine forever.*

PSALM 73:26

PAUL ANDERSON WAS once known as the strongest man who ever lived. The Olympic champ broke eighteen American records and eight world records, and he was listed in *The Guinness Book of World Records* for lifting 6,270 pounds in the back lift.

Like many athletes, Paul used his platform as the strongest man in the world to promote a message. He didn't focus on advocating a product or world peace or another cause. Instead, he used his fame to point to someone who really deserves the fame and adoration: Jesus Christ.

Paul was the strongest man who ever lived, but he still had to look to God for strength and power.

Where do you find your strength? By keeping in shape? By eating right?

It's great to have a physically fit body, but as Paul told people, it's not an end in itself. The only one you can truly entrust your life to in this world is God. He will be your strength in every area of your life, no matter what shape you're in. Are you relying on him?

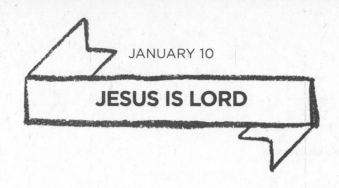

JESUS IS LORD

God elevated [Christ Jesus] to the place of highest honor and gave him the name above all other names, that at the name of Jesus every knee should bow, in heaven and on earth and under the earth, and every tongue declare that Jesus Christ is Lord, to the glory of God the Father.

PHILIPPIANS 2:9-11

SOMETIMES PEOPLE JUST don't have any respect for Jesus.

Doesn't it aggravate you when they use his name in vain or disparage or ridicule him? It's hard to remember to pray that people will find out the truth and seek forgiveness for their sin.

Thankfully, this disrespect won't last forever. God assures all of us that eventually Jesus will be recognized for who he is. His glorious act of saving the world will be known and revered from one end of the earth to the other. No one will fail to understand his greatness, perfection, love, and goodness. No one will ever ridicule him again.

Though we must live in this corrupt world, hearing the insults and taunts of unbelievers about the person we know as the greatest person who ever lived, one day everything will change. Our Lord will reveal himself. All those people will see their folly and bow down, realizing their mistake. At the same time, we will see our Lord exalted and blessed in ways only he deserves. Count on it. Today's Bible promise is that although Jesus may be taking the brunt of verbal shots now, one day he will gain the glory he has deserved ever since he created our world.

WHERE IS GOD?

*Those who have been ransomed by the LORD will return. They will
enter Jerusalem singing, crowned with everlasting joy. Sorrow and
mourning will disappear, and they will be filled with joy and gladness.*

ISAIAH 51:11

HAVE YOU EVER felt distant from God?

If so, you can probably relate to how the Israelites felt at different times over the years. Here they were, God's people, yet they were far from the God of their forefathers. Physically, they were in exile, even removed from the land he'd given them.

But the separation wasn't forever. The Scripture above speaks of an eventual return to the land God had given them and to the God who had given them the land. Isaiah prophesied that these men and women would enter Jerusalem singing and joyful—filled with gladness.

Perhaps most of us go through times when we feel separated from God. At times we get distracted by busy lives, earthly concerns, fears, and other hindrances.

But when we face those times of feeling distant, we can cling to the promise in today's verse. We can come back to God. Whether we've been "away" for days or for years, we can return to him, entering his presence with the joy of repenting and renewing our relationship with him.

Do you feel distant from God? He's waiting with open arms to fill you with the joy of his presence again.

ABBA

Because we are his children, God has sent the Spirit of his
Son into our hearts, prompting us to call out, "Abba, Father."
Now you are no longer a slave but God's own child. And
since you are his child, God has made you his heir.

GALATIANS 4:6-7

THE RELIGION OF Islam portrays Allah as an aloof, distant potentate who has no personal connection with his followers. Hinduism features millions of gods, few of whom are "nice," let alone good or gracious. Buddhism doesn't even have a god in its belief system. Other religions—such as Jehovah's Witnesses and Mormonism—teach that we can achieve godhood or that we must work for our salvation, or they promote views of a god that is not the God of the Bible.

One of the great truths about God is that he is personal. He wants us to know him intimately and deeply. In fact, one of the first things that happens to a new believer is what the verses above refer to: we begin responding to God as "Abba, Father."

Abba is the Aramaic term for "Daddy" or "Papa." It's an intimate word, reserved for those who would crawl into God's lap, look into his face, and say, "Daddy, can you help me with this problem?"

God promises that he will personally make himself real to us and that we can experience an intimacy with him that is unparalleled in our world. Today, bask in your relationship with a personal God.

DELIVERANCE

*Strengthen those who have tired hands, and encourage those
who have weak knees. Say to those with fearful hearts,
"Be strong, and do not fear, for your God is coming to
destroy your enemies. He is coming to save you."*

ISAIAH 35:3-4

WHEN THE ISRAELITES learned that the Ninevite army was approaching, many undoubtedly lost courage. Already weary, they shrank from the task of fighting the Ninevites. As they watched the horizon for the dust of the attacking hordes, their spirits quaked, and many felt tempted to sink into despair and terror (see 2 Kings 19).

Isaiah records, though, that King Hezekiah called on God for help. And as a result, he received the promise that God would fight for the Israelites because they trusted in him.

When Sennacherib of Nineveh came to attack Jerusalem, more than 185,000 soldiers rallied outside the walls. God kept his promise, and in the night he sent an avenging angel. The next morning, everyone in the army lay dead, and Sennacherib escaped in defeat.

God originally sent the Ninevites to punish the Israelites for their sin. However, when they repented and turned to God, he relented and saved them. Where do you find yourself today? Do you sense God's displeasure for something in your life? Turn back to him in faith. Call on him for forgiveness and help, even if you've created the mess you're in. He will give you the power to prevail and will fight your battles for you.

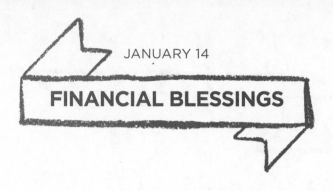

JANUARY 14

FINANCIAL BLESSINGS

God will generously provide all you need. Then you will always have
everything you need and plenty left over to share with others.
2 CORINTHIANS 9:8

HAVE YOU EVER considered that one reason God blesses people financially is so they can bless others with their wealth? That's the point of this
passage. God meets the needs of those who give, but part of the reason
he blesses them is so that they can help others.

How else would God work in the world? Certainly, everyone doesn't
make the same income. Many times, good people suffer reversals that
could leave them homeless. Some Christians think that they don't have
to do anything—the church will help these people. But what if you just
made a lot of money in a stock windfall? Received an inheritance? Benefited from something else? Is hoarding that money or putting it into
an account for retirement always the best thing to do?

Not according to this passage. Part of the reason you may have
received a sum of money is so you can help others in need. God always
works through his people to meet such situations. Could it be that he is
blessing you right now so that you can bless others? His promise is that
as you learn to give, and possibly to sacrifice, God will bless you even
more because he sees that you are a faithful servant he can trust with
larger sums.

JUSTICE

*God blesses those who hunger and thirst for
justice, for they will be satisfied.*

MATTHEW 5:6

AROUND THIS TIME of year, we celebrate the life and work of Dr. Martin Luther King Jr. He sought justice for all African Americans, and he wanted them to be treated like other God-created humans, with equal rights before the law. Dr. King was highly effective at motivating people of all races, and he accomplished much in moving our country to establish a more just and righteous system of laws that support freedom and equality.

To be sure, this world has many injustices. People still face danger because of their race, gender, or Christian beliefs. Tyranny destroys multitudes. There are people who, in their greed, strip others of dignity, possessions, and power. These are not the kinds of people God blesses.

On the other hand, God does bless those who long for righteousness in the world. In a way that only God can do, he will satisfy those who work for justice, defend the poor, help the victims of crime, bring those who violate the law to their just ends, and strive for freedom of worship where Christians are persecuted.

Do you have a passion for justice? Do you hunger and thirst for goodness in the world? Keep working for it. You'll find ultimate justice in God's Kingdom. And until then, as you seek to bring about fair treatment and righteousness in the world, God will bless you in incomparable ways.

LOOKING AHEAD

*This world is not our permanent home; we are
looking forward to a home yet to come.*

HEBREWS 13:14

"WHAT IN LIFE gives you the best feelings?" one young man asked his mom.

He was surprised when she responded, "Coming home after a long trip and seeing our house and family and everything looking great."

Most of us can identify. A home represents comfort, safety, security, and feelings of joy and love. Our memories are stored there. From the pictures on the walls to the CD collection next to the stereo to the hobby materials in the basement, home is where the heart is.

Now, think about the fact that God has actually prepared a home for you in heaven that will be far better than anything you can imagine! The Scripture above doesn't spell out exactly what we'll experience, but God has planned something so marvelous we can't even begin to picture it. Will our homes in heaven have pictures on the walls? Comfy furniture with a wide-screen TV, a stocked refrigerator, and the old jukebox in the corner?

Who knows? But you can be sure if God promises that we should all prepare to be astonished (see 1 Corinthians 2:9), you can count on heaven being something amazing. God intends to give you a place to live in that will be the final and fullest fulfillment of all your homey dreams.

GOD'S SECRETS

*Ask me and I will tell you remarkable secrets you
do not know about things to come.*

JEREMIAH 33:3

DON'T WE ALL love to hear secrets? How quickly we open our ears when we think someone is going to tell one!

Did you know that even God has secrets to tell?

His secrets aren't gossip or rumors, as many of the secrets we hear are; his secrets are truthful things that the rest of the world doesn't know about.

Perhaps you've had this experience with God's secrets: you're reading in the Bible, and suddenly some verse seems to explode. Now you understand that truth in a way you've never grasped before. That's one of God's secrets. He's just let you in on something only we Christians will ever understand.

Or perhaps you're talking with a friend, and suddenly he or she says something that lets you see deep into his or her heart in a way you have never seen that person before. For a second you get a glimpse of how deeply he or she feels or believes something, and it shows you a side of that person that's precious and beautiful.

Those are God's kinds of secrets too. There are many more. How do you get them? Ask God to give you eyes to see such things. He promises that if you ask, he will give you those insights.

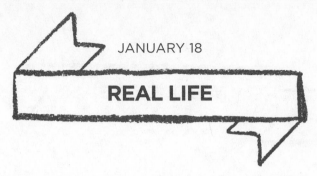

REAL LIFE

The disciples saw Jesus do many other miraculous signs in addition to the ones recorded in this book. But these are written so that you may continue to believe that Jesus is the Messiah, the Son of God, and that by believing in him you will have life by the power of his name.

JOHN 20:30-31

WHAT IS THIS life John speaks of?

Ryan experienced it sometime after he became a Christian. "One day I started to notice the beauty of creation. I was amazed. Then I started to notice the beauty of people. How they were constructed. Their faces. Every one of them was unique. I also sensed God was there as I talked to him in prayer. I no longer felt alone, although I'd felt intense loneliness for years before my conversion. I could sense the Holy Spirit deep within my being, talking to me, listening when I prayed. It was totally awesome."

In time, Ryan noticed something else: how he felt a strange peace even when problems blew up in his face and could have seriously messed up his life. "It just was so gripping. I didn't scream and yell, for once. I turned to God. It wasn't like he zapped everything and made it perfect or anything. It's just that I knew he was there, my situation was in his hands, and he would lead me through it. That was powerful comfort and strength."

Those are the kinds of things that change merely existing into truly living a supernatural, engrossing, freeing, abundant life. And we can experience this only through Christ. Walking with him. Spending time in prayer. Learning about him. Growing close.

Draw near to him, and you'll find him drawing near to you. That's the life God promises you.

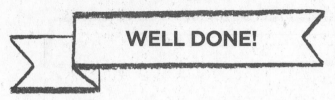

WELL DONE!

The master was full of praise. "Well done, my good and faithful
servant. You have been faithful in handling this small amount, so now
I will give you many more responsibilities. Let's celebrate together!"

MATTHEW 25:21

DON'T YOU LOVE to be praised for a job well done? From parents to corporations, we're discovering the value of lauding people for doing good work. In fact, many offices have forms employees can fill out to give applause where it's due.

Just hearing that someone else has noticed we've accomplished a feat well not only encourages us to work harder but also often makes the work we've done seem worth the effort.

This Scripture verse seems to show us two promises. The more obvious one is that if we are dependable in the smaller tasks God gives us, he'll bless us with more challenges and opportunities.

The second promise is that we can also count on God to notice. Even if a job is so small that no one else would notice what we did, God sees it. He celebrates even our smaller accomplishments with us. And he seems to appreciate them. After all, the one giving this illustration is the same one who pointed out that if we give just a cup of water in his name, we will have a reward.

Today, keep fulfilling with excellence the small responsibilities God has given you. Know that they're significant in his Kingdom. And enjoy celebrating your successes with him.

REAL FAITH

*All these people earned a good reputation because of their faith,
yet none of them received all that God had promised.*

HEBREWS 11:39

WHEN WE FIRST come to trust Christ, we often have little idea of what we're getting into. We don't physically see him or feel him. We simply take what the Bible says and stake our lives on it. When we make decisions in faith, we often feel as if we're "shooting in the dark," having no idea where those decisions will lead. Faith can take us on an unexpected journey. We may enjoy experiences we never dreamed possible. And, of course, there are also times when life looks scary and we need to depend on that faith to support us.

Think about those people of faith referred to in the verse. They rarely had the Scriptures to encourage them, surely not what we have today. They were often rejected, hated, tortured, and killed. Some faced lions. Others died by the sword or by incineration.

What held these people together at those times? Faith. They saw something beyond this world. They saw God and his Kingdom. They saw his promises.

Faith is like a sixth sense. By means of faith, you understand and become convinced of realities unbelievers could never grasp. Where does it come from? The Bible says over and over that our faith is part and parcel of being a Christian, a gift of God.

Do you see with the eyes of faith? The main thing to know is that faith will sustain you through everything. And then one day you will see God, and your faith will be rewarded with tangible reality.

CAPTIVATED

*Thank God! He has made us his captives and continues to lead us
along in Christ's triumphal procession. Now he uses us to spread
the knowledge of Christ everywhere, like a sweet perfume.*

2 CORINTHIANS 2:14

WHEN ROMAN GENERALS returned from conquests throughout Europe, they would lead a procession through Rome. The captives came behind— some in chains, some bound, some even in cages.

But some captives found new joy in their relationship with Rome. Perhaps in their homeland they had experienced hard lives, suffered abuse, and endured hatred. Under the Romans they found freedom and hope. Thus, their joy. They ran along in the procession, casting flowers and fragrant spices into the crowds lining the streets. They filled the air with a sweet aroma, and their joy was palpable.

Paul makes the analogy that we are God's joyful captives. We run about in the procession, spreading a beautiful fragrance to those who watch, making them wish they could join. Some do, becoming believers as we are. And they also experience the freedom and joy of belonging to a great King.

God promises that if you walk with him, you will experience this joy and peace. Do you have this joy, and do you spread this aroma to those you know and love?

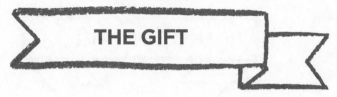

THE GIFT

*The wages of sin is death, but the free gift of God is
eternal life through Christ Jesus our Lord.*

ROMANS 6:23

WHEN WAS THE last time you received a gift?

Did the giver ask you to pay him or her back? To do something in return? Unless it's a marketing ploy, anything that's called a gift is usually free.

Sometimes, gifts are about the only things in life that come with no strings attached. Few items, possessions, sources of help and strength, or anything else come without a price tag. We're used to paying for whatever we get.

But this verse tells us that eternal life, the spiritual salvation that comes from Jesus, is a "free gift."

Think about it. This gift from God to us—which includes forgiveness of sin, eternal life, salvation, a home in heaven, the power of the Spirit, God's presence in our lives here on earth—is truly free. We can do nothing to merit or earn it. We can't work for a week at hard labor and receive it as wages for a job well done. We can't reach into our wallets and pull out a donation to gain it. We can't even do something spiritual, such as praying for hours on end or beating ourselves with a whip to show our repentance, to get God's attention and approval.

No, God's gift to us is free. All we can do is give him our sins, open our hands and our hearts, and say, "I accept. Thank you." It's true. God offers his Kingdom, love, and eternal friendship for nothing more than a statement of faith.

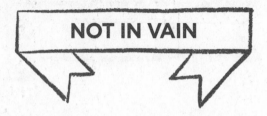

NOT IN VAIN

Be strong and immovable. Always work enthusiastically for the Lord,
for you know that nothing you do for the Lord is ever useless.

1 CORINTHIANS 15:58

MARABEL DIDN'T HAVE many talents or gifts. She couldn't teach or preach. She was no writer or singer or actor. She didn't draw well, and her menial job was far from glamorous.

But she did have one gift: she could cook meals like no one else. At one time or another, she had tried many other church activities such as teaching, singing in the choir, working on the drama team. But in time she found her real ministry was cooking for banquets and other meals at church.

That wasn't all. She helped at the local rescue mission and took meals to shut-ins and other people going through tough times. She also invited church visitors, neighbors, and others to come to her home and enjoy various feasts she prepared.

When her new pastor asked her one day, "What do you do for the Lord?" Marabel just shrugged and said, "Not much." But over time he learned about all she really did.

It doesn't much matter what your gifts are. All that matters is that you use them for the Lord. God promises that nothing you ever do for him will be "useless." And he will honor you for your service.

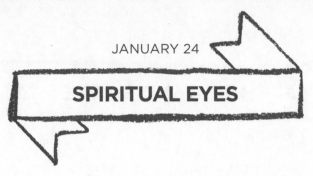

SPIRITUAL EYES

*Our present troubles are small and won't last very long. Yet they
produce for us a glory that vastly outweighs them and will last
forever! So we don't look at the troubles we can see now; rather, we
fix our gaze on things that cannot be seen. For the things we see now
will soon be gone, but the things we cannot see will last forever.*

2 CORINTHIANS 4:17-18

WHAT DOES IT mean to see with spiritual eyes? What will you observe if
you look at the world and life through such orbs?

For one thing, you will focus not on this world but on the next world.
No matter what this world throws at you, if you have spiritual eyes, you
see beyond it: "I won't worry, because one day God will rescue me from
this mess, and I'll live with him in a far better place forever."

For another, you realize that no matter how badly you're treated now,
one day these tough times will be over, and in God's new world, you'll be
treated like a family member and a prince or a princess.

Forget any dreams of becoming a member of the House of Windsor
or enjoying a weekend in the Lincoln Bedroom at the White House. You
have a home in heaven that will be grander than anything a billionaire
could experience on earth.

Spiritual eyes also change your perception of others. You see more
than the surface of the people around you. You see them as God's creations, either in need of redemption (in which case, you'll want them
to hear about Jesus) or as people who have been redeemed—and you
welcome them as brothers and sisters in Christ.

Are you seeing the world through spiritual eyes?

HELP AND SHARE

*Don't forget to do good and to share with those in
need. These are the sacrifices that please God.*

HEBREWS 13:16

DOING GOOD AND *SHARING.* These simple words define the actions that
are the essence of Christian living.

Think of all the opportunities you have every day to do good and
share. Maybe you could say a kind word to a coworker or tell your son's
soccer coach how much you appreciate his work. Perhaps someone has
a financial need and you had a windfall this past month, so you can help
out. Maybe you can assist a neighbor who is struggling with some serious
troubles.

God puts such opportunities in your path because he wants you to
rise to the occasion. Will your efforts cost you? Sometimes. Will things
automatically go right? Not always. Does God promise that everyone you
encourage or help will come to a great relationship with Jesus? Not necessarily. But he does promise that when you do good, he will be pleased.
And when he is pleased with you, he blesses you in some way that will be
meaningful and, sometimes, even fun for you.

Today, look for opportunities to bless others. They'll be pleased and
so will God.

GOD DELIVERS

The righteous person faces many troubles, but the
LORD comes to the rescue each time.

PSALM 34:19

ONE OF AMERICA'S favorite fictional film characters is Indiana Jones, and one of the greatest movies of all time, according to the popularity charts, is *Raiders of the Lost Ark*.

It's interesting to note just how many times the heroine, Marion, gets into trouble. First, Indy rescues Marion from Germans. Then from a burning building. Then from bad guys at the market—a couple of times. Then, when she is missing, he finds her and promises to rescue her. Then he saves her from snakes. Then from a moving plane. Then from Germans again. And on and on. But each time the heroine faces troubles, the hero rescues her *again*. He doesn't complain—doesn't say, "Stay out of trouble, for heaven's sake, can't you?"

No, the hero willingly saves her again and again.

The best hero that the cinema can create is nothing compared to the Lord!

It doesn't matter how many times we face troubles or make wrong choices and end up in hot water—God will still rescue us, time and time again. He never complains. Never threatens not to be there the next time. He just rescues us.

If you're in trouble today, don't struggle trying to extricate yourself—call on your personal spiritual rescue squad. If you're not in trouble, spend a little time praising and thanking the Lord for the times he's been your hero!

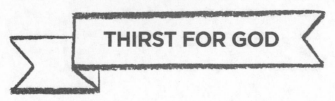

THIRST FOR GOD

[God] said, "It is finished! I am the Alpha and the Omega—the Beginning and the End. To all who are thirsty I will give freely from the springs of the water of life. All who are victorious will inherit all these blessings, and I will be their God, and they will be my children."

REVELATION 21:6-7

HAVE YOU EVER been truly thirsty? A relentless thirst can drive you crazy, especially if you have no way to fill that need at the moment. Our bodies can last awhile without food, but they can't go without water.

Even though physical thirst can be bad, spiritual thirst can be far worse. Spiritually, we can be desperate at a far deeper level. We know that eventually death looms in the future, and we don't know what's beyond that final door.

We also feel a spiritual thirst for the meaning of life, for a sense of purpose and fulfillment. Sometimes spiritual thirst involves not knowing what we want to do with our lives. All our dreams seem so elusive.

When Jesus spoke of thirst, he referred to a desperation for God—as well as for meaning, purpose, hope, joy, love, and knowledge of what lies beyond the grave. When a person comes to Jesus, the beautiful truth and promise is that he will satisfy your thirst. He will not only give you eternal life but also show you your purpose, tell you what he wants you to do in this world, and give you a deep sense of joy and fulfillment in life.

Have you called out to him to satisfy your thirst? If you do, he promises to satisfy it.

SEEING GOD'S GLORY

*All of us who have had that veil removed can see and reflect the
glory of the Lord. And the Lord—who is the Spirit—makes us more
and more like him as we are changed into his glorious image.*

2 CORINTHIANS 3:18

AFTER MOSES SPENT time with God in the tent of meeting, his face literally glowed from the encounter. It shone so brightly that when he stepped out of the tent, people could not look at him directly. He learned that if he wanted to go out in public after worshiping, he had to place a veil over his face so people could stand to look at him.

That was then, though, and this is now. Today, God puts that same glorious glow on some of us who worship him with fervor, intimacy, and true abandon. To the world, we just look happy, enjoy life, and talk about God's greatness. We don't glow literally, but something about us is different. One man said of Christians, "Something about their eyes is different."

What is it? He expounded, "It's like they have this inner light, like there's real joy and peace inside them."

Would you like to have that kind of glory of God evident in your life? Meet with the Lord daily. Get to know him intimately. Your life, he promises, will reflect his glory; you will bask in it, and the world will see it.

BECOMING HOLY

May the God of peace make you holy in every way, and may your whole spirit and soul and body be kept blameless until our Lord Jesus Christ comes again. God will make this happen, for he who calls you is faithful.

1 THESSALONIANS 5:23-24

HOW DOES A Christian become a holy, godly person?

Probably most of us were not angels before our conversions—or even after. In 1 Corinthians, Paul acknowledges that many of the people in the Corinthian church committed all kinds of sins, from drunkenness, cheating, swindling, and theft to sexual sins, impurity, coveting, and lying.

Clearly, that society was not much different from ours, and some of those Christians were still living lifestyles that match some of our own.

Somehow, though, God takes us just as we are at salvation and moves us in the direction of goodness, faithfulness, and self-control. The Spirit works in us to perfect us. No matter what we've done, no matter how young or old we are, he starts where we are and begins the process of transforming us into Christ's image.

God never intended to save us and then leave us in our old sinful condition. No, he plans to make us fit for his new heaven. And that will take a lot of honing and changing. This happens day by day as we walk in the power of the Spirit. His promise is to get you there. So trust him as he works in you. He's perfecting you for eternal life in a heaven of righteousness, peace, and joy.

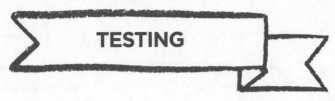

TESTING

*When you go through deep waters, I will be with you. When
you go through rivers of difficulty, you will not drown.
When you walk through the fire of oppression, you will
not be burned up; the flames will not consume you.*

ISAIAH 43:2

AS SIX-YEAR-OLD KATIE stood on the sidelines preparing to play dodge-ball, Janie looked down at her daughter and said, "But it's not that hard, honey. Just go in the middle and try to avoid getting hit by the ball."

"But I'm afraid," Katie said. "I'm afraid that it will hurt me."

"It's a rubber ball," Janie answered. "It's soft, and it doesn't hurt. Look, I'll go get one."

Even after Janie showed her the ball, Katie was unconvinced. "Okay," her mom said, "let's stand on the sidelines and watch, and you can see what happens. I'll hold your hand the whole time."

Katie eventually got the courage to join the game. But what was the key? Her mother's concern and presence and assurances.

That's precisely what God promises. He will be with you through every circumstance of life. When you know you're not facing the problem alone, when you know that the awesome God of the universe is at your side, you become courageous. And you can face anything.

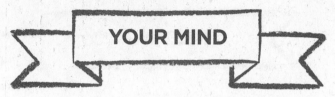

YOUR MIND

Fix your thoughts on what is true, and honorable, and right, and pure, and lovely, and admirable. Think about things that are excellent and worthy of praise. . . . Then the God of peace will be with you.

PHILIPPIANS 4:8-9

WHAT KINDS OF thoughts do you let course through your mind each day?

Many of your thoughts may be right on track with God. But Christians do struggle with thoughts and images that come from the culture they live in or from the time before they met Christ. How does a person extinguish those bad thoughts and feelings?

Today's verses are the antidote. Gene worked on his thoughts by memorizing Scripture. Carla dealt with her thoughts by refusing to listen to them and then meditating on something good—a praise song, a word such as *peace*, or a Bible verse. James fought off bad thoughts by praying and setting his mind on God.

There are many methods. God wants you to "fix your thoughts" on certain things—not the junk and garbage of the past or our culture, but on the good things of life and God's Word: what's true and honorable and right. What's pure and lovely and admirable. Things that are excellent and praiseworthy. How do you get your thoughts "fixed" on such things? You focus your mind and heart on them. You simply pray, "God, help me think thoughts that honor you." And then you make your mind dwell on the good things of God's character and all he has done for you and others in your world. His promise is that his presence will be with you and bear peacefulness in your life.

FEBRUARY

ANSWERS BEFORE YOU PRAY

*[God said,] "I will answer them before they even call
to me. While they are still talking about their needs,
I will go ahead and answer their prayers!"*

ISAIAH 65:24

HAVE YOU EVER barely voiced a prayer when you received the answer? Have you ever been about to cry out to God, and lo, the situation was fixed right before your eyes?

This has probably happened to all of us. God knows our prayers even before we utter them. He understands our needs. He goes ahead of us and plans to meet those needs even before we've thought about them. His plan encompasses our whole future, even into eternity.

That doesn't mean we shouldn't pray, but it's a great promise nonetheless. God cares enough to plan his actions in light of our needs even before we've thought about them or prayed about them.

God cares so much about each of us that he is intimately involved in every aspect of our lives. He promises to hear us even before we speak and to start working even before we've reached the point of need. He delights in answering our prayers and demonstrating his power.

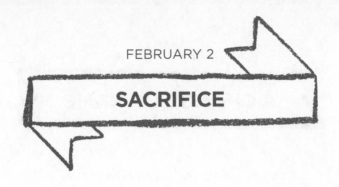

SACRIFICE

We know what real love is because Jesus gave up his life for us. So we also ought to give up our lives for our brothers and sisters. If someone has enough money to live well and sees a brother or sister in need but shows no compassion—how can God's love be in that person?

1 JOHN 3:16-17

WE SELDOM ENJOY sacrificing for others. Many of us don't want to come out of our comfort zones to do something that may cost us emotionally, physically, or monetarily. Too often, when someone presents a need, our first thought is, *Let so-and-so handle it. He's good at it* or *Let the Help Fund person at church handle it. There is money for just that purpose.*

Becoming like Jesus in character, though, means that God expects us all to learn to sacrifice for others, especially for other believers. From minor inconveniences to major investments, Christians make all kinds of sacrifices every day. Perhaps you know of a need right now that you could meet if you just decided to give up your complacency.

God will call upon each of us to sacrifice at times. If we claim to love God, he expects us to share his love with others.

A CHANGE OF NAME

*Never again will you be called "The Forsaken City" or
"The Desolate Land." Your new name will be "The City
of God's Delight" and "The Bride of God," for the LORD
delights in you and will claim you as his bride.*

ISAIAH 62:4

GOD HAS CHANGED many names in biblical history. *Abram* ("father")
became *Abraham* ("father of nations"). *Jacob* ("cheat") became *Israel* ("God
strives") after he wrestled all night with God to gain God's blessing. *Simon*
became *Peter*, which means "rock."

When God changed the name of someone or something, it usually
carried great significance. In the above passage, we see the city of Jerusalem, devastated by the Babylonians, being called "The Forsaken City."
People from neighboring nations believed that God had forsaken the
Jews and derisively called their capital city that. But God had no intention
of leaving the Jews desolate. So Isaiah wrote that the new name would be
"The City of God's Delight." That's certainly a nicer term.

You also have a new description as a Christian. From "lost" to
"found." From "slave" to "free." From "Gentile" to "Friend of God."
And God says in Revelation that one day we will have new names only he
will call us (see Revelation 2:17). It's a great promise of God's love and
the fact that you belong to him.

HONORING GOD

Honor the LORD with your wealth and with the
best part of everything you produce.

PROVERBS 3:9

GIVING OF OUR finances and other assets can be one of the most difficult responsibilities of the Christian life. We work hard. Often we labor in adverse conditions. Why should we give 10 percent or more away when we could use the money for things that help us to survive or that would make our lives more enjoyable?

But think of who gave you your abilities, your talents, your job, even your commitment and desire to do it well.

One man who worked a menial job made only several hundred dollars a week. It wasn't hard to give 10 percent of that to his church. But then he invented something that sent the level of his wealth into orbit. He began making millions. Suddenly, giving a tenth seemed much more difficult than the thirty or so dollars he had given in his former job.

So he made a proposal to God. "How about if I just go back to giving what I was giving back then?"

God said, "Fine. I'll take you back to making that amount too."

Suddenly, the man got it. No, he wanted the increased income, and he would give the Lord his due.

God does not need your money. But you need to give it—to become a player in his Kingdom's work. His promise is that he will not only reward you handsomely later for your sacrifices but also bless you for it now.

POWER IN WEAKNESS

[God] said, "My grace is all you need. My power works best in weakness." So now I am glad to boast about my weaknesses, so that the power of Christ can work through me. That's why I take pleasure in my weaknesses, and in the insults, hardships, persecutions, and troubles that I suffer for Christ. For when I am weak, then I am strong.

2 CORINTHIANS 12:9-10

CLARA WAS EXPERIENCING a strange mix of emotions. On one hand, she was in a hospital bed, hardly able to bear the pain and to breathe. But she was also enjoying her interaction with others as she witnessed to several nurses and attendants. While she rested, she read her Bible. Some of those who came into her room asked her why she read it, which gave her another chance to explain why she believed in Jesus.

She almost felt as if those weeks in a hospital bed were the most fruitful of her life. When she discovered these Scripture verses written by Paul, she began to understand. Coming to the end of herself, realizing she really could do nothing, made her rely on God more than ever. And others noticed that she was relying on God.

Though we don't have to end up in a hospital bed to discover the power of God's strength when we're weak, he promises that if we realize our lack of ability and let him work through us, he will do so in ways we can't imagine. Just as he did with Clara and with Paul.

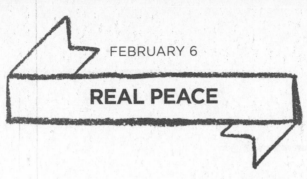

FEBRUARY 6

REAL PEACE

I have told you all this so that you may have peace in me.
Here on earth you will have many trials and sorrows. But
take heart, because I have overcome the world.

JOHN 16:33

HOW DO WE find peace of mind in the midst of the circumstances many of us encounter? A single mom faces a pile of bills. Though she knows and trusts Jesus, it's hard for her not to give in to despair when the financial deadlines approach and no help has appeared.

An older man gets his walking papers at the job he's given himself to for years. Now he knows he may be too old to find something comparable. He believes in the Lord, but hanging in there month after month with no job prospects gets harder and harder.

You can name any number of circumstances and you probably know people in the midst of them. How do Christians maintain their balance in such times? God never promises we won't face hard times—even bitterly hard times—in this world.

What he does promise, though, is to give us peace in the midst of trials. What is that peace? Philippians 4:6-7 speaks of it as a supernatural, incomprehensible peace that the world cannot grasp but the Christian can. It's the peace Christ gives to us because we know he will be there with us, will meet our basic needs in the midst of troubles, and will get us to our destination—heaven—safely.

That's powerful peace. Do you need some now? Just ask.

GOD'S ANGER

Go and give this message to Israel. This is what the LORD
says: "O Israel, my faithless people, come home to me again,
for I am merciful. I will not be angry with you forever."
JEREMIAH 3:12

MANY PEOPLE WHO read the Bible are startled by how angry God sometimes appears. He was so angry at the world of Noah's time that he
destroyed everything in a flood except for Noah and his family and one
or more pairs of every breed of animal.

He punished the builders of the tower of Babel with an inability to
communicate and sent them to the ends of the earth.

During Israel's journey from Egypt to the Promised Land, God
judged the people for their sin. Thousands died.

The fact is, sin makes God angry.

However, that doesn't mean God will hammer you for every infrac-
tion. Study those biblical situations, and you will see that God warned
those people many times before he acted. In many cases He remained
patient for years, but the people eventually reached a point of no return.

What hope can you have in the midst of such power? Simply this:
repent. Believe in God. Run to him and admit your wrongdoing. He
will forgive you, forget his anger, and eagerly embrace you. God is always
merciful. While he does judge sin and punish evildoers, he first calls out
to us repeatedly that if we turn to him, he will relent and have mercy. Is
God calling you today?

GOD'S MASTERPIECES

*We are God's masterpiece. He has created us anew in Christ Jesus,
so we can do the good things he planned for us long ago.*

EPHESIANS 2:10

TEN-YEAR-OLD RICKY LOVES to create masterpieces. They are formed from Bionicle parts. Bionicles are the older kids' answer to Legos—each kit of pieces makes one mechanical-type warrior.

However, Ricky uses the pieces to create his own warriors. He studies long and hard and takes a lot of time while he creates and puts different pieces together in different ways. His endeavors may look haphazard, but they're not. After he's finished crafting one of these warriors, he can tell you exactly what purposes the different parts serve.

Ricky is like most artists at work when they're creating a new, special piece. They concentrate and work hard to make their masterpieces just right. They go to extra effort and take time to build perfection. And when they're finished, they're proud of their creations—for good reason!

The Scripture above reminds us that *we* are God's masterpieces. He is the artist, and we are the outstanding works of his hands. Like Ricky and his Bionicles, God has created us to fit a purpose. He has developed our unique sets of abilities, temperaments, and personalities to fill a niche in his world in the time and place in which we live.

God doesn't make junk. He creates only masterpieces. So today, remember his promise that you're special and that he has a plan for your life.

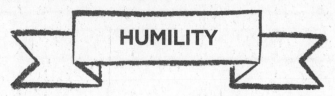

HUMILITY

You rescue the humble, but you humiliate the proud. You light
a lamp for me. The LORD, my God, lights up my darkness.
PSALM 18:27-28

HUMILITY IS ONE of those traits that are so hard to come by. Some say the moment you think you have it, you've lost it. In fact, when you truly do demonstrate humility, you probably won't even know it. In fact, you may think you're showing only pride and arrogance, when in the eyes of others you may be truly humble and gentle in ways that amaze them.

How does that work? When you learn true humility, you become others centered. You stop thinking of yourself all the time—how an event affects you, how a situation can mess up your life. Instead, you look at the needs of others, and you get involved trying to meet those needs. You care about people, and that care leads you to take action. When you've taken action, you might feel as if you didn't do enough. But the people you helped will see the truth: you're a person who really loves and cares, and that will thrill them and glorify God at the same time.

It also means you will sometimes get into trouble. Your care, love, and willingness to help others will make some people angry. They might not like your reaching out like that. And they might attack you for it.

That's where this verse comes in: God promises to rescue the humble. Every time.

GOD IS NEAR

*If I ride the wings of the morning, if I dwell by the farthest oceans, even
there your hand will guide me, and your strength will support me.*

PSALM 139:9-10

CHARLES FACED AN unhappy situation. Because of some shenanigans
in the courts, someone charged him with a crime he hadn't committed, and he ended up in prison. He felt his testimony as a Christian
was compromised and he could never speak for Christ again. But while
there, he decided to spend time in prayer and found God speaking to
his heart to start a Bible study with like-minded inmates. In time, several
men met when they had the chance. Charles realized that even in prison,
God was there.

In this psalm, David speaks about God's nearness. He uses images
of heaven, hell, darkness, and the deepest places of the ocean. In every
remote place, he realizes God is there because God is everywhere—he is
omnipresent.

Theologically, God's omnipresence means that he is in every place in
every time in his full person. He doesn't divide himself and send a millionth of himself one place and another millionth somewhere else. No,
he is completely with you and him and her, all the time and all at once,
regardless of whether it's morning in Pakistan or you're in the farthest
ocean by Antarctica.

This means not only that you can't escape God but also that God will
never escape you, either. His promise is that he's here with you, right
now and always, with his whole being, not just part of himself. So no
matter what you have on your mind, he's with you to listen or to act or
to meet a need.

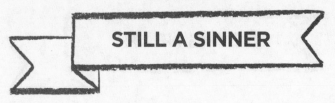

STILL A SINNER

Prepare your minds for action and exercise self-control. Put all your hope in the gracious salvation that will come to you when Jesus Christ is revealed to the world. So you must live as God's obedient children. Don't slip back into your old ways of living to satisfy your own desires. You didn't know any better then.

1 PETER 1:13-14

BECOMING A CHRISTIAN, trusting Christ, and even walking closely with him doesn't mean you won't make mistakes, commit errors, or even sin. Satan is always lurking, looking for any and every opportunity to lead you astray.

That's why we have to be vigilant. How do we do that? By becoming obedient in every way the Bible calls us to. Like Marcus. One day he came upon something he'd stolen long ago from a family. God seemed to say he had to send it back. That's what he did, worrying that the family would hate him. Instead, they thanked him and invited him to come visit!

Are you struggling with telling small lies to escape from inconvenient situations? Stop! Obey God's Word, and speak the truth. Have you succumbed to Satan's temptation to pad your expense account? Stop! Listen to God's Word, and apply it.

One of the primary reasons God wants us to read, memorize, study, and meditate on his Word is so we will know what he wants of us. We cannot apply what we don't know. We can't know until we start to read his Word regularly, every day if possible.

God wants us to obey him, not just to avoid sin but also to gain his daily blessings on our lives. He promises always to reward good behavior with his gifts. So obey all you can. And then obey some more.

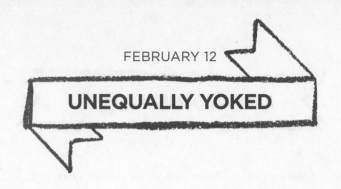

UNEQUALLY YOKED

If a believing woman has a husband who is not a believer and he is willing to continue living with her, she must not leave him. For the believing wife brings holiness to her marriage, and the believing husband brings holiness to his marriage. Otherwise, your children would not be holy, but now they are holy.

1 CORINTHIANS 7:13-14

AFTER JENNIE CAME to Christ and her life changed, she faced the fact that she was married to a man who didn't know Jesus. Jennie's husband drank often, gambled occasionally, and could get mean in an argument. Jennie's own mother counseled her to divorce him. But the verses above held her back. Wanting to please the Lord, she stuck it out in a tough marriage because she knew what his Word says.

Over the years, she didn't see much progress in her husband's spiritual life. However, her three children committed themselves to the Lord at early ages. One even became a missionary when he reached adulthood. Because of her faithfulness to her husband and to God's Word, she often thought that God rewarded her with children who kept the faith even in hard times.

Late in life, the miracle happened. Jennie's husband began seeking the Lord. In time, he accepted Christ and became a strong member of the congregation Jennie had attended for years.

While not all unequally yoked husbands and wives see their spouses come to Christ, God does reward their faithfulness. If that's your situation, hang in there. God knows and understands your pain and confusion. He will hear your cries for help and send you blessings.

NOW AND LATER

*Now we see things imperfectly, like puzzling reflections in a
mirror, but then we will see everything with perfect clarity. All
that I know now is partial and incomplete, but then I will know
everything completely, just as God now knows me completely.*

1 CORINTHIANS 13:12

HAVE YOU EVER wished someone, just one person, could know and understand how you really feel about various issues in life?

Norm found such things difficult too. But one day he joined a grief group in his church, because he'd recently lost his wife. There he poured out his feelings, and many people identified with what he said. But the thing that helped him the most was prayer, drawing near to God. He said, "That's when I knew someone knew everything inside of me. That really encouraged me."

Many Christians find it hard to articulate their encouragement beyond the usual platitudes. But the trite remarks don't always go to the depths of our thoughts and feelings. We are left still wanting to be fully known and understood.

In this world, it is impossible to be known and to know others to that degree. It can never happen in this world because there is too much sin and hatred and violence, which separate all of us. But did you know that one day in heaven we will know one another, God, and everything else with "perfect clarity"? In heaven we will be perfect, never thinking a sinful thought and having deep and powerful feelings we can communicate, as well as fuller knowledge of things that are eternal.

The promise here is that one day we won't have to worry about faulty communication or a failure to communicate. No, we will know so perfectly that no mistake or false judgment will ever be possible again.

GOD'S LOVE

This is how God loved the world: He gave his one and only Son, so
that everyone who believes in him will not perish but have eternal life.

JOHN 3:16

THIS FAMOUS VERSE tells us a great deal in one sentence.

First, it reveals that God loves us. Each of us. No matter where we are, what we've done, how old or young we are, or what we believe about him. If we need assurance that he cares about us personally, this verse gives it completely.

Second, the verse shows us that God paid the price for our redemption, gladly and with finality. God doesn't love only his followers. Instead, he fixed the most basic problem that keeps all of humanity from enjoying fellowship with him: sin. Jesus paid the death penalty that we would otherwise have to pay ourselves. He made it possible for us to be forgiven and to live in heaven.

Third, this verse says that God offers this salvation to all people, anywhere, at any time. We must only have faith. Just believe it. Accept that Jesus died for our sins, that God loves us.

Last, this verse shows that God gives us the ultimate reward and gift—eternal life—for the simple act of believing. This is the greatest gift ever for the smallest action on our part.

You don't have to climb Mount Everest. You needn't become a superhero to gain heaven. All you have to do is believe in Jesus as Savior and Lord.

FOREVER STARTS NOW

You will show me the way of life, granting me the joy of your
presence and the pleasures of living with you forever.

PSALM 16:11

BEING IN LOVE is so exciting!

When you're in love, you just can't wait to talk to your sweetie. And to spend time with him or her is the joy of living! It seems as if no matter how much time people in love spend together, it's never enough. The time passes—hours seem like only moments, and you both long for time to stand still while you're together.

If you're married, remember those days when you dawdled at chores, your mind on your sweetheart? Remember imagining what it would be like to live with the person you love—*for always*? What joy when that day finally came!

When we enter a relationship with Christ, we become part of his bride, the church. We sometimes imagine what heaven will be like when we're all together. We picture the mansion he's preparing for us. We envision how it will be when we're finally with him forever.

The truth is, the joyous promise of the Christian life is that forever begins while we're still on this earth. Sure, we'll live with Christ and be his bride in heaven someday. But until then, he'll live within us, on earth. As we invite him to take charge, he'll be part of our days like a beloved spouse—helping us, looking out for our best interests, and just enjoying being with us.

Let's take some time today to enjoy his presence in our lives, since our forever together has already begun!

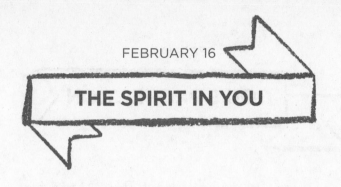

THE SPIRIT IN YOU

I will pour out my Spirit upon all people. Your sons
and daughters will prophesy. Your young men will see
visions, and your old men will dream dreams.

ACTS 2:17

SOMETIMES PEOPLE IN the Christian world don't agree about precisely how a person receives the Spirit. Does he automatically indwell us after salvation? Or do we have to do something to get the Spirit into our lives?

Peter's words, quoted from Joel 2:28, are reassuring. They tell us that the Spirit will be poured out upon all people who believe in Jesus. Some strange phenomena may follow—young men having visions that probably would provide guidance and hope in a situation, and old men dreaming dreams that teach them something deeper of God.

Do you wonder if the Spirit is in your heart and life? Here's the test: Have you put your faith in Christ? Has your life changed—in big or small ways—under his power? Have you repented of things you know are wrong? Have you discovered certain talents and abilities for serving God that you never noticed before?

God promises to give his Spirit as his personal representative to all his people. He will withhold him from no one who truly believes.

GOD'S PROTECTION

*I love you, LORD; you are my strength. The LORD is my rock, my
fortress, and my savior; my God is my rock, in whom I find protection.
He is my shield, the power that saves me, and my place of safety.*

PSALM 18:1-2

LOOK AT THAT collection of terms related to security: "strength," "rock,"
"fortress," "savior," "shield," "power," and "place of safety." Pretty amazing list, isn't it? Do all those words really describe the God we love and
worship?

A Christian in the early church, persecuted and pursued, sought
shelter and a hiding place. He came upon a cave and took refuge inside.
He watched the entrance. There, a spider began weaving a web, right
across the mouth of the cave. When his pursuers came, they saw the spider web and moved on, thinking that if the one they were pursuing was
in there, he would have broken it going in.

Not everything in life goes perfectly. But when you think of the times
you have faced real danger or enemy forces, how many times did you find
that God was there, a close friend, a surrounding fortress?

In the ancient world, a fortress was just about the only safe place in the
land. Marauding hordes, armies of the night, bandits, robber gangs—all
of them roamed about, looking for victims.

But for believers, God is the fortress that surrounds us wherever we
are—in the car, at home, on the street, in the darkness of night. God is
there. Trust him.

EXPERIENCING CHRIST

*I want to know Christ and experience the mighty power that raised him
from the dead. I want to suffer with him, sharing in his death, so that
one way or another I will experience the resurrection from the dead!*

PHILIPPIANS 3:10-11

WHAT DO YOU most want to experience in life? Riding every roller coaster in the world at least once? Becoming president of the United States? Being the best in your career? Finding personal fulfillment?

All of us have dreams—large or small—that drive us. For many of us, these desires are little more than wants and really don't amount to much. How many times have you heard a Hollywood star or sports great confess that attaining fame, wealth, notoriety, or power isn't all it's cracked up to be? Some famous people have even ended up committing suicide because they found that the fulfillment of their dreams just wasn't what they expected or even needed.

Too often, Satan tempts us to give our lives to things that simply don't matter in the long run. Paul, in these verses, points out what drove him. Did he long for fame as a missionary? Was his goal to hang as many converts' names on his belt as he could? Was it to preach to crowds of thousands and get a standing ovation each time?

Not at all. His motivating force was that he wanted to "know Christ," "experience [his] mighty power," and "suffer with him," thus sharing in his death. We, too, should die to all those lesser goals in this life, even if we have to make painful choices. Because when we share in Christ's death, we will also be raised with him!

THE PATHS HE SMOOTHES

For those who are righteous, the way is not steep and
rough. You are a God who does what is right, and
you smooth out the path ahead of them.

ISAIAH 26:7

EVERY WEEK OF the summer, three hundred excited teenagers poured into the youth camp ready to have the time of their lives. Horses galloped across the pasture; motorbikes buzzed down the road; kids jumped onto huge inflatable rafts floating on the lake or shouted to one another while they practiced their high dives; soccer games filled the fields.

But behind the soccer fields was a sanctuary where these kids could find quiet time—acres of wooded land where creatures danced and the sun played peekaboo through the trees. Best of all, these acres of trees offered winding paths. Originally pounded into the ground by horses' hooves, the paths were often narrow and filled with debris a walker needed to step around. Sometimes the paths went up small hills that required a little bit of effort to climb.

Perhaps paths like those are reflections of the promise in today's verse. Realistically, none of us has a perfect path in life. At times we hit the debris of heartache and problems, or the path of trust seems to get narrow. We may even have to pant up a hill. But the challenges we face are endurable, which is nothing compared to how they'd be if the Lord didn't walk before us.

So get away from the frenetic activity of life and walk quietly with the Lord. Remember his promise to clear the path before you, and enjoy the walk!

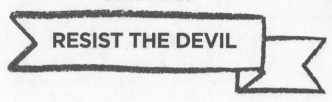

RESIST THE DEVIL

Humble yourselves before God. Resist the
devil, and he will flee from you.
JAMES 4:7

THE DEVIL COMES to each of us with different tactics and strategies. Some people give in to the temptation to commit flagrant sin, such as adultery, stealing, lying, hatred, jealousy, and so on. Others give in to his tricks to get them focused on the wrong things, such as money or power in business. Still others might be deceived into believing falsehoods by those who promote many ways to God or into thinking that by doing good they can make themselves pleasing to God without believing in Christ.

Amber seemed to experience all those kinds of temptations in her life. In fact, she seemed to careen from one temptation to the next. First, she believed the lie that having sex outside of marriage is okay. But in time, jealousy, anger, and hatred began to intrude. Then she broke up with her boyfriend. Finally, Satan really moved in on her, accusing her of blowing it.

Satan uses all these tactics on all of us at one time or another. Through Scripture, though, Amber found forgiveness and learned to tell the devil to "go away" when the bad thoughts and temptations returned.

How does one deal with such attacks? James says it simply: "Resist." How do you do that? Quote the Bible. Run if you're tempted beyond what you think you can stand. Stop and pray and ask God to deal with Satan.

When you feel the devil trying to lead you down an evil path, resist. The Bible promises he will flee. Every time.

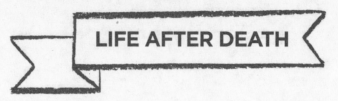

LIFE AFTER DEATH

*God has made everything beautiful for its own time. He has
planted eternity in the human heart, but even so, people cannot
see the whole scope of God's work from beginning to end.*

ECCLESIASTES 3:11

EVERY HUMAN LONGS for and hopes for something beyond this world. Most people simply do not believe death can be the end. They feel something *must* lie beyond life on this earth. And most religions are based on some kind of promise that life exists after death.

This verse explains why we experience such a strong belief in life after death. God has "planted eternity in the human heart." God has fixed the idea and hope of eternal life in the human soul for one reason: to drive us to find out the truth about him. The fear of death and the longing for something more are primary reasons people come to Christ in the first place. They seek what he alone can give: forgiveness and a home in heaven for all eternity.

That's part of what God has made "beautiful for its own time." This means that somehow God's plan is perfect. Everything happens right on time in God's plan. Your own search for hope and eternity happened just as God planned it. He promises that nothing happens in this world by accident. All of it is part of his grand scheme to save the world—and to draw you to himself.

As we walk through our days, we can trust that God has planned perfectly for each of us from here to eternity.

PURITY

God blesses those whose hearts are pure, for they will see God.

MATTHEW 5:8

THE GLASS DOOR was absolutely disgusting. It revealed traces of dirty toddler fingers down low and fingerprints from older, bigger people up higher. Smeared mud and other gunk made the window look as if a dirty dog had pressed against it. And no one could guess what probably caused other marks.

The dirt was almost as effective as a curtain. No one could have clearly seen through that glass door! It would definitely take some heavy-duty window cleaner—several applications—and some real scrubbing to be able to see through that glass again.

Have you ever felt as if your heart is gunked up? Maybe you feel it has some smears of envy or prints of disobedience or just spiritual dirt in it. When our hearts are dirty, it's harder for us to see God. Our view of him is blocked by the dirt of sinful actions, bad attitudes, or lack of faith dwelling inside. When we clear away the gunk, we can once again see God and follow him. Sometimes we just need the spiritual equivalent of a shot of Windex and the wipe of a paper towel to get back to purity. At other times we need several applications of a stronger cleanser and some real work.

Need some spiritual Windex? Let's make sure our hearts are as clean as can be.

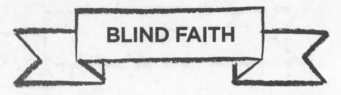

BLIND FAITH

Jesus told him, "You believe because you have seen me.
Blessed are those who believe without seeing me."

JOHN 20:29

MISSOURI IS KNOWN as the "Show-Me" state. Sometime in history, the state got a reputation of having skeptical, stubborn people. Missourians wouldn't just believe what they were told; they demanded proof before they took someone's word for matters.

Though many people consider themselves skeptics, they don't really have a hard time believing in what they haven't seen. For instance, you might not have seen the North Pole or the South Pole, but you probably still believe they exist. You have faith that people who have mapped out these areas were accurate.

Likewise, we may not see the engine on a plane, but we believe the plane will fly. We don't ask to see the pilot's license to prove that he or she is qualified to transport us.

But when it comes to Christianity, normally trusting people often turn skeptical. They demand proof that God exists and that the Bible's words are true. Like Thomas, who was skeptical of Christ's resurrection until he saw the wounds in Jesus' hands and side, they want proof they can see and touch. Actually, it takes more faith to believe in non-Christian gods or man-made answers to spiritual questions—such as the theory of evolution—than it does to believe in Jesus and what the Bible tells us.

Sometimes we have to just believe, whether or not we see or understand all that's going on, especially in spiritual matters. When we do so, we'll experience special blessings.

LISTEN UP

My child, listen to what I say, and treasure my commands. Tune your ears to wisdom, and concentrate on understanding. Cry out for insight, and ask for understanding. Search for them as you would for silver; seek them like hidden treasures. Then you will understand what it means to fear the LORD, and you will gain knowledge of God.

PROVERBS 2:1-5

SOLOMON WROTE THIS to his son, advising him to take to heart all his father had to teach. Three words stand out: first, *wisdom*, which is the ability to solve problems skillfully; second, *insight*, the power to see beneath the superficiality of things; and third, *understanding*, the power to see the big picture, what God is really doing in the whole world.

We should seek these abilities just as we'd seek treasures of silver and gold. Gaining wisdom, insight, and understanding will give us true reverence and respect for God. They will help us see what God is doing in our lives and in the lives of others. These characteristics help us realize how much God loves us. And through them, we gain a depth of understanding about God and his work.

Do you want to know God more deeply? Study his Word. Seek wisdom, insight, and understanding from it. God will reward you with not only knowledge of truth but also personal knowledge of himself.

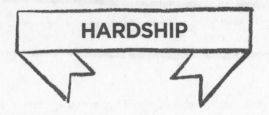

HARDSHIP

You have allowed me to suffer much hardship, but you will restore
me to life again and lift me up from the depths of the earth.

PSALM 71:20

WE ALL KNOW people who've suffered true hardship. Perhaps they go for years without seeing any success in their business. Or maybe they fight a disease, only to succumb in the end. Others live in homes where strife abounds. They pray and try to be kind and gentle, but the situations deteriorate.

Are you facing hardships like these? These problems and others like them can wear you down. They can make you feel as though God has vanished or has ceased caring or is punishing you for some sin from long ago. You may even feel guilty and broken. As the passage above says, God sometimes allows us to go through physical or emotional depths for long periods of time, sometimes for years.

Why? Over and over the Bible tells us that God allows such troubles to come upon us for at least two reasons: to build us up, teaching us to persevere, and also to show his glory by rescuing us, restoring us, and lifting us "from the depths of the earth."

That doesn't mean a struggle doesn't hurt or doesn't wear you down. But keep your eyes on God; he will restore you just as he restored Job and will bless you for your commitment and endurance.

FOOLISH CHILDREN

A youngster's heart is filled with foolishness, but
physical discipline will drive it far away.

PROVERBS 22:15

SARAH, A TODDLER, spotted her father's toolbox, opened it, and spread the tools all over the floor. She thought they looked beautiful and ran to find Daddy. "Look what I did!" she told him.

Daddy wasn't pleased. He gently warned her to put all the tools back and never to do that again. "Next time, I'll have to punish you," he told her.

Sarah obeyed, and soon the mess was cleaned up.

On another front, seventeen-year-old Joseph came home one day with some things he thought looked beautiful: a tattoo on his back and a stud in his nose.

"What have you done?" his mother cried, horrified. Joseph explained, "Everybody has them. They're cool."

"We already told you that you couldn't do this," his mom responded. He was instantly grounded.

While all parents won't deal with such infractions the same way, the problem is pretty much the same: children do childish things. They don't think logically about many things that seem so appealing.

How does a parent deal with such foolishness? Laugh it off? Or shrug and wonder what can be done?

No. The Bible says to discipline your children if you don't want them to repeat their foolish decisions. How that discipline is carried out is rather broad and may be different for different personalities and situations.

Develop your own discipline policies and responses before God. But remember that just letting your children do as they want will lead only to ultimately dangerous behavior patterns. God promises to work through your discipline and give your child a chance.

COME CLOSE

Come close to God, and God will come close to you.
Wash your hands, you sinners; purify your hearts, for
your loyalty is divided between God and the world.

JAMES 4:8

AN OLD BUMPER sticker asked, "If God seems far away, who moved?"
The implication is that *you* moved. God didn't, because he's consistent
and eternal—he stays the same.

Harper had been a Christian since his teens, but during college he
seemed to move away from God. As he entered the job market, got married, and started a family, he realized he needed to get back into church.
At this point, he wasn't sure he could. He was afraid that perhaps God
was angry with him and wouldn't give him another chance.

But Harper did take his family to church. And there he learned about
things such as repentance, confession of sin, and coming back to God.
He followed through, and instantly he discovered a real relationship with
God. Walking with God wasn't always easy, but Harper's life, under God's
guidance, got better and better.

Many of us will face times in life when God does seem distant. Sometimes we may even feel as if he has vanished from our lives or written us
off. But God promises he will never leave or desert those who belong
to him.

How do you return to spiritual closeness with God? Call on him.
"Come close," as the Scripture says. Spend time with him. Seek him with
all your heart. Wait on him to respond. God promises that no one who
comes to him like that will ever be turned away.

GOD STILL ANSWERS

We will receive from him whatever we ask because we
obey him and do the things that please him.

1 JOHN 3:22

DOES GOD ANSWER prayer?

Many people today, even Christians, feel that God's answers are few and far between. Many consider prayer a waste of time. When we do get an answer, often we tell ourselves it's nothing more than mere coincidence or the law of averages.

A study was done several years ago to research the effects of prayer on sick people. One group of participants prayed for a number of ill people. The other didn't pray at all for a second group. Result: no real difference in the number of people who recovered. Thus, the people conducting the study reported that prayer had no visible effect.

However, wasn't the whole idea flawed from the beginning? Would God normally respond to such a manipulative technique? And what of the beliefs of the people who were prayed for, and the commitment of those praying?

In fact, those are important factors, mentioned in the verse above. John states that God gives us whatever we ask for. Wonderful. Let's get praying! But then he adds the kicker. Why does God give us what we ask for? Because "we obey him" and "do the things that please him." So there are requirements.

Are you praying and not seeing answers regularly? The question then is, are you obeying God and doing the things that please him? If you are, he will be more inclined to give you what you've prayed for.

MARCH

KINDNESS

Never let loyalty and kindness leave you! Tie them around your neck
as a reminder. Write them deep within your heart. Then you will find
favor with both God and people, and you will earn a good reputation.

PROVERBS 3:3-4

YEARS AGO, A book encouraged people to practice "random acts of kindness." This has spun off to other books and to websites where people can tell about how others have blessed them through kind acts.

Perhaps not surprising is how many people in these books and websites mention church, faith, or Christianity in the same breath as the acts of kindness they've experienced.

The Scripture verses above remind us of the importance of being kind to others. When we are kind, not only is God pleased with us, but others are too. It's also a great way to reach out to people who need to know God and his touch. As we make it a habit to speak kind words and to do caring, courteous, and compassionate acts, we get a reputation. And perhaps we never reflect our caring God better than when we're mirroring his compassionate nature.

When we want to reach others with the gospel, the first thing we can do is show them how kind Christians can be.

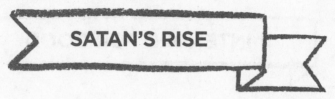

SATAN'S RISE

The man of lawlessness will be revealed, but the Lord Jesus will kill him with the breath of his mouth and destroy him by the splendor of his coming.

2 THESSALONIANS 2:8

THE WORLD HAS its share of formidable people. If we look at the social landscape, we see renegade despots and others threatening those who would uphold peace. From Iran to North Korea to Venezuela and other nations, we see leaders breathing all kinds of threats against those in the free world. Many are empty threats, but they still inspire fear.

The verse above reminds us that even the most powerful people will face and answer to the awesome, almighty God. The "man of lawlessness" referred to in this Scripture is traditionally believed to be the Antichrist, who will appear in the end times of our world and wield great power over those who are living at that time. He will persecute and kill many Christians. And he will be the worst of the worst.

But notice how God will deal with him: a sword battle à la Star Wars? A huge gunfight at the OK Corral? The firing of cruise missiles and nuclear warheads? No, it's the mere "breath of his mouth." Martin Luther wrote of it in the great hymn "A Mighty Fortress Is Our God" when he said, "One little word shall fell him."

Imagine it! The Antichrist will have incredible power, yet all God does is breathe a word and he's gone! He is more powerful than the world's most evil leaders, including the Antichrist. This great God is the one who promises to be with you through everything!

INTENDED FOR GOOD

[Joseph said,] "You intended to harm me, but God
intended it all for good. He brought me to this position
so I could save the lives of many people."

GENESIS 50:20

JOSEPH SPOKE THESE words to his brothers after Jacob, their father, died. The brothers greatly feared Joseph would take revenge for selling him into slavery when he was a youngster. He used these words to reassure them.

But for us, the story and words of Joseph reveal a tremendous truth and promise of God.

Joseph went through hard times. A slave. A prisoner. In all of it, though, God led him. Ultimately, he became the prime minister of the greatest nation on earth at that time. Undoubtedly he asked God many questions as he went along. These words reveal Joseph's understanding of his plight. He could see the plan God had all along—to use him to save lives, not only among the Egyptians but also in his own family.

Have you faced difficult, distressing, and even unfair situations? Do you wonder why God has let you go through them? Hold on tight to your faith in God. He has a plan and a purpose. Others may plan evil against you, but if you're righteous and God allows it to happen, that means he will use it to bring something positive out of it. God promises that he will work everything in our lives together for our good (see Romans 8:28).

THE SHIELD

Hold up the shield of faith to stop the fiery arrows of the devil. Put on salvation as your helmet, and take the sword of the Spirit, which is the word of God.

EPHESIANS 6:16-17

HOW DO CHRISTIANS defeat the devil as he tries to tempt, deceive, accuse, and trick us into sin? Paul lists the equipment a Roman soldier was to fight with and gives a spiritual application to each piece.

In the verses above, we see three defensive weapons that represent elements of our arsenal against satanic attack. The first one is the "shield of faith." The Roman shield protected a soldier against arrows, spears, and swords launched at him. Similarly, when we hold up faith as a shield in front of us, it wards off the accusations of the devil when he tries to attack us with guilt, fear, and anger. The "helmet" of salvation defends our minds against the doubts and worries Satan will try to hammer into us. Last, the "sword of the Spirit" is our primary weapon, which we can use both offensively and defensively. Through quoting, obeying, and applying Scripture to the tricky situations Satan throws into our path, we send him running for cover. Without these pieces of armor, we are sitting ducks. But as we use these tools, God promises to defeat Satan when he attacks our lives.

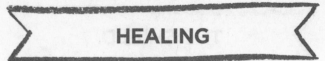

HEALING

*O LORD, if you heal me, I will be truly healed; if you save
me, I will be truly saved. My praises are for you alone!*

JEREMIAH 17:14

AFTER THE DOCTOR looked over Judy's body, palpated various sites, studied her with his stethoscope and other instruments, and went over the scans with her, he finally sat down and said, "It is completely inexplicable. I'd say you're entirely healed. No sign of the cancer. No sign of any disease. You're as good as new."

Judy breathed with relief as the doctor said, "I just don't understand what happened."

Nervously, she looked into her lap. "You won't believe it when I tell you, but I prayed. I got every person I know praying, even on the Internet. My small group at church. Friends. Family. We prayed and didn't give up. I guess all I can say is God, for some reason, chose to make me well."

Opening a Bible she always carried in her purse, Judy read the above verse from Jeremiah. "I told God I wanted true healing, not just survival. I wanted to be healthy again. And he did it."

While not all people are healed—God always reserves the right to do his will in his people—when God does heal, it's often complete. God does use doctors to bring Christians back to health. But Christians who depend only on doctors and modern medicine are fooling themselves. God is the one who ultimately heals us physically and even emotionally. Seek him, and he will surely hear your pleas. Wait on him, and whether you end up whole in this world or perfect in the next, God *will* heal you.

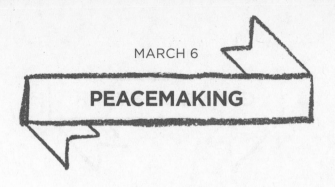

PEACEMAKING

*God blesses those who work for peace, for they
will be called the children of God.*

MATTHEW 5:9

PEACEMAKING IS A big issue in our world. In fact, one of the highest awards any human can receive is the Nobel Peace Prize, which gives recognition for work to make the world a better place in which to live.

Dissipating some of the strife in the world is not an easy thing to do. Just think how difficult it was for Henry Kissinger to achieve agreements among the enemies in Vietnam. Or consider how many times a president has attempted to reconcile the Jews and the Arabs. Think of how many wars have been fought to try to bring peace. This all shows that human peace is fragile and temporary.

In contrast, what is God's award to people who help others work through differences of opinion, arguments, enmity, jealousy, and other problems? God says such people will be "called the children of God." Earthly prizes for peace will eventually be destroyed, but God's reward for peacemaking lives forever in our lives and in the lives of those we help.

Are you a peacemaker in your area of influence? Do your best to be one. It's your role as a child of God in a strife-torn world.

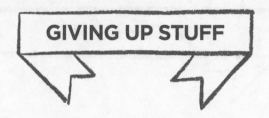

GIVING UP STUFF

*"Yes," Jesus replied, "and I assure you that everyone who has
given up house or brothers or sisters or mother or father or
children or property, for my sake and for the Good News, will
receive now in return a hundred times as many houses, brothers,
sisters, mothers, children, and property—along with persecution.
And in the world to come that person will have eternal life."*

MARK 10:29-30

MANY TIMES WHEN a Christian gives up everything for Jesus, people are shocked, even those who say they're Christians. A wealthy businessman decides to give all his money away and go and serve as a missionary. A doctor leaves his practice to do surgery on needy people in Africa. A young woman tells a young man no, she won't marry him because he's not called to youth ministry as she is.

One man, with a prospering veterinary practice, and his wife decided that they were called to go to a foreign land and practice there as missionaries. Friends and family all objected, but the couple knew they had to obey God. Today they report what a wise decision it was, as they ministered not just to animals but also to many people they would never have met otherwise, even helping people who were ill.

To some Christians, leaving everything behind doesn't make much sense. One man, when asked why he couldn't be a missionary, said, "I like air-conditioning too much." Every Christian, though, will have to give up things to serve Christ wholeheartedly. From sins, to money, to careers, to the type of community you live in—God may call you to give up something valuable to you. What will you do? Say no and go your own way? Or say yes, not knowing where he might take you?

When we give up our own comfort or an entire lifestyle to serve God, he will ultimately provide rewards and blessings a hundred times over for our commitment.

NOT UNDERSTANDING EVERYTHING

*Trust in the LORD with all your heart; do not depend
on your own understanding. Seek his will in all you
do, and he will show you which path to take.*

PROVERBS 3:5-6

WHEN HIS SISTER went to college, fourth grader Evan didn't quite understand why she was going. Finally one day after his sister had been gone a few weeks, he told his parents, "I know why Alison went to college."

"Why?" his dad asked.

"Because she wanted to get away from home, and that's the only way she could get a car of her own. They give cars to people at college."

For the price of tuition, maybe students *should* receive a car from the college, but that's beside the point! At ten, the young boy's logic wasn't developed. Kids that age frequently make guesses and assumptions about how different aspects of life work, but their understanding is often flawed.

By the time we reach adulthood, most of us are pretty good at figuring things out. But in some areas our understanding may still be limited or flawed.

That's the joy of the promise in the verses above. God doesn't expect us to understand everything perfectly. In fact, he warns us *not* to depend on our own understanding but to depend on his perfect knowledge. We don't just go our merry way, operating on what we assume or think to be true—we're to look for God's guidance. He wants to lead us.

Next time we start to set our own course, let's pause and pray. Let's follow God's compass when we're wondering which way to walk.

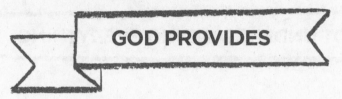

GOD PROVIDES

*[All creatures] depend on you to give them food as they
need it. When you supply it, they gather it. You open your
hand to feed them, and they are richly satisfied.*

PSALM 104:27-28

TOO MANY PEOPLE today place their trust in science, technology, and advances that have made our lives easier. Unlike the farmer of years ago—who thanked God for the rain that made his crops grow, for the crops themselves, and for the harvest at the end—we tend to think God isn't involved in the process of our getting what we need to survive.

A man came to breakfast one morning and announced he was a "self-made man." His wife regarded him with a smile and said, "Well, you have just relieved God of a tremendous responsibility."

We may think we tilled the fields and produced the crops or made ourselves rich and prosperous, but today's Scripture verses point to the real truth: God gave us the ability to till those fields and produce the crops. In the end, the good things in life are all from him, even if some think they've done it all themselves.

Real satisfaction in life, though—that's the tricky part. And that's the end result of his gifts. Is satisfaction found in living in a nice home or having a filet mignon set down before you? To be richly satisfied is to know the one who provides these things and the love for us that is behind the provision.

Do you want that kind of satisfaction? Then thank God now for his blessings, and recognize that all good things are from him.

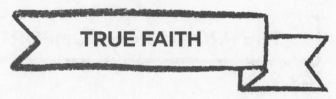

TRUE FAITH

The Scriptures tell us, "Abraham believed God, and God counted him as righteous because of his faith."

ROMANS 4:3

IF YOU LOOK at Abraham's life, you might wonder what was so great about his faith. After all, God visited him, spoke to him out loud, and was his friend. But those things happened *after* Abraham expressed his faith in God. When God called him, however, he obeyed, "without knowing where he was going" (Hebrews 11:8).

Faith is the essential ingredient. Some may ask, "Why do we need what Jesus did on the cross?" Basically, there are two things that happen the moment we express faith in him. First, we receive complete and final forgiveness for all our sins. They're wiped away.

The second part of the faith transaction is that when we believe in Jesus, he not only wipes away our sins, promising never to hold us accountable for them again, but he also gives us something—his own righteousness. He takes our sins. He gives us his perfection, his good deeds, and his perfect life. That is how faith makes us righteous. By believing in God, as today's Scripture verse says Abraham did, we gain the righteousness that results in God's favor.

When you believe in Jesus, the promise is not only that you are cleaned up from all the gunk in your life but also that you are clothed in the white robes of righteousness.

THE PROMISE OF COMFORT

Even when I walk through the darkest valley, I will not be afraid, for
you are close beside me. Your rod and your staff protect and comfort me.

PSALM 23:4

IT WAS ELEVEN at night when seven-year-old Liz was awakened by her dog barking at her bedroom window. Liz peeked out to see a man walking toward the front door. Dad was already taking care of the matter, but instantly Liz dashed into Mom's room. And, of course, Mom not only reassured Liz of her protection but also quieted her fears.

Comforting others is such a big part of life. It is so important that we comfort children after the painful and frightening moments in their lives and that we comfort friends when they face challenges, giving them hope that they will prevail. Encouragement during difficult times helps remind others that they're not alone in what they're experiencing. It brings them reassurance that others care.

That's what's special about this promise in the Bible. It reminds us not only that God is concerned about our spiritual and physical well-being but also that he cares about our emotional stability. He is concerned when we're afraid. He understands when we doubt. He is near when we're heartbroken and uncertain. He is ready and willing to reassure and comfort us, to remind us that he will work all things out in the long run.

The God who created us—including our emotions—promises not only to protect us from harm but also to lavish on us the emotional support we need in life's dark moments.

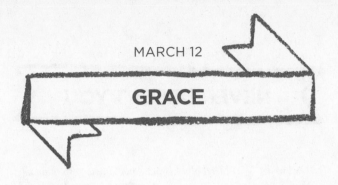

GRACE

God is so rich in mercy, and he loved us so much, that even though we
were dead because of our sins, he gave us life when he raised Christ
from the dead. (It is only by God's grace that you have been saved!)
For he raised us from the dead along with Christ and seated us with
him in the heavenly realms because we are united with Christ Jesus.

EPHESIANS 2:4-6

HAVE YOU EVER thought about how great God's grace is? His grace provided our earth, so filled with variety and diversity and amazing wonders. Grace gave us our bodies, minds, and hearts. God's grace has supplied each of us with unique abilities and talents to help us find a sense of self-worth and fulfillment in this world. His grace meets our needs daily, giving us the food, shelter, and other sustenance we need to survive. As C. H. Spurgeon, a great preacher of the late nineteenth century, wrote, it's "all of grace."

But what is the greatest grace of all? This passage tells us: "It is only by God's grace that you have been saved."

Many Christians don't really understand what God did to ensure that they would not only hear the gospel but also respond positively to it. The result is that our real life from now on is hidden with Christ in heaven (see Colossians 3:3) and that Christ is living in us here on earth. We are resurrected spiritually when he gives us the grace to receive him.

God's grace not only covers our sins but also draws us to God and meets the other needs in our lives. Thanks to his grace, he provides what we need for everything we face in life.

NEVER DESERT YOU

*[God said,] "I will lead blind Israel down a new path, guiding
them along an unfamiliar way. I will brighten the darkness
before them and smooth out the road ahead of them. Yes,
I will indeed do these things; I will not forsake them."*

ISAIAH 42:16

QUINTON'S MOM TOLD him and his two younger siblings that she needed to go to the front of the restaurant to pay the bill. She left the three children in their booth, promising to be right back.

Quinton knew his mother was probably just at the front of the restaurant, but he began to get scared. What if his mom's plan was to desert him and the others? What if they were now homeless? Where would they go? What could they do?

His terror mounted, and by the time his mom returned, he and the two others were in tears. Their relief, though, was great when they saw their mom.

Have you ever feared being left alone? rejected?

Though this sometimes happens in our world, it never happens with God. He promises that he will never leave us, never give up on us, never forget us. You can trust that when God brought you to faith, he made an eternal pact with you. That can never change.

Next time you're tempted to feel alone because you're not familiar with the road you're on, remember that God is there leading you. He's the light on your path and the one who makes a bumpy road smooth.

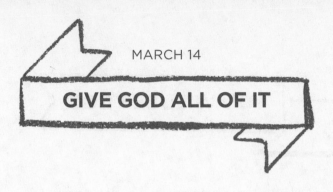

GIVE GOD ALL OF IT

Give all your worries and cares to God, for he cares about you.
1 PETER 5:7

WORRY CAN BURY you. Jeremy faced a job layoff and mounting bills and had a car that was on its last miles. He fretted about it constantly, until one day in his devotions he came across this verse from 1 Peter. He mentioned it to his wife. "Claire, have you ever read this?"

She nodded but said she found it difficult to apply. "So do I," Jeremy said. "What if we pray about this together? Give everything to the Lord. Let's do an experiment and see what happens. Every time something hits you or me that gets us worried, let's stop right then and pray about it, giving it to the Lord."

Claire agreed. About three months later, Jeremy read this verse again and remembered his prayers of some time earlier. Prayers related to worry had actually tapered off. Why? Because the promise that God takes our cares when we give them to him had lessened Jeremy's anxiety. Claire said, "You know, the same thing has happened to me. I guess it really works."

Try it. Every time you face a situation where your first reaction is to worry and fret, stop there, and give the problem to the Lord. Wait and see. He provides for those he cares for, and he cares for you!

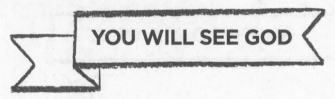

YOU WILL SEE GOD

God blesses those whose hearts are pure, for they will see God.
MATTHEW 5:8

HAVE YOU EVER wondered what a pure heart might do for your life?

Purity is a word that's often used in the area of sexuality, such as when a man or woman abstains from sex until marriage or remains faithful in marriage. But purity means more than that. It's something that we can practice regardless of our age, marital status, or life situation. God values purity.

What exactly is purity? In short, it's being clean on the inside. It goes beyond a sexual connotation. For instance, when pride or bitterness fills your mind, you snuff it out, refusing to dwell on it. When others curse, swear, put down, gossip, and otherwise tear up everyone else in their world, the pure refuse to participate. Instead, they keep their dignity, speak words of grace and kindness, and offer love and helping hands to those who have needs. They don't allow their eyes to lust after the material things of this world.

Here on earth, none of us will ever achieve perfect purity. But it's something to work toward. Fill your mind, heart, and life with good things, good habits, good words, and good deeds, and one day you will know God's smile of approval.

FAITHFUL

If we endure hardship, we will reign with him. . . . If we are
unfaithful, he remains faithful, for he cannot deny who he is.

2 TIMOTHY 2:12-13

YELLOWSTONE PARK—LOCATED in Montana, Wyoming, and Idaho—was established in 1872, making it America's oldest national park. Though the park boasts more than three hundred geysers, probably the most famous is Old Faithful. This geyser erupts, on average, every seventy-four minutes and can be counted on to expel 3,700 to 8,400 gallons of 204-degree water each time.

Though there are some variables in the time between eruptions (from 60 to 110 minutes apart) and the amount of water expelled each time, the geyser faithfully shoots off seventeen times a day. That's why it's called Old Faithful. No matter how the years and seasons change or how many tourists come and go, the geyser sticks to seventeen eruptions a day.

One of the attributes of God is that he remains the same. Seasons, years, and people change, but God doesn't. His character cannot vary. And one of the areas in which he is unchanging is his faithfulness.

Even when we're fickle and when we struggle in our relationship with God, he is there for us—still caring for us and watching us grow and eager to commune with us. So ask God to help you be more consistent in serving him. He will be there to help you in your struggles and will draw you closer to himself. Knowing he is faithful, we can endure every hardship, because we know we will reign with him in heaven one day.

Have you thanked him for his faithfulness recently?

FORGIVENESS

He forgives all my sins and heals all my diseases.

PSALM 103:3

WHEN WE TRUST in Christ, how many of our sins does God forgive? All of them.

Think about it for a moment. What if God said, "Okay, you've trusted my Son now. I give you four 'Get out of Jail Free' cards. You also have five hundred 'I Forgive Whatever You've Done' tickets. And I'll also let you get by with breaking my Ten Commandments thirty-two times a year."

Where would we all be under such a system? If you're like most of us, you'd run through all those cards and tickets in no time.

But God never puts limits on his forgiveness. It's complete. Total. Past, present, future. It covers every wrongdoing. Jesus paid for all of them.

We sometimes say that God's patience does run out. The Bible shows times when God's patience ran out with people: the people of Noah's time, Samson, King Saul, Judas Iscariot.

But the question is, Did any of them ask for forgiveness? Did any stop in their tracks, think about what they'd done, and cry out to God, "Okay, I see it now. I've done some wrong things. But I'm through with that. Will you forgive me and give me another chance?"

Would God have answered, "All right, just one more chance"? No, he would have drawn each of them back into his arms, assuring them that all was forgiven and that the only thing needed if they sinned again would be to come back and get right with him.

Do you need another—or even still another—chance? God has it covered.

GIVING TO THE KINGDOM

*Honor the LORD with your wealth and with the best part
of everything you produce. Then he will fill your barns with
grain, and your vats will overflow with good wine.*

PROVERBS 3:9-10

STATISTICS REPORT THAT most church members give less than 4 percent of their income to church and charities. Many pastors make the case that tithing—giving a minimum of 10 percent of our income to the church— is God's mandate for our giving. Other pastors feel tithing was an Old Testament concept, whereas "proportional giving" is the principle in the New Testament. That means we give as we are able, whether that's more or less than the 10-percent benchmark.

The powerful Scripture passage above, from the writings of Solomon, is another way of looking at giving. What does it mean to "honor [God] with your wealth"? It means to show respect, thanks, and reverence to God for what he has done in your life by giving back to him. Let's create an analogy: suppose someone rescued you from a horrible death, showered you with gifts, adopted you into his family, and made you his personal heir. Would you think it an appropriate level of honor to give that person a piece of chocolate from a dollar store?

That kind of paints a picture, doesn't it? Take a look at your life. What blessings has God given you? List them all. Then look at your income, your talents, your time, and your power to serve. How are you showing God honor? When you honor him appropriately, his promise is to "pour out a blessing so great you won't have enough room to take it in!" as Malachi 3:10 says.

GOD CAME

*I waited patiently for the LORD to help me, and he turned
to me and heard my cry. He lifted me out of the pit of
despair, out of the mud and the mire. He set my feet on
solid ground and steadied me as I walked along.*

PSALM 40:1-2

"HELP!"

Anytime that cry fills the air, people turn to look. "Help!" means a person has reached the end of his or her abilities. It's a call for reinforcements—right away! It is usually a desperate pleading.

Probably the shortest prayer any of us has prayed at one time or another is, "Lord, help!"

Psalm 40 gives meaning to that prayer. Here, David experienced perilous circumstances, though we don't know what, and he cried out to God. Perhaps this psalm was written while David was on the run from King Saul, who was trying to kill him. Maybe it was in days of despair over family problems. Perhaps it was amid battles David led. David had apparently waited patiently for some time. But he told himself to keep the faith.

Then God acted. He pulled David out of the depression, which might have felt like being stuck in mud or being pulled under by quicksand. God moved him onto solid ground and steadied him as he walked away, the problem apparently dealt with.

You can count on God to do the same for you. You might have to wait for a while. But God's relief and help will come.

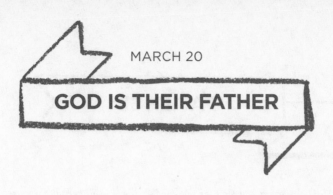

GOD IS THEIR FATHER

Father to the fatherless, defender of widows—
this is God, whose dwelling is holy.

PSALM 68:5

TERESA HAS A ministry in her church, helping orphans find adoptive parents. She finds that many Christians are reluctant to adopt today because of the horror stories they hear—especially about kids from foreign countries. In some cases, those kids have been abused in their homelands. If and when they are adopted, they bring plenty of emotional baggage with them, even at age one or two years.

But Teresa repeatedly says it's all worth the effort. And she speaks knowledgeably. She has two adopted kids—a girl from China and a boy from Kazakhstan. After the adoptions, at great expense, she and her husband discovered that both children had developed serious medical and emotional problems from difficulties they encountered before Teresa and her husband took them in.

As Teresa prays about kids who need parents, the verse above is one of her favorites. She feels that even kids who do not find homes have a blessing: God is a father to the fatherless. He is there with them, no matter how troubled their circumstances.

God's heart is too great to overlook a single child, with or without a family. His promise is to take those fatherless children and make them his own in a special, loving way.

And the overriding promise we all can enjoy is that God is the father and protector of those who are weak. Anytime we feel weak and vulnerable, we can depend on him to take care of us.

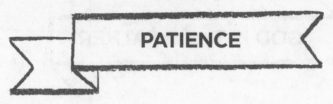

PATIENCE

*Be patient as you wait for the Lord's return. Consider the farmers
who patiently wait for the rains in the fall and in the spring. They
eagerly look for the valuable harvest to ripen. You, too, must be
patient. Take courage, for the coming of the Lord is near.*

JAMES 5:7-8

PATIENCE IS SO hard to learn. For Lindsey, the challenge involved learning not to lose her temper with her two young children, who constantly pressed her about their real and imagined needs. For Charles, it was his boss at work, who often made him stay late when he wanted to go home. For Christy, it was the girls in her Sunday school class. Did they ever listen to anything she said?

So many of us struggle with being patient. But how does God teach us patience? Often he does so by putting us in situations where we *have* to be patient. He wants us to learn and grow in this character trait, so he frequently puts us in circumstances that push our patience to the limit.

We have so many things to learn in this world. Are you developing in the area of patience? If not, don't be surprised if God lets you encounter situations that strengthen your patience. His encouragement is to "take courage." One day the Lord will return and reward you for your patient faithfulness.

PRAISE HIM

*Sing to the LORD! Praise the LORD! For though I was
poor and needy, he rescued me from my oppressors.*

JEREMIAH 20:13

WHY DO CHRISTIANS sing to God and praise him in church and elsewhere? It's not because God needs the encouragement or the compliments. It's not even because God just enjoys hearing our praise. Ultimately, it's because God deserves that kind of response for all the good things he does for us.

Did you have a nice breakfast this morning? Why not praise God for the variety he gave you? Did work go well today? Did you solve a problem or two? Doesn't the God who gave you your mind and ability to solve problems deserve more than a nod now and then? Did you come home to a family? If so, did they materialize out of nowhere? No. The Bible says they're gifts from God to you because he loves you. Like Jeremiah, we're all poor and needy in some area. But we praise even in time of need, confident that God is our provider.

God does not need, require, or demand our praise. He can get along quite well without it. But when you have a friend who gives you good gifts, don't you say thank you?

God promises to bless us all through the day. Why not take a moment to bless him right now with a word of thanks or praise or a song of joy?

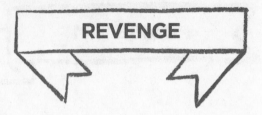

REVENGE

Don't repay evil for evil. Don't retaliate with insults when people insult you. Instead, pay them back with a blessing. That is what God has called you to do, and he will grant you his blessing.

1 PETER 3:9

THE DRIVER OF the Chevy van didn't mean to do something wrong. He was driving on an unfamiliar road, didn't know his lane had ended, and accidentally cut off the Ford truck behind him.

If the van driver hadn't known before what he did, he quickly found out. When he reached the next stoplight, the driver of the truck got out of his car and began pounding on the van driver's window.

Road rage is a problem. According to one study, more than half of United States citizens encounter road rage in one way or another, and many of these experiences are serious incidents.

Those involved in road rage may not always be as clueless as the van driver. Most of us have probably been tempted at one time or another to respond in anger when we receive an insult from another vehicle driver.

When we're the recipients of an evil action or insult—on the road or off it—what's the right thing to do? One website recommends that we keep an "I'm sorry" sign in our cars to hold up when we encounter road rage.

But when it comes to the rubber of wickedness meeting the road of life, God's Word tells us to return blessings for insults, to pay back others with goodness and kindness. They may or may not be affected by our positive behavior, but that doesn't matter. What does matter is the promise God has made to us: as we bless others, he will bless us.

HE DIED FOR US

Jesus gave his life for our sins, just as God our Father planned,
in order to rescue us from this evil world in which we live.

GALATIANS 1:4

WHAT DOES IT mean when we say Jesus gave his life for our sins? Most Christians understand that Jesus paid the penalty for our sins when he died on the cross. But what exactly does "gave his life" mean? How costly was that sacrifice?

Some theologians believe that when Jesus cried out, "My God, my God, why have you abandoned me?" (Matthew 27:46), he was experiencing the pain of separation from his Father as he took on responsibility for all the sins of humankind—including yours and mine.

Jesus paid a steep price to give you spiritual life—his own life for yours. Because he was willing to die, we have both new life here on earth and God's promise that one day we will see and know him fully for all eternity when we go to heaven.

Have you claimed the promise of the life Jesus came to give? He also came to give you entry into heaven, where you will experience an unbelievably great time for all eternity. No one else in history could have made that possible.

Jesus also came to make your present life better, full of peace and joy. You don't have to be overwhelmed by the challenges and difficulties and evil of this world. Instead, you can live on a higher spiritual plane because of one man: Jesus.

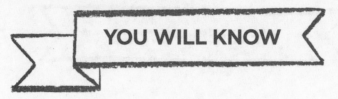

YOU WILL KNOW

You will know that I am among my people Israel,
that I am the LORD your God, and there is no other.
Never again will my people be disgraced.

JOEL 2:27

MANY TIMES THROUGHOUT history, the people of Israel experienced disgrace. Even before it became a nation, the three patriarchs—Abraham, Isaac, and Jacob—committed sin at various times, causing shame. After Joseph saved his family from the famine, the Hebrews ended up in Egypt in slavery for four centuries. During the years of the judges, the Israelites went from top to bottom many times, largely because of failing to obey God and sinning repeatedly. Under its first kings, there was so much turmoil and rebellion that Israel split into two nations; then both of those nations, Israel and Judah, were carried off into slavery at different times because God had to discipline them for their repeated and stubborn behavior.

With the coming of Jesus, Israel had its best opportunity yet for redemption, hope, and glory. However, most of the people failed to recognize him, and in less than fifty years the Israelites would again be scattered throughout the world, rejected, hated, and despised.

But God, in spite of knowing what his people would do, offered them hope in this passage in Joel. He promised Israel that one day the world would see God's power revealed in them.

Even though we Christians, too, continually turn away from God, he promises that when we again return to him to believe and trust, we will find him compassionate, merciful, and welcoming.

KEEP TRUSTING

Do not throw away this confident trust in the Lord. Remember
the great reward it brings you! Patient endurance is what
you need now, so that you will continue to do God's will.
Then you will receive all that he has promised. "For in just a
little while, the Coming One will come and not delay."

HEBREWS 10:35-37

HOW MANY CHRISTIANS today look forward to Jesus' coming? All through the ages, Christians have awaited that moment. This passage is one reason. "For in just a little while," the writer says.

The timing of Jesus' second coming has always been in question for believers. From the writings in the New Testament, one could easily get the impression that the disciples thought Jesus might come at any moment. St. Augustine, in the 400s, thought Jesus might come in his lifetime. Martin Luther in the 1500s also thought Jesus might come soon. In our own time, many have even predicted a specific time when they thought the Bible indicated Jesus had to come.

They've all been wrong. But one thing is right: Jesus will come back. And when you look at it from God's perspective—that a few thousand years are like a day—it makes sense. And for us who have eternal life, Jesus' coming is only a short time away compared to all the time we will have with him in heaven.

Look up, and keep looking there. One guarantee beyond death and taxes is that Jesus is coming back. Live as if he's coming in just a little while.

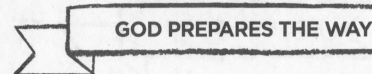

GOD PREPARES THE WAY

*Be strong and courageous! Do not be afraid and do not
panic before them. For the LORD your God will personally go
ahead of you. He will neither fail you nor abandon you.*
DEUTERONOMY 31:6

WHEN RICK STARTED his new job, he had great misgivings. He had been
transferred to another department within his company. He had heard
much about the crew that worked there. They were vulgar and nasty and
engaged in backbiting; they had the worst reputation in the whole company. Part of the reason Rick was sent there was to clean up the crew.

But Rick wasn't sure he was up to it. He began praying about the situation every day. What he asked for was just one opportunity every day to
build a friend in the group.

What he hadn't counted on was the truth of this verse. God *had* gone
before him in that group and made them very open to the kind of integrity and friendship Rick could give. In time, Rick built a number of solid
friendships with his coworkers. They began to function like a real team.
No one but Rick had any idea how it had happened, except the comments
kept referring to Rick and his kind, nurturing personality.

You may think a work, church, or home situation is impossible. But
remember this verse and its promise: God is there, and he has gone
ahead, paving the way for you in ways you can't even imagine. Trust him
to help you succeed in your mission of building his Kingdom.

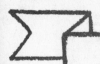

THE IDEA OF MARRIAGE

A man leaves his father and mother and is joined to
his wife, and the two are united into one.

GENESIS 2:24

WHERE DID THE idea of marriage come from? Who invented it?

Those who support the idea of evolution would have us believe that marriage came about as lesser animals evolved into thinking people. The socialization necessary to the success of the human race demanded it.

Others might say marriage developed strictly from the need to survive. Women needed protection. Men needed sex. As a moral consciousness developed, people naturally gravitated toward the union of marriage.

But this is all hypothetical. The Bible offers a precise and exact reason: it is the way God made us. Male and female. One man, one woman. A boy grows into a man, finds the woman of his dreams, leaves his home, sets up his own place, and they link for the duration of their lives.

It makes sense, doesn't it? If you subscribe to other theories, why would a man settle down with one woman? Why would women not work together to protect themselves? Why wouldn't it involve the whole village? No, God created the family unit as the single primary social structure. He knew we'd function best that way. It's worked for millennia. And God promises to bless marriage if we follow the Bible's blueprint.

THE MAN OF SORROWS

He was despised and rejected—a man of sorrows, acquainted
with deepest grief. We turned our backs on him and looked
the other way. He was despised, and we did not care.

ISAIAH 53:3

HAVE YOU EVER seriously considered what Jesus went through to pay for the sins of the world—yours in particular? We can read these poetic words and think about the truths behind them, but let's look closer:

Despised: Jesus was God incarnate, and yet human beings treated him like dirt.

Rejected: Have you ever been on the receiving end of others' scorn and ridicule? "Idiot!" "Fool!" "Jerk!" Imagine how it hurt the God who loved those people to hear them throw hateful words in his face.

A man of sorrows, acquainted with deepest grief: Jesus hurt at the sight of people throwing away with both hands the salvation he came to give. How much would it hurt you to see a son or daughter stomp into the dirt a check for money it took you years to earn and wanted to give as a blessing?

Turned our backs, looked the other way, did not care: Have you ever cried out to someone you loved and watched him or her walk away as if you were nothing?

Hateful, hurtful actions. Yet Jesus didn't stop in his mission. He never gave up and said we weren't worth it. He pressed on to the end, knowing that one day we might wake up and see his love for what it really is. His promise to those who do not reject him is found in John 1:12: "To all who believed him and accepted him, he gave the right to become children of God."

BEYOND THE HERE AND NOW

*All praise to God, the Father of our Lord Jesus Christ. It is by his
great mercy that we have been born again, because God raised Jesus
Christ from the dead. Now we live with great expectation, and we
have a priceless inheritance—an inheritance that is kept in heaven for
you, pure and undefiled, beyond the reach of change and decay.*

1 PETER 1:3-4

THE OLD COUPLE had lived very modestly all their lives. They never col-
lected many possessions, and they never threw out things that still had
some wear in them. When they didn't need certain items anymore, they
put them into a basement-level garage until someday when they might
be needed or wanted by the couple or their children.

But the couple never thought about the leaky foundation and damp-
ness in their basement. When they died and their children cleaned out
the basement, the pile of rust-corroded and decayed furniture, tools,
and other household goods filled a good part of the driveway. Not much
of an inheritance!

The inheritance most people leave or receive is all here on earth—
where it will end up, eventually, in a pile of trash or destroyed.

But this verse promises us something beyond the here and now,
something lasting, something eternal. As we live for God, we have an
inheritance in heaven—the inheritance of salvation and being the Father's
child, the inheritance of rewards for what we've done here on earth.

Where's your focus? On enjoying and building an earthly inheritance? Or on an inheritance that will never decay?

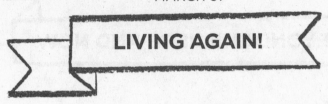

LIVING AGAIN!

Those who die in the LORD will live; their bodies will rise again! Those who sleep in the earth will rise up and sing for joy! For your life-giving light will fall like dew on your people in the place of the dead!

ISAIAH 26:19

FOR YEARS, WILLIAM had watched as his father's abilities became more limited. It was a sad day when William had to help his dad enter a senior living center. Even then William visited his mom at his parents' home every day.

Finally, the organs in his dad's body started wearing out. William never knew when he woke up in the morning what the day would bring—frequently a trip to the ER was in store.

As he watched his father's health fade, William kept his Facebook friends informed. He shared updates on his father's status, including the amusing moments of a macho Irish dad who had Alzheimer's disease, as well as the prayer needs.

Dozens of people cried with William the day his dad's body gave out for good. But for William and his dad, the story doesn't end there. The story doesn't end there for any of us who have put our faith in Jesus. Instead, the end of life on this earth is actually the beginning of our lives in heaven, the continuation of our lives in Christ. And what a joyous continuation it is!

When we lose the ones we love so dearly, they're not really lost. In fact, we're the ones who are still misplaced—these loved ones who put their faith in Christ are home for good. And God has promised that we'll see them again.

Of course William misses his dad's presence on earth, and his friends ache with him. But he also looks forward to the day when he can see his dad doing an Irish jig of joy as he worships his Savior.

APRIL

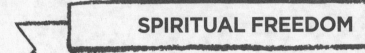

SPIRITUAL FREEDOM

*Under the old system, the blood of goats and bulls and the
ashes of a heifer could cleanse people's bodies from ceremonial
impurity. Just think how much more the blood of Christ will
purify our consciences from sinful deeds so that we can worship
the living God. For by the power of the eternal Spirit, Christ
offered himself to God as a perfect sacrifice for our sins.*

HEBREWS 9:13-14

BLOOD IS VERY important in the scope of humanity. Why is so much
emphasis put on blood? Because the life of all creatures is in the blood.
Without blood, our bodies would die.

Why is blood so important to God? Perhaps it's because life—both
earthly and eternal life—*is* in the blood. It's blood that nourishes our
bodies, cleanses them, and keeps them healthy and functional. The shed-
ding of Christ's blood is the way we will be cleansed from all sin. When
Jesus died for us, the offering of his blood was what cleansed us on the
inside—spiritual blood that is applied to us by the Spirit when we believe
in Christ.

The promise related to Jesus' blood represents purity, hope, freedom,
and fulfillment. Because Jesus gave his life and blood, we are cleansed
of all sin and set free from its power over us. We are made new, into
creatures that are holy and acceptable in God's eyes. Because of Christ's
sacrifice, we will be given incorruptible bodies to live in heaven with
him for eternity.

Jesus' sacrifice makes this promise: when you believe in him, you are
made righteous in God's eyes because his righteousness is put in you. You
no longer need to feel guilty over the sins of your past. You no longer
need to wonder if you are going to "make it into heaven." Because of
Christ's sacrifice and our belief in him, we are spiritually free and headed
toward perfection in heaven.

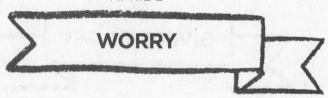

WORRY

Do not dread the disease that stalks in darkness, nor the disaster that strikes at midday. Though a thousand fall at your side, though ten thousand are dying around you, these evils will not touch you.

PSALM 91:6-7

IF YOU ARE a parent or a grandparent, do you ever worry that one of your little ones might be abducted? Have you ever entered a restaurant as the news was broadcast of a slaughter at another nearby eating place? Ever think twice about taking a road trip, for fear that a sleepy trucker will cross the center line and smash your car and you and your family?

Such things do happen sometimes. But the probability of such accidents happening to us is slim, and most of us are never touched personally by violent crime. Why is that? One reason is that we belong to God, and he promises to care for us in this often harsh world. None of us has any reason to quake in fear or to worry continuously or to obsess about hypothetical scenarios that could leave us maimed or dead.

Psalm 91 is a fantastic picture of God's continuing watch over his loved ones. We needn't live in fear. We should never sit at home terrified to go out because we might find the "bullet with our name on it." God wants us to live in the knowledge that he watches over us, he protects his own, and he cares for each of us.

Even when bad things do happen to God's people, his promise is that he'll be there with us. He's always watching and sheltering us in his arms of love and grace.

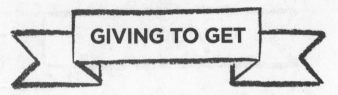

GIVING TO GET

Remember this—a farmer who plants only a few seeds will get a small crop. But the one who plants generously will get a generous crop.

2 CORINTHIANS 9:6

IN HIS FIRST working years, Glenn could barely afford to give 10 percent of his income to his church and to other organizations he supported. He found, though, that God always rewarded his faithfulness—he never lacked money to pay for his family's needs.

Over time, he found more and more needs coming his way: a missionary couple who lost several supporters and were short in their finances, a parachurch organization that had helped Glenn in his college years so he felt an obligation to donate to it, and several situations in his own church to which he wanted to respond. His 10 percent grew to 15 percent and then 20 percent. His wife felt he gave too much, but it seemed that God always blessed them for their sacrifices.

Then one year, three missionaries Glenn supported visited his church. They all gave testimony to how the church's resources and those of people in it had kept them from having to stop ministering. Now they were seeing a great harvest come in after years of work.

God doesn't always reward givers in monetary or tangible blessings or by showing them the results of their sacrifices. But the promise is always true: the more you give, the more harvest there will be—if not now, certainly later.

LOVING WITHOUT SEEING

You love [Jesus Christ] even though you have never seen
him. Though you do not see him now, you trust him; and
you rejoice with a glorious, inexpressible joy. The reward
for trusting him will be the salvation of your souls.

1 PETER 1:8-9

HOW CAN WE love someone we can't even see? How can Christians trust
a person who is invisible?

By faith. By faith, we know Jesus is with us, watching, helping, guiding, empowering. By faith, we believe that this world is not the end—that
God will take us to a place where we will never suffer again.

When Jill became a Christian, the first thing she said was, "I've met
God. He's real. He's there. I know it. He talks to me. He listens to me.
It's the most amazing thing." Some of her friends thought she was a little
crazy. But that's what faith does—it opens our eyes so we see the truth
about our world, about God, about life.

Some call such things foolishness or just plain stupidity. They say
we've deluded ourselves. They tell us to get with it and realize this world
is all there is.

But they're the ones who are deluded. Though we can't see God, we
sense him in our hearts and in our lives, working around us and in us.
Though we don't always know what he is doing or will do, we trust his
promises in the Bible that he will get us through and be with us every step
of the way. Others can then see our inexpressible joy, and though they
can't see the source, they know God is real.

JOY IN THE MORNING

His anger lasts only a moment, but his favor lasts a lifetime! Weeping may last through the night, but joy comes with the morning.

PSALM 30:5

HAVE YOU EVER wept over a problem for a whole night? A week? A month? Probably few of us have ever wept more than an hour at a time. But there are many situations that do drive us to weeping: the loss of a loved one. Our house burned and all our possessions gone. Our beloved child turning from God. A pet dying in the street, killed by a speeding driver. Struggling and fighting and working and seeing no end to the strain.

Weeping is a very natural and normal human response to conditions we feel we cannot bear. But God understands. When we weep, he does not reel off a bunch of Bible verses; he weeps with us. When we're ready to accept his words, he gives them to us.

And the fact is that often joy does come in the morning. A new day, sunlight, seeing things with a new perspective, or gaining some insight from the Spirit during our time in the dark often returns us to optimism and hope. God promises never to leave us weeping for so long that we give up. He wants us to trust him and to let our tears be the means to reflection, prayer, and looking to him. His promise is to give us the strength that empowers us to face the trial once more, this time with hope, endurance, and the certainty that joy will come "with the morning."

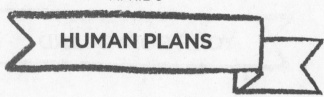

HUMAN PLANS

You can make many plans, but the LORD's purpose will prevail.

PROVERBS 19:21

AL PLANNED TO make a million dollars by the time he was twenty-five years old. He laid out the steps that would lead him to success in reaching his goal. He figured out what career to enter, decided what kind of training he'd need for that career, and started taking necessary classes.

Sure enough, Al excelled. Besides making careful plans, he had natural ability. He began evaluating which specific businesses would get him to his goal of a million dollars the quickest.

But then, in the middle of Al's course of action, something happened: he met Jesus. He started reading his Bible and going to church and praying. He started thinking about all the people who did not know Jesus.

Al continued along the course he'd set, but he lost his enthusiasm. One night at church, Al went forward for prayer. He dedicated his life to the Lord. And he went a step further. He stopped focusing on making a million dollars and accepted God's challenge to try to reach a million people—one at a time—through starting a small ministry.

How many times do we, like Al, make our plans, plowing through life? Al was seeking the Lord, and his heart was tender enough to change direction when God spoke.

Nothing is wrong with making plans, but God promises that what he wants to happen will happen—whether it's through our plans or whether we have to change our plans. The key is to keep our hearts pliable and our minds open to him.

YOUR BODYGUARD

He will order his angels to protect you wherever you go.
PSALM 91:11

HAVE YOU EVER looked at a photo of a rich or famous person or a political figure and noticed the people standing around him or her? Yes, celebrities are usually surrounded by throngs of admirers, but some of the people in the photo are probably bodyguards.

Bodyguards are professionals, often highly trained in areas such as protection, first aid, firearms, crowd screening and control, unarmed combat, and other skills. They also must have good hearing and eyesight and be attentive and observant. When on duty, a bodyguard has to be alert every moment.

Did you know that Christians have God-given bodyguards in this world? The Bible tells us that we are surrounded by angels who are protecting and watching over us. We may not see these angels, but there are many stories of believers who have experienced some problem or situation that reversed itself without explanation. They claim angels did it!

God has revealed in the Bible that angels have just that purpose. Hebrews 1:14 says they're "servants." Other passages refer to guardians and those who stand watch to protect us from evil. Today's passage is direct about it. God "will order his angels to protect you wherever you go."

Isn't that a comfort? Doesn't that thrill you? One day we shall all know and see exactly what those angels did for us. Although they're invisible and often forgotten, don't forget this truth: God promises many ways to protect us from our enemies, from evil, and from disaster. Although that doesn't mean he won't allow some things to occur for our growth and spiritual development, the promise is that he cares for us immensely. And so does that angel watching over you right now.

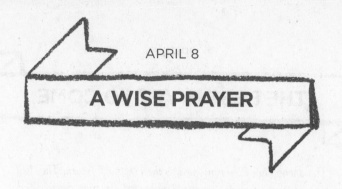

A WISE PRAYER

*I pray that your love will overflow more and more, and that you will
keep on growing in knowledge and understanding. For I want you to
understand what really matters, so that you may live pure and blameless
lives until the day of Christ's return. May you always be filled with the
fruit of your salvation—the righteous character produced in your life
by Jesus Christ—for this will bring much glory and praise to God.*

PHILIPPIANS 1:9-11

THIS IS ONE of those tremendous prayers Paul prayed for his converts. In
it we see Paul's heart, what he truly wanted most for those people. Notice
what he prays for. Not financial or material success. Not healing from
every kind of affliction. Not a spouse or a family or even that believers
would find the right church to attend.

No, Paul was concerned about spiritual realities. He wanted those
following Christ to overflow with love toward one another in the church
and outside it. He wanted them to comprehend "what really matters."
This would lead them to live "pure and blameless lives until the day of
Christ's return." Above all, he wanted believers to have righteous character—demonstrating goodness, holiness, and justice to the world.

It's so easy for us to slip into the mundane in our prayers. How much
time, though, do we pray about "what really matters"? If you take this
kind of praying seriously, God will bring the fruit of righteousness into
your life. Be the kind of person described in the verses above, and you'll
be able to truly change your world.

THE BEST IS YET TO COME

Those who have been ransomed by the LORD will return. They will enter Jerusalem singing, crowned with everlasting joy. Sorrow and mourning will disappear, and they will be filled with joy and gladness.

ISAIAH 35:10

DO YOU EVER wish you could sing a little better? That you could worship God with more fervency and enthusiasm?

Many Christians struggle with those issues as they attend church, try to share with others, and attempt to live the kinds of lives that glorify God. The struggle is often tremendous. With all the pressures most people face today, we often give in to small temptations, and we end up regretting and feeling guilty.

One day, though, when we reach heaven, that entire struggle will be over. We will be perfect, never again to make a mistake or sin. It's not that we'll be turned into spiritual zombies, either. It's simply that God will give us the power through our new spiritual bodies, minds, wills, and environment to live lives that are perfect.

If you've been ransomed (saved) by the Lord, his promise is that the best is yet to come.

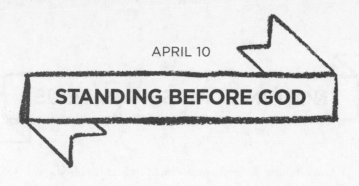

STANDING BEFORE GOD

*All who are victorious will be clothed in white. I will never
erase their names from the Book of Life, but I will announce
before my Father and his angels that they are mine.*

REVELATION 3:5

IMAGINE THE SITUATION. You're out there in the crowd. Just standing and watching. Wondering what will happen next.

The president of the United States stands at the podium. He seems to be looking around. Then suddenly, his eyes stare into yours. He calls you to come forward, and a second later you're standing up there with him for all to see. Before he asks a question, though, or tells you to speak, he begins reeling off all your great achievements, from the time you refused to tell a lie as a first grader to how you saved that little boy from drowning last year. He recounts your exploits, reminding the crowd repeatedly that you are his friend, you've been loyal, and he wants to reward you with every good thing the good old USA has to offer.

Think that's a fantasy? Perhaps in this world. But in the next one, for all of us who have allied ourselves with Jesus, that day will come. We will stand before the whole creation, and Jesus will speak of his friendship with us, his love for us, and his intent to bless us beyond anything we could imagine.

Never stop doing good. Keep fighting the good fight. Don't give up on Jesus no matter what. His promise is that he will make all your trials here and now worth it all on that great day.

NOTHING CAN SEPARATE US

I am convinced that nothing can ever separate us from God's love.
Neither death nor life, neither angels nor demons, neither our fears for
today nor our worries about tomorrow—not even the powers of hell
can separate us from God's love. No power in the sky above or in the
earth below—indeed, nothing in all creation will ever be able to separate
us from the love of God that is revealed in Christ Jesus our Lord.

ROMANS 8:38-39

DO YOU EVER fear that something or someone could separate you from God? That some atheist will come along and talk you out of your faith? That some terrible circumstance will make you lose your faith?

Look at the list Paul gives in these verses of things that cannot touch you. Neither death nor life can rip you away from God. Angels and demons are impotent against you. God will always be there. The fears of today and worries about tomorrow can't fell you either. You have your roots deep in Christ. Nor can the powers of hell put a wall between you and God. God's love is stronger than all of these.

Beyond these things, no power in the sky above or earth below can mess with you. God will see you through everything. In fact, Paul doesn't want us to fear anything in creation. The only person we need to fear is God himself. And that kind of fear is really trust and awe because he promises to stick with us forever.

THE CROWN OF GLORY

When the Great Shepherd appears, you will receive
a crown of never-ending glory and honor.

1 PETER 5:4

LEADERSHIP IN A church can be a daunting task, whether someone is part of a paid staff or in a volunteer position. Christians can be wonderful to work with, and they can also be as difficult as any other humans!

Many full-time leaders give up after a few years, having found the ministry and managing a group of believers just too difficult. The failure rate for people in full-time ministry is very high. Discouragement is always pawing at the door. Satan loves to knock these people down and out.

God has some strong words for such leaders. Working in church leadership is not a position to enter lightly. You don't take on expanding God's Kingdom on a whim. At the same time, though, God does remind us that he holds some great rewards for those who serve.

Years ago, a missionary couple returned from Africa on the same ship as Teddy Roosevelt, who was returning from a safari. As the ship arrived in the harbor, the news reporters, crowds, and well-wishers all gave Teddy a grand reception. For the missionaries? No one. The man turned to his wife and said, "Here we are, coming home, and there's no one here to even greet us. Was it all a waste?"

The wife sagely replied, giving him a hug, "Honey, we're not home yet."

What a powerful truth! God does not promise anyone success on this earth. But to those who serve faithfully, the eternal rewards will simply never stop.

GIVING STRENGTH

You cause grass to grow for the livestock and plants for people to use.
You allow them to produce food from the earth—wine to make them
glad, olive oil to soothe their skin, and bread to give them strength.

PSALM 104:14-15

MICHELLE SIGHED AS she sent her husband to the store again. Sure, she'd thought of the big things before the baby came home—the crib, the car seat, and the diapers.

But she'd never stopped to realize that it would be handy to have more than one cute set of sheets for the crib—one to put on it while the dirty one was in the laundry. Somehow, she'd forgotten that she might need some diaper-rash ointment. And she never thought about needing an aspirator until her baby got sick. She didn't even know how to use a humidifier, let alone realize her baby might need one. Then it was teething gel. Soon her husband knew the layout of the baby and health aisles at the store better than he knew the halls in his office building!

Taking care of a person's health and well-being takes a lot of work. Today's Scripture verses point out how God has thought of everything his people need. He knew we'd need food, thus he created plants and animals. And the animals would need to eat, to grow healthy and tasty for us, thus grass. He put some greens on the earth to maintain our diets and made the earth able to produce the food we'd need.

God didn't leave it at keeping our stomachs full. He thought about our happiness, our comfort, and our strength.

And he's still preparing for our health and well-being. Let's rest in the promise that he will take care of us physically and emotionally—as well as spiritually!

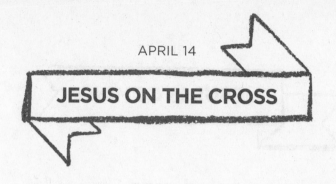

JESUS ON THE CROSS

He personally carried our sins in his body on the cross so that we can be
dead to sin and live for what is right. By his wounds you are healed.

1 PETER 2:24

SALVATION DIDN'T COME without a price. You didn't have to pay a thing. But Jesus paid everything so that you can live.

Take a look at the Savior hanging on that cross. If you saw the movie *The Passion of the Christ*, you probably have a much clearer and more graphic idea of what Jesus went through to redeem us. There was the spitting, the ridicule, the sneers, the slaps in the face, the insults, the threats, and the taunts. Imagine going through that. Many of us get hurt just by an unkind word. Jesus was assaulted with a barrage of unkind, hateful, and nasty words, smacks, and punches.

Next came the whipping. How many of us had to turn away from the screen during the portrayal of that part of Jesus' payment for our sins? It was brutal, debilitating, and obscene. Yet he endured it for us.

Finally, there was the cross. What horror and agony must Jesus have felt as his own Father left him and he was forced to cry, "My God, my God, why have you abandoned me?" (Mark 15:34). They'd never been apart before. Ever. Not for a minute. Yet in that moment, Jesus experienced the anguish and separation from his beloved Father that those who don't know Christ will suffer eternally in hell.

Perhaps now is a good time to bow your head and thank Jesus for all he did to heal your soul.

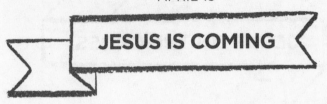

JESUS IS COMING

*There is more than enough room in my Father's home. If this
were not so, would I have told you that I am going to prepare
a place for you? When everything is ready, I will come and
get you, so that you will always be with me where I am.*

JOHN 14:2-3

IN THE JEWISH culture of Jesus' day, when a man and woman became betrothed, the man would start working on the home he and his beloved would share. Imagine the bridegroom's excitement as he planned the love nest. He planned sturdy walls and a strong roof to protect his wife from the elements of nature. Imagine the little details he added to give his wife small comforts—details that he thought through just because he loved her and wanted their home to be as much of a "palace" as possible for her.

When the bridegroom had completed the home, then came the next stage—the man would go for his bride, wed her, and they'd move into the home to be together for the rest of their lives.

What a picture of how Christ cares for us! When we become betrothed to Christ by giving our lives to him, work starts on our heavenly palaces. Our Beloved prepares a home for us that includes the creature comforts he knows will show us how much he loves us and has thought about our happiness. Imagine how amazing that custom-built home will be!

Finally the day will come when Christ comes to claim us, to take us to this home so we can live with him—happily ever after. It's a promise we can look forward to!

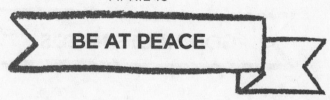

BE AT PEACE

*Do all that you can to live in peace with everyone. Dear friends,
never take revenge. Leave that to the righteous anger of God. For the
Scriptures say, "I will take revenge; I will pay them back," says the LORD.*

ROMANS 12:18-19

REVENGE IS A big theme in literature, movies, television, and relationships. The reason some people commit terrible crimes is to get revenge on those who have wronged them. Statistics reveal that more murders are committed against relatives than against strangers. Revenge is the primary motivation of the devil, the enemy of God, and he tempts people to seek revenge every day. Even Christians can fall for its subtle enticements.

This passage teaches us that as Christians we are to try to "live in peace with everyone." Granted, there are some people who will never be at peace with us personally. That doesn't mean we don't try to find common ground or work toward reconciliation. God wants us to be a true people of peace—peacemakers—and people who build relationships of trust and love rather than sow hatred and anger.

What should you do when someone wrongs you and refuses to apologize, make up, and rebuild trust? There's one basic principle: leave all judgments to God. That doesn't mean you can't solicit help from the authorities—the law, the courts, and so on—when necessary. But it does mean that you refuse to take matters into your own hands and try to physically, financially, emotionally, or personally damage the offending party.

Give God time and opportunity to work on your behalf. You will be amazed at what he does when you trust him.

GOD MEETS NEEDS

[Jesus said,] "Don't worry . . . saying, 'What will we eat? What will we drink? What will we wear?' These things dominate the thoughts of unbelievers, but your heavenly Father already knows all your needs."

MATTHEW 6:31-32

CAROL STARED AT her bank account. How could she pay the bills again this month? She had a daughter in college and two younger kids still in school. Her finances were stretched to the limit. She worried about it constantly. She wasn't putting away a cent for the family's future, and it seemed she was always in survival mode.

One day, though, she came across this great passage, in which Jesus spoke about worry and anxiety. She said to herself, *Okay, God says he'll meet my needs. So I'll leave them in his hands.* She began to work with a new outlook: God would provide for her and her family because he loved them, and Carol would stop worrying about money all the time.

She forgot about that prayer for a while until one day she noted she had saved more than two thousand dollars in one account, had been contributing to her company's 401(k) plan, and her company was thriving. At bonus time, she nervously opened her gift check. What she read astonished her: because of her hard work and trustworthiness, the company president had given her a check for more than ten thousand dollars. Nervously, she asked him if it was a mistake. "No," he said. "You deserve it. You're a great worker. And I don't see you wasting time on gossip and nonsense. I respect that."

God promises to meet all our needs. The great thing is, he meets the basics and then goes way beyond that.

KIDS ARE STUBBORN

Direct your children onto the right path, and when
they are older, they will not leave it.

PROVERBS 22:6

AUTHOR AND BIBLICAL counselor Dr. Henry Brandt used to ask parents, "How long do you have to tell a child to keep his room clean, or make his bed, or brush his teeth?"

Many parents said it took a lot of telling. "Twenty-one years," Brandt used to say with a smile. "You have to keep reminding those kids until they grow up. They won't get it the first, second, or hundredth time around."

It's so true. Parents must reinforce their instructions with repeated warnings, corrections, directions, and so on, to teach their children to live righteously on their own. What's the upside of this? God promises that your efforts will not go unrewarded. He tells us over and over that eventually our kids will get the many things we want to teach them, and when they finally grow up, they will do those things naturally without prompting.

Don't give up, even with stubborn kids. You may have to repeat those directions until you're blue in the face, but God is faithful. You can trust that what you have taught and built into their lives will influence them, even if it takes twenty-one years.

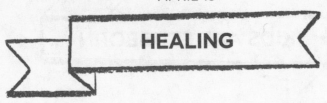

HEALING

Are any of you sick? You should call for the elders of the church to come
and pray over you, anointing you with oil in the name of the Lord.
Such a prayer offered in faith will heal the sick, and the Lord will make
you well. And if you have committed any sins, you will be forgiven.

JAMES 5:14-15

A WOMAN NAMED Sally has had a healing ministry for many years. As she
has prayed for God to heal people physically and emotionally, she has
seen some amazing results.

Sally tells one story about a woman who had suffered from migraine
headaches all her life. When she met with Sally, she explained she wanted
freedom from those headaches. As Sally prayed with this woman, she felt
led to ask a series of questions that led to the woman's revealing, for the
first time in her life, some sexual abuse she had suffered as a fourteen-
year-old girl. The woman said that when she told her mother what had
happened, she was told never to speak of it again because the abuser was
a relative.

The woman kept her promise until that day in Sally's apartment.
As Sally led the woman in forgiving her abuser and her mother for
their exploitation and lack of concern, the woman stopped and said,
"My headache is gone." From that moment on she never had another
migraine.

Not all healings work like this one, but God certainly promises to
heal. Sometimes that healing comes in ways we don't expect, but we can
be sure that, whatever happens, God will raise our lives to a new level in
response to our prayers.

PERSEVERANCE

Those who trust in the LORD will find new strength. They
will soar high on wings like eagles. They will run and
not grow weary. They will walk and not faint.

ISAIAH 40:31

KEEP MOVING. *You have too much to do to relax.*

How many times have you told yourself this on a busy day? And how many busy days do you have each week?

We only have twenty-four hours each day, and we're so used to filling that time with things we *have* to do. So what do we do when our waking hours are filled with necessary activities and responsibilities? Studies over several years have shown that we're taking more and more time away from the hours we should be sleeping. As a result, we're more prone to illness, and we're tired—too tired to care about things we might care about otherwise. Too tired to relax and renew. Sometimes we're too weary to even have the energy for God.

How can we keep going when we just want to drop?

Today's Scripture verse gives us the promise that, as we trust God, we'll find renewed strength. It's no accident that this verse uses eagles as an illustration. Even the smallest eagles have longer and broader wings than other birds, especially other birds of prey. As a result, they have more direct and faster flight.

As we look to God to help us soar, he may show us how to streamline our flights so we're exerting less energy or not stopping at certain points along the way. He may give us supernatural strength. But no matter how he helps us, we can count on his promise to keep us going—not just physically but emotionally and spiritually as well.

YOU KNOW WHERE TO FIND HIM

I love all who love me. Those who search will surely find me.

PROVERBS 8:17

WHEN YOU WERE little, did you enjoy playing hide-and-seek?

Well, if you don't have kids or grandkids around right now, you can rest assured: it's still one of the most popular games for the younger set.

Some form of hide-and-seek is played in most countries of the world. Some sources have the game dating back at least as far as the 1600s.

Some older kids really pride themselves on being able to hide in indiscernible places. On the other end of the spectrum are the young ones. Perhaps you've played hide-and-seek with a little one. He or she will "hide" in someplace terribly obvious like a bathtub or behind a chair, in full view. The young ones become terribly excited when we pretend we can't find them.

Their giggles make the game almost as much fun for us as it is for them!

When we're seeking God, he's not one of those master hiders that we have to search and search to find. Instead, he's easily found. He's right there in front of us, like those toddlers, just waiting for our eyes to focus on him.

God promises that when we look for him, we'll find him. Whether we're seeking his comfort, his guidance, his forgiveness, or even just his fellowship, he's available. He's waiting and longing for your relationship to grow. Open your heart and gaze with the eyes of faith; he promises you won't be disappointed.

Don't let anything hold you back from seeking him today.

APRIL 22

GOD SAVES

He redeems me from death and crowns me with love and tender mercies.

PSALM 103:4

ATHEIST RICHARD DAWKINS wrote in *The God Delusion* that the God of the Old Testament is a "most unpleasant character." Dawkins cataloged God's supposed sins—making him responsible for genocides, murders, homophobia, sexual prudery, and other things he says he finds in the Bible. You have to wonder, though, if Dawkins has ever read words like those of Psalm 103.

While the Bible does sometimes bewilder us, it can be understood and honestly explained if one is willing to study and learn. Much more often you find words and passages like those in Psalm 103, which lists many of the benefits and blessings God bestows on us. In the above verse we read, "He redeems me from death." Jesus accomplished that when he died on the cross for our sins and then rose again, sending death back to its hole forever. Those of us who trust Jesus know the confidence and hope that one day, though we may die physically in this world, in the next we will be alive forever in a world that contains none of the evil of this one.

God redeems us not only from physical death but also from spiritual death, emotional death, and all the other kinds of death we experience in this world. When we truly encounter the God of the Bible, we don't find him "unpleasant," but rather a tender Father who "crowns [us] with love and tender mercies." That's the God true Christians know, love, and tell the world about.

FOLLOWING THE LEADERS

In the same way, you who are younger must accept the authority
of the elders. And all of you, dress yourselves in humility as you
relate to one another, for "God opposes the proud but gives grace
to the humble." So humble yourselves under the mighty power
of God, and at the right time he will lift you up in honor.

1 PETER 5:5-6

JOHN WESLEY WAS a proud man. He traveled by ship to America in the early 1700s, bent on converting the masses to the truth of God. But there wasn't only the problem of his pride—John Wesley wasn't even converted to God yet.

After his total failure as an evangelist on that trip, Wesley traveled to America again to give it another try. On the ship were a number of Moravians, committed believers who held strongly to the idea of a personal relationship with God, and Wesley realized that his pride and lack of a true conversion were holding him back. Later, in a church in Aldersgate, England, Wesley listened to a reading of Martin Luther's commentary on the book of Romans. While listening, Wesley expressed true faith in God and felt his heart "strangely warmed," a phrase Luther had used to describe his own conversion experience.

His pride vanished, his heart relationship with God flourished, and he went on to become one of the great evangelists of the 1700s, establishing Methodism, which later became one of the major denominations of Christianity.

Are you proud in heart? Then you will not feel closeness with God. When we're proud, we don't see our need of God. We won't successfully live the Christian life. But when we are willing to leave our pride behind, self is out of the way, and God is able to "lift [us] up" and use our service.

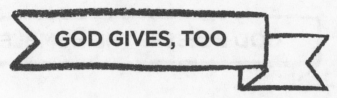

GOD GIVES, TOO

Give, and you will receive. Your gift will return to you
in full—pressed down, shaken together to make room for
more, running over, and poured into your lap. The amount
you give will determine the amount you get back.

LUKE 6:38

A YOUNG CHRISTIAN walked into church one morning, intending to give five dollars of the fifty dollars he'd been paid the night before for some work he'd done. As he opened his wallet, though, it seemed the Spirit spoke to his heart and told him to give the full fifty dollars.

A little astonished, he prayed about it, and the Spirit seemed only to confirm the directive. A humble man, he finally wrapped the fifty dollars in a one-dollar bill and dropped the packet into the offering plate. He felt a little miffed after church, but he told himself God had good reason for the addition.

On the way home from church, his father, who was one of the counters, said, "It was really remarkable. We didn't think we'd make the budget. But then we found fifty dollars wrapped in a one-dollar bill. It put us over the top."

The young man said nothing, thinking to himself that God had done something remarkable. The next day he was offered an extra job that would net him $150.

God simply will not be outgiven, and his promise is to reward those who give liberally and sacrificially.

GOD BLESSES THE HUMBLE

God blesses those who are humble, for they will inherit the whole earth.
MATTHEW 5:5

THE WORD TRANSLATED "humble" here is an interesting one. It could also mean "meek" or "gentle." The image often given is of a horse that is gentle and mild tempered, even though it's a huge animal and could easily stomp the life out of anyone who rode it. Some have talked about this kind of humility as "power under control," which is appropriately illustrated by a gentle horse.

Similarly, people who have great power in their minds and thoughts but control that power will inherit the earth. These are the kinds of people who can lead others, guide them into God's wisdom and blessing, and gently prod them to do good.

Think of what such people could accomplish in the world—those who motivate not by threats, dire warnings, or force but by kindly and gently taking charge and enabling people to find how they best fit into our world. They could change everything. And that's why Jesus promises such people will inherit the earth.

OBEDIENCE

Does anyone want to live a life that is long and prosperous? Then keep
your tongue from speaking evil and your lips from telling lies! Turn away
from evil and do good. Search for peace, and work to maintain it.

PSALM 34:12-14

EVERYONE ON EARTH might answer the question "What do you most want?" with "To live a long, happy, and fulfilling life." But how do we do such a thing? Where do we get the wisdom to actually experience such a life?

To be sure, God warns all Christians that when we truly seek to live out Christian values and truth in the world, we will be persecuted (see 2 Timothy 3:12). We're in the middle of a war between good and evil, God's values and truth versus the lies of the devil.

God promises to bless us if we obey his laws. So what should we do to take hold of that kind of abundant life? The passage from Psalm 34 offers us several lines of action: one, don't speak evil words, about others or about God. Two, don't tell lies. Simply refuse to fudge on the truth about anything and everything. Three, refuse to do evil, even if it costs you. Four, do good, everywhere you can. Five, try to find a peaceful solution in any situation. And six, work at maintaining such peace.

It's a rather amazing formula, isn't it? But it's not really a formula. It's more a plan of action, a personal MO, a mission statement. Why not make it yours by self-examination, starting today, in every relationship you have?

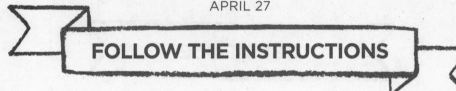

FOLLOW THE INSTRUCTIONS

*Study this Book of Instruction continually. Meditate on it day
and night so you will be sure to obey everything written in it.
Only then will you prosper and succeed in all you do.*

JOSHUA 1:8

HOW OFTEN DO you rip into a new electronic device, appliance, or other household tool and just start using it, while the instructions sit unused? Why is it that so many of us hate to read the instructions? Perhaps we think they're a waste of time, or that surely our new items can't be complicated enough to need directions. Or we may consider an instruction manual something to open only when we hit a trouble spot.

On the contrary, instructions can often save us time. They can give us an overview of the product. And a good instruction manual is often developed *because* of questions and problems other people have had—to answer questions before we ask them. Instruction guides can also help us know how to get the optimum performance from our purchase from the very start.

The verse above likens the Bible to an instruction manual. Perhaps that's why we Christians should make sure we're consistently reading it—and, even more, studying it. If we read it and take it to heart, it can help us know how to not only survive but also truly find success and live an optimum Christian experience.

Keep studying that Instruction Manual—you'll never regret it!

FORGIVING GOD'S WAY

I have swept away your sins like a cloud. I have scattered
your offenses like the morning mist. Oh, return to
me, for I have paid the price to set you free.

ISAIAH 44:22

HOW COMPLETE IS God's forgiveness?

One day, while watching the clouds drift across the sky, Scott was reading his Bible and came to this passage. He had struggled with the issue of forgiveness, worried that although God had cast away most of his sins, perhaps some new ones had stuck. And he was afraid that one day God would make him face the truth: he wasn't really forgiven.

Scott had faith, though, and he asked God to help him understand the truth of his forgiveness. Was it total? Did it cover everything? Did Jesus' death put every sin away for all time?

As he stared at the sky full of clouds, a wind came up, and in a matter of minutes the sky became clear and blue, empty of every cloud. Scott returned to the passage, and his heart responded: God had indeed taken his sins and swept them away "like a cloud." They were gone. The record was clear, perfect.

If you ever doubt the level of God's forgiveness, take this truth to heart. The promises of God state repeatedly that he has swept away all your sins, from the first to the last.

NATIONAL SIN

If my people who are called by my name will humble themselves and
pray and seek my face and turn from their wicked ways, I will hear
from heaven and will forgive their sins and restore their land.

2 CHRONICLES 7:14

MANY CHRISTIANS WHO love their nation and its people will value the words in the verse above as a tremendous promise of healing and blessing from God.

Such a person was Danyel, an African who won a scholarship to the United States and became a doctor. As he began to practice, he found the work lucrative. But he also felt a need to minister to his own people, who lived in poverty, had few doctors or medicines, and had little hope of ever earning one-tenth of what Danyel made in a year. Moreover, his people were stricken with diseases and with the common sins of all cultures.

Danyel began to pray. Few of his friends agreed that he needed to return to his homeland. But he felt called to his people, and he continued praying for them. He put together a mission project that gathered funds, medicines, and other resources, and he moved back to Africa and lived in a hut like those of his people. With his help, many people found not only physical healing but also spiritual healing.

This passage speaks to the issue of changing the direction of one's nation. In Danyel's case, his fellow villagers began developing their own businesses so they could meet their own needs and even prosper. Through Danyel, God healed their diseases and blessed their new faith.

When you look at the United States of America, where do you see us today? Can you begin praying that we will turn from our evil ways back to God, and ask him to heal our land and bless us again?

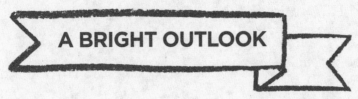

A BRIGHT OUTLOOK

*Those who look to [the Lord] for help will be radiant with
joy; no shadow of shame will darken their faces.*

PSALM 34:5

WE'VE ALL SEEN the photos of those apprehended for trial in the midst of a crowd of police and media, whether accused murderers or Wall Street moguls. They are trying to shield their faces from the glare of the cameras. Some may be innocent of the charges and are merely attempting to escape notoriety, but the guilty are covered in shame. Not so for those who look to the Lord.

When we as believers look into ourselves and see our guilt of many offenses, we, too, want to hide, to cover up our sins and put on a cloak of deception to conceal our wrongdoing. But when we look up and out of ourselves and seek God's forgiveness, love, and grace, his glory shines down upon us, and we, in turn, radiate his love to others. The apostle John tells us that when we walk in the light (of his presence), the blood of Jesus Christ cleanses us from all sin.

So if you have sinned, don't run away or try to cover it up. Look directly into the light of the Lord's glory and feel his healing burn away the filth and darkness of sin and replace it with the purity of his own righteousness. Although we are sinners like murderers and the embezzlers on Wall Street, we have one advantage: if we are redeemed by Jesus Christ, he has brought those sins into the radiance of his glory and wiped them away forever. That is a cause for radiant joy!

MAY

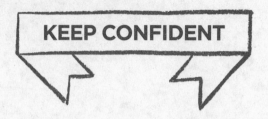

KEEP CONFIDENT

Patient endurance is what you need now, so that you will continue
to do God's will. Then you will receive all that he has promised.

HEBREWS 10:36

THE BOSTON RED SOX have taken some hard hits. For eighty-six years they languished and did not win a World Series. But then in 2004, facing the awesome St. Louis Cardinals, they did it. They won. The Red Sox won again in 2007 and 2013.

How many fans gave up over those eighty-six years, calling the Red Sox "losers"? How many prayed for a victory, just one, and never saw it, dying without ever seeing their beloved team triumph? But for some, the miracle happened, and the town went crazy.

Enduring, persevering, hanging in there is one of the hardest things to do in life. It means to try, try, and try again, even if defeated every time. Some eventually do give up. They turn to alcohol or bitterness or other destructive means of avoiding or dealing with their pain.

Christians are not immune. The Christian life is a marathon, and it takes much determination and endurance to reach the end whole. Don't give up the struggle. Refuse to throw in the towel. Keep in the race. If you do press on, God will reward you one day, and that reward will literally be out of this world.

DON'T FEAR

Don't be afraid, for I am with you. Don't be discouraged,
for I am your God. I will strengthen you and help you.
I will hold you up with my victorious right hand.

ISAIAH 41:10

FEAR CAN PARALYZE a person, even a Christian. Worry about anything, and everything, can waylay you quickly.

The antidote is a passage such as the one above. This is one of those great promises of the Bible that many Christians memorize early on in their faith. It's so full of great spiritual power that you should get it right now firmly treasured in your heart so you can refer to it at any moment.

Just look at what it says. First, God is with you. Considering he's the biggest guy on the block, that should be strong assurance. Second, he says, "I am your God." That means the only true God is the one you worship and trust. No one can stop or derail him. Third, he will "strengthen you and help you." Who better to do that than the almighty, all-knowing, all-wise, and all-present one? Last, he says he will "hold you up with [his] victorious right hand." The immense right hand of God holds up small, insignificant you. You cannot be anything but victorious.

Are you afraid? Discouraged? Feeling weak and overwhelmed? Get this verse into your heart, and then ask God to make the promise a reality in your life. It's a promise he will never fail to keep.

OLD LIFE GONE

Anyone who belongs to Christ has become a new person.
The old life is gone; a new life has begun!
2 CORINTHIANS 5:17

JULIE LISTENED RAPTLY to the Bible study leader. She called herself a seeker and wasn't really sure about this "Jesus thing." But as she listened to the leader talk about this passage, something ignited in her. She so wanted to be a new person. Her life was filled with bad decisions, mistakes, and sins she knew she never should have committed, and she wished for a new start.

She held up her hand. "Is this what being born again is all about?"

"Absolutely," the teacher responded. "Just like a newborn baby, unseen before, so God in Christ starts us over at that moment, and we are new on the inside."

Julie immediately said she wanted that—she would become a Christian if someone showed her how. The leader led her in prayer, and from that day on, Julie was a new person, with different values, different desires, and a new power to overcome her old ways.

The promise here is not just that you get a new start in life, or a second chance. No, Paul says you become utterly new on the inside. You are no longer an unforgiven sinner, broken, full of guilt, insecure, and struggling with all kinds of sins. Instead, God takes you and leads you in a totally different direction. Your life will never be the same again.

SET YOUR FACE

Because the Sovereign LORD helps me, I will not be disgraced.
Therefore, I have set my face like a stone, determined to do
his will. And I know that I will not be put to shame.

ISAIAH 50:7

STONE MOUNTAIN PARK is a popular attraction outside of Atlanta. The park boasts authentic plantation buildings, a pioneer village, a museum, a steamboat, a train, a laser show, and more. But the center and highlight of the park is Stone Mountain itself.

Some people say Stone Mountain is the largest exposed granite stone in the world. It has no trees or vegetation atop it—or not enough to matter. It's a big rock standing 825 feet high, and its top is 1,683 feet above sea level. On one side of the mountain is the world's largest relief sculpture, depicting three confederate heroes on their horses.

No matter how many times you visit the mountain or how long you gaze at the carving, it stays the same. The generals' faces will forever look in the same direction they're facing. Stone faces don't have the option of turning around and looking back the other way.

When it comes to following the Lord, Scripture tells us our "faces" should be like those in this carving—set in one direction, the direction of following the Lord.

When we're tempted to let ourselves be distracted by sin and other problems, let's remember those confederate generals and keep our direction set, determined to do God's will! We will not be put to shame.

IN THE PRESENCE OF GOD

Let us go right into the presence of God with sincere hearts fully trusting him. For our guilty consciences have been sprinkled with Christ's blood to make us clean, and our bodies have been washed with pure water.

HEBREWS 10:22

IN THE DAYS when Jesus was on the earth, one of the great problems for all Jews was the sense of God's aloofness. No one could go into the presence of God in the Temple except the high priest. He could do that only once a year, on the Day of Atonement, and when he went in, it was to make a special blood offering for the sins of the nation.

Every Jew who came into the Temple saw that separation. God was distinct, separate, utterly removed from his people.

But Jesus broke down that barrier. In Matthew 27:51, Matthew says that when Jesus died, the curtain, or veil, that separated the outer court from the inner court where God dwelled was torn in two. This symbolized the fact that anyone could now come in faith into God's presence.

When you pray and when you worship, you literally enter the presence of God. You can't see him, but you are there. You have a personal relationship with him in which he is your Father. What a great promise it is that we have access to the living God at any time, anywhere.

DEPENDENCE ON GOD

God blesses those who are poor and realize their need
for him, for the Kingdom of Heaven is theirs.

MATTHEW 5:3

SOME CALL THESE verses the "Be-attitudes" after their Latin name, the *Beatitudes*. In a sense, they're the kinds of attitudes and ways of looking at and dealing with life that God most wants us to employ in our daily living. What do they mean?

Let's take the first one. To be "poor and realize their need for him" just about says it all. This beatitude is about humility before God and your recognition of your need of him—his support, his blessings, and everything else under the sun. Those who think of themselves as "self-made" and who "need no one and nothing" are the antithesis of this kind of person. They will never get anything from God. He will leave them to their own resources because that's the way they want it.

But the humble person who recognizes dependence on God for everything will find not only God's blessing but the promise of the Kingdom itself. All it takes is humility, acknowledging your need, and wow!—you've got the resources of heaven at your feet!

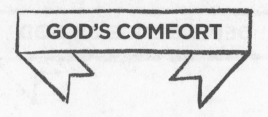

GOD'S COMFORT

We are confident that as you share in our sufferings,
you will also share in the comfort God gives us.
2 CORINTHIANS 1:7

IF YOU HAVE ever seen the movie or read the book *The Hiding Place*, you know the trials Corrie ten Boom and her family endured at the hands of the Nazis during World War II. Their "crime" had been to harbor Jewish people in their home. Corrie and her sister, Betsie, were interned in Ravensbrück, a women's concentration camp, where death and torture were the daily fare of the inmates.

When Betsie died from a horrible whipping and general sickness during her time there, Corrie almost fell into despair. But God did a number of things to comfort her. Among them, in one wintry call to attention, a little bird came and sang to the inmates as they stood freezing in the cold. On another occasion, she felt God had even sent the lice in their barracks to keep the guards from stepping in and breaking up their Bible studies. Because Betsie had been such a woman of faith, when she died, the mortician prepared her body so that in Corrie's mind Betsie looked like a queen, even though dead.

God doesn't always give us comfort in our sufferings the way we might ask or wish. But his comfort always comes, and it's often far better and more powerful than any we might imagine. As you go through times of trouble, look for God's comfort to come, as he has promised.

BE KIND TO THE POOR

Oh, the joys of those who are kind to the poor! The LORD
rescues them when they are in trouble. The LORD protects
them and keeps them alive. He gives them prosperity in the
land and rescues them from their enemies. The LORD nurses
them when they are sick and restores them to health.

PSALM 41:1-3

YOU'VE PROBABLY SEEN them, standing at intersections and holding signs saying they'll work for food. Beggars will walk the streets and step right up to you and ask for a dollar or two. In some countries, they're everywhere: on every corner, in every neighborhood. Some just sit and stare vacantly, clearly hungry, clearly in despair, just hoping for the next handout.

Do we ignore them? Write them off as alcoholics or druggies who take whatever we might give them and throw it away on their addiction? The truth is, God doesn't call you to be responsible for how the poor use your handouts. He simply asks that you notice them and, when you can, give them something to meet their needs.

There are hundreds of organizations out there that minister to the poor of all nations, from the United States to many we've never heard of. Giving to those organizations or even directly to the poor is not wasted money or a waste of time. God's promise is that he will bless your efforts and use your resources to feed and care for the needy. Stop walking by them. God will bless you for your compassion and love.

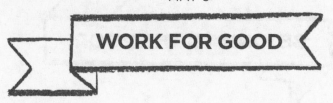

WORK FOR GOOD

We know that God causes everything to work together for the good of those who love God and are called according to his purpose for them.

ROMANS 8:28

PERHAPS THE GREATEST promise in all of Scripture, today's verse assures us of several things. One is that God really is in charge of the events in our lives. That doesn't necessarily mean that he causes them. But everything that happens to us is known to God and under his control.

Think of people such as Moses, who killed an Egyptian taskmaster. Moses fled from Pharaoh and spent the next forty years in the desert as a lowly shepherd. But God had not forgotten him. In fact, God probably used that time to help build qualities such as perseverance, determination, and humility into Moses' life. After those forty years, when God called Moses to return to Egypt, he went, and he became one of the greatest leaders in human history.

The second truth in the verse above relates to the word *everything*. Nothing in your life happens by accident. Nothing.

A third truth is that God makes everything "work together for . . . good." Somehow, even the bad things in our lives can be stitched together by God for our good. We may not see it right away, but he will make it all clear in time.

Last, he does this only for his children. Just as with Moses, God will work for good in our lives when bad things happen.

It's a great truth to hold on to in good times and bad. It's a promise that we can trust no matter how difficult things seem at any given moment.

IN THE LIGHT

Once you were full of darkness, but now you have
light from the Lord. So live as people of light!
EPHESIANS 5:8

HAVE YOU EVER stepped into a dark bathroom in a hotel, switched on the light, and seen ugly things scatter? It can be a jarring experience, but in places where bugs, cockroaches, spiders, and other insects find a home, they often come out at night. Why? Because there is safety for them in the dark.

In the same way, much of the havoc people wreak on others is done in the dark. Not necessarily in the dark of night, but in places where others cannot see or intrude. Robbers go into dark houses to do their dirty work. Adulterers find out-of-the-way places to carry out their trysts. Murderers generally try to find moments when people are not prepared, behind closed doors and out of sight.

What things did you used to do in the dark? God says that if you're a Christian, you're a new person now—a person of light. Walk in that light. Live openly, without guilt or regret. Do your good deeds everywhere you can. God promises that your life in the light will preach more effectively than simply saying good words.

GOD'S ON YOUR SIDE

*My enemies will retreat when I call to you for
help. This I know: God is on my side!*

PSALM 56:9

SUE DIDN'T KNOW what hit her. One minute she was enjoying her job as
a middle school special-needs teacher and receiving praise from parents
and administration alike. The next minute Jeni, the new district supervisor, began stirring up trouble. Jeni suggested that Sue try procedures
that she was already using—and she wouldn't listen when Sue pointed
that out. Though Sue had served wonderfully as a special-needs teacher
for seven years, thanks to Jeni's unfair criticism, Sue's principal began
to doubt Sue's ability.

The teacher's aides who worked with the students in Sue's class seemed
to smell blood and decided to get in on the act. Sue cared about them
and had gone overboard to be a good supervisor to them for seven years
—even covering for their lateness and other problems. Yet they suddenly
turned on her too.

Even one of the parents started blaming Sue for her son's Down syn-
drome. Everywhere she turned, it seemed that Sue was facing people who
were suddenly against her.

How did Sue respond to this conflict? She enveloped herself in prayer
more than ever before. She prayed for the young district supervisor and
her aides. Though she'd always prayed for her employees, students, and
students' families, she now prayed even more fervently for those who had
become her enemies. Soon things began to turn around in her favor.

Sue learned that the promises of God hold true. Even though others
may be against us, when we call upon him, he will vanquish our enemies
and uphold us with his might and power.

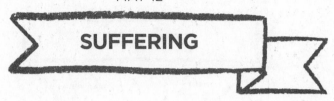

SUFFERING

*What we suffer now is nothing compared to
the glory he will reveal to us later.*

ROMANS 8:18

MANY CHRISTIANS EXPERIENCE suffering every day. Perhaps they struggle with chronic illnesses, addictions, financial problems they simply can't solve, or other situations that leave them weary and broken.

Some suffering is more emotional in nature. One man who runs a home business has worked for years to make a good profit. Yet sometimes it looks as though things are getting worse instead of better, and he wonders how he'll provide for his family.

A woman married to an alcoholic prays daily for her husband's salvation. She tearfully stumbles into her weekly support group feeling she really has no hope.

Others suffer in silence, never telling their friends or relatives what it's really like to live in their skins. One man, blind and suffering from chronic pain, gets little help from doctors. They simply don't know how to help him.

Similarly, Paul knew what it was to suffer. You can read about the things he went through in 2 Corinthians 11:23-29. His difficulties ranged from being beaten with rods three different times to being stoned. Yet Paul kept looking up. What did he see? As this passage says, he realized that no matter what he faced in this world, it didn't compare at all to the greatness of the next.

God promises to take you out of this world to another, where every hope is fulfilled. So refuse to look at your troubles and think that they will go on forever. They won't.

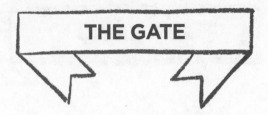

THE GATE

*[Jesus said,] "I am the gate. Those who come in through me will be
saved. They will come and go freely and will find good pastures."*
JOHN 10:9

TO MAKE PLAIN his truth and ideas, Jesus often gave his listeners analo-
gies, word pictures, parables and stories, and various other examples that
explained some of the hard issues of Scripture. This verse is one of them.
Jesus wanted us to think of him as a gate. If we walk up to him, push open
the gate, and walk through, we will find salvation.

Instantly, like sheep, we find that Jesus is the gate to blessings in this
world and the next. Our vistas become clear. We find freedom in the
world to do what we most want to do, to seek fulfillment of our dreams,
and to enjoy life to the fullest.

The foundation, though, is Jesus. He is the gate. No one else is, or
could be, that gate. We must go through his gate. Believe in him. Trust
him. Acknowledge him. Follow him. In other passages, Jesus makes clear
that there are many false gates in this world. Only the one true gate leads
to fulfillment and joy: Jesus himself.

Jesus' great promise is that real blessing is to be found only in him.
He is the way to all the hopes and dreams and blessings you seek, and he
will give them to you freely and willingly.

MAY 14

A PLACE OF SAFETY

*I will sing about your power. Each morning I will sing
with joy about your unfailing love. For you have been
my refuge, a place of safety when I am in distress.*

PSALM 59:16

"I REALLY JUST need to talk to someone about the challenges we're facing," Anita told her friend Zeta.

"Go ahead. I'm all ears," Zeta encouraged. "And besides that, I'm a safe person to talk to. My house is a safe place. You can say what you want, and it will stay right here."

With that reassurance, Anita poured out her heart.

We all need people like Zeta and the safe places they offer. Places where we won't be threatened or face danger, emotionally or even physically. Places where we can live in the freedom of being ourselves. Places where we can go to regroup, revive, and maybe even heal when we feel out of sorts with the world.

God offers us that kind of place. When we feel emotionally beaten, he tells us to come to him for safety and rest. When we've been fighting spiritual battles, holding out against the wiles of Satan, God tells us to take refuge in him. When we're threatened by others seemingly stronger than ourselves, he is our defender and protector.

We can trust God to be our fortress because he made us for himself. We are his lambs, and he tells us it's his job to keep the wolves at bay.

As we realize that God offers us a place of safety, we can cheerfully, confidently face whatever the day may bring.

SHARING HIS GLORY

Since we are his children, we are his heirs. In fact,
together with Christ we are heirs of God's glory.
ROMANS 8:17

DAN SAT NERVOUSLY with several others as he listened to the lawyer for his deceased friend's estate read the will. Since Bruce had died without a family, none of his friends or neighbors knew what he might have willed to any of them.

In time, the will mentioned Dan and advised that he'd be receiving a substantial bequest from Bruce's estate. Dan was overjoyed, and he promptly went out and partied.

Finding yourself an heir to someone's fortune can be a big moment for anyone. But what if you discovered that one day you would inherit God's fortune? Since he owns the whole universe, that could be a tidy sum indeed.

What might God give us? The Bible speaks of such things as vast wealth, mansions, positions of honor and authority, the right to eat from certain food-producing trees, and so on. But what about talents, gifts of character, or the opportunity to sit with Jesus on his throne?

Do any of those things sound awesome to you? There's one more we've forgotten: the promise that God will also let us share his glory. What does that mean? No one can be completely sure, but God's glory is the respect, honor, reverence, and love due him because he's the greatest being in existence.

WIPE AWAY YOUR TEARS

*He will wipe every tear from their eyes, and there will be no more
death or sorrow or crying or pain. All these things are gone forever.*
REVELATION 21:4

IT'S HARD TO imagine a world without tears, death, sorrow, and pain,
but that is what God promises in this passage. At times, it seems almost
too good to be true. How can being in heaven possibly take away the pain
of loss, the horrors of persecution and torture that some Christians face,
and just the plain grief that comes to all of us?

God has revealed several ways heaven will be wonderful: first, heaven
will be so incredible that we can't even imagine it now, and when we get
there, everything we went through on earth will pale in comparison. The
pain will be forgotten. Have you ever experienced the birth of a child?
The pain is tremendous. But how quickly it is forgotten when that tiny,
lovely child is placed in your arms!

A second aspect of heaven is that God's comfort will be supernaturally
powerful, greater even than the comforts he showed us on earth. Some
have written of how God came to them in a time of pain and suffering.
Even a moment of his amazing love can help so much.

No matter how bad it has been for you here on earth, God's promise
is that one day, all sorrow will be a thing of the past—forgotten, healed,
left behind.

GOD GIVES JUSTICE

Look at my servant, whom I strengthen. He is my chosen one,
who pleases me. I have put my Spirit upon him. He will bring
justice to the nations. He will not shout or raise his voice in public.
He will not crush the weakest reed or put out a flickering candle.
He will bring justice to all who have been wronged. He will not
falter or lose heart until justice prevails throughout the earth.
Even distant lands beyond the sea will wait for his instruction.

ISAIAH 42:1-4

YEARS AGO, A popular Christian song told us that "Jesus is the answer" to all the problems of the world. It's still true. Who is the answer to the lack of justice in our world? To its cruelty? To how so many people are oppressed, hated, tortured? To the way some nations carelessly oppress or destroy their own people?

For those who seek justice in our world, Jesus remains the only viable answer. No other person or god promises real hope to those who live under tyranny or who have been hurt, wounded, or put down by their culture.

But Jesus isn't only a dispenser of justice. From the Scripture above, we learn of his compassion, his gentleness, his care for people. He would never inflict pain or destroy someone emotionally for no apparent reason. He looks over the world for people who believe in him and are oppressed to give them help and comfort. The truth is that no injustice in this world will be overlooked or forgotten. Every child of God will see justice done. That's God's solemn promise.

THE CHAIN

*These are the gifts Christ gave to the church: the apostles, the prophets,
the evangelists, and the pastors and teachers. Their responsibility is
to equip God's people to do his work and build up the church, the
body of Christ. This will continue until we all come to such unity in
our faith and knowledge of God's Son that we will be mature in the
Lord, measuring up to the full and complete standard of Christ.*

EPHESIANS 4:11-13

WHAT A DIFFERENCE ten years can make! Especially in a family.

If you're a parent, you can probably remember when it seemed that
your kids squabbled nonstop. But what a difference after the kids start
maturing! Then family times can become relaxing times of enjoying one
another's company. As they mature, children start to live up to a different
standard—they start acting like adults. At various times, the Bible writers
refer to quarreling believers as "little children." Sometimes believers in
churches have to mature, just as children do!

How do we reach that stage of maturity? So many times we go to
church looking for what *we* can get out of it and expecting the church to
be structured the way *we* want.

Instead, perhaps we should focus on how we can serve others through
the distinct abilities God has given us. As we minister to others, we
mature and grow personally. And as a result, God's promise is that we
affect the whole church in a positive way.

Just as a chain is only as strong as its weakest link, our churches are
only as strong as the weakest believer. Let's use our gifts to build a church
full of fruitful, effective, mature Christians.

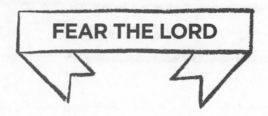

FEAR THE LORD

Charm is deceptive, and beauty does not last; but a
woman who fears the LORD will be greatly praised.

PROVERBS 31:30

MANY WOMEN, EVEN Christian women, can be discouraged by the pictures of beautiful models on magazine covers. No matter a model's age, her wrinkle-free face, full hair, and slim figure can make women feel as if they don't measure up.

But this world has a serious problem: all of us age. Photoshop eliminates signs of aging, but all of us wrinkle, dry up, lose our looks, and become less—or physically more!—than what we were.

What makes the difference among God's people as they age? Fearing the Lord, according to this proverb. What separates those who will be praised all their lives from the rest is not charm, beauty, or anything physical. Rather it's their inner selves, their character.

Do you see yourself as a person who "fears the LORD"? What does that mean? It signifies respect, reverence, awe, obedience to his Word, faith, and other godly attitudes and habits. These are the qualities that distinguish you from those who do not fear the Lord. At the heart of the matter is your inner self. What resides there? God promises that you will be praised to the end of your days because of your reverence for God more than for any charm or beauty you possessed in your youth.

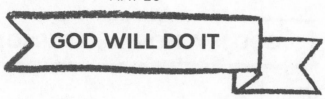

GOD WILL DO IT

You can ask for anything in my name, and I will do it,
so that the Son can bring glory to the Father.
JOHN 14:13

WHEN YOU ASK people to tell you their stories of answered prayer, you never know what you'll hear, but you can be sure that you'll get a great variety of responses and that you will be amazed at the scope of God's power and love.

There are healings from physical infirmities. Financial miracles. Restoration of relationships. Spiritual growth. You'll hear all that and much more when you start inquiring about answered prayers.

And it's no wonder, considering the enormity of the promise we find in this verse. Jesus told his listeners they could ask for *anything* in his name and he would do it.

Does that mean God's like a slot machine—you put your prayer in and get your riches out? The key is to ask in Jesus' name with a pure heart and unselfish motives. Another key is to ask for something that will bring glory to the Father.

Just think. We have unlimited access to the one who has unlimited power. He not only *allows* us to bring our needs and issues to him but also *encourages* us to. He wants us to ask so that he can answer. He wants to say yes!

If you have a hard time believing that God wants to do good things in your life, even grant your heart's desires, just ask others about how he's answered prayers in their lives. Memorize today's verse. And ask him in confident faith. Ask in Jesus' name, and just see what he'll do to bless you and glorify his Father.

GOD IS A MORNING PERSON

Great is his faithfulness; his mercies begin afresh each morning.
LAMENTATIONS 3:23

CHARLIE WAS NOT a morning person, and he let everyone know it. He joked that his midmorning third cup of coffee was the magic elixir to get him in high gear. He often felt overwhelmed by his problems at home and at work, taxing his strength and exhausting him. Yet his wife, Amber, seemed to roll with the punches and was able to handle all that came at her.

One night as Amber was getting into bed, Charlie asked his wife, "How do you pull it off, Amber?" So she told him her secret—just like manna in the desert, God had a fresh batch of mercy for her every morning before she started her day. He was faithful in terms of equipping her to handle life's stresses after she had communed with him and "fed" on his Word.

Charlie decided to go to bed a bit earlier and see if getting up early enough to spend time with God would work for him, too. After a few mornings with his new routine, Charlie found that his days didn't seem so exhausting—physically or spiritually. He found new mercies ready and waiting at the start of each day.

See how faithful God is as you start each day with him. He never slumbers or sleeps, and he can't wait for you to spend some intimate time with him. He loves it when you let him know he's the first thought in your day. And he promises to show you bountiful mercies when you do.

Feed on the Word of God. He promises blessings beyond anything you could imagine.

HARVESTING

*Those who plant in tears will harvest with shouts of joy. They weep as
they go to plant their seed, but they sing as they return with the harvest.*

PSALM 126:5-6

PLANTING SEASON DOESN'T always look perfect. Rains might not come.
The seeds can be eaten by crows and other birds. Other predators can
turn a hopeful crop into a disaster. That's the risk of farming.

The image in today's verses goes beyond agriculture, though. It paral-
lels what happens when you plant the seed of God's Word in the hearts of
those you love and hope it will bear a harvest. Often such plantings are
done with tears. We admonish friends or relatives, "Please listen to this.
It's a matter of life and death." They may laugh in our faces. They may
even pity us for our strange beliefs. But we know the truth: those who
reject Christ will face a dark eternity.

That's where the tears come in. We so desperately want to see people
saved, brought into the fold, and made a part of our eternal family. And
many times, it's years before we see the harvest. How many people have
you prayed for since you became a Christian—perhaps for decades—with
no apparent change or interest on their part?

God's promise, though, is that the harvest is coming. One day, you
will see many of those seeds come to fruition. So don't despair. Keep
planting. God will not waste the seed you have obediently scattered. The
harvest is out there, and one day you will see the fruit of your labor.

GOD'S SPIRIT IS WITH US

*My Spirit remains among you, just as I promised when
you came out of Egypt. So do not be afraid.*

HAGGAI 2:5

HAGGAI IS ONE of the shortest books in the Bible. The book was an announcement to the Israelites that it was time to rebuild the Lord's Temple in Jerusalem.

God knew this was not going to be a particularly easy job for the Israelites. After all, the former glorious Temple had been in ruins for quite some time, and there were enemies all around. The Israelites were weak from being disciplined, and they had meager resources. Some would have serious doubts that a splendid Temple could be rebuilt in their lifetimes.

God gives us challenging tasks to do, just as he did with the Israelites. They may seem completely out of our reach. Some of us may just give up, thinking the job is impossible or we don't have the needed skills.

But no job is impossible when God tells us it's part of his plan and it's time to do it. Yes, it may be difficult, and God may be the first to acknowledge that! But just as he promised to be with the Israelites when they left Egypt and when they were called to rebuild the Temple, he is with us in life's tough assignments. His Spirit empowers us with his wisdom and perseverance.

We can complete any task God calls us to because he's always there—to protect, equip, and sustain us.

BLESSINGS FOR ENDURANCE

*God blesses those who patiently endure testing and
temptation. Afterward they will receive the crown of life
that God has promised to those who love him.*

JAMES 1:12

THREE-YEAR-OLD TYLER IS not very patient. He gets frustrated when
he has to wait. Sometimes as the frustration builds, he behaves in inappropriate ways. And that just gets him into trouble.

Over and over again, Tyler's parents try to teach him to be patient, to
endure the slowness of certain aspects of life, so he won't get frustrated
and throw a temper tantrum. Some days, though, they wonder if Tyler,
in his immaturity, will ever learn.

We adults at times don't seem to make a lot more progress than Tyler.
Patience isn't easy for any of us. Especially when we're enduring the tough
stuff of life. We just want it to be over . . . now! We want God to answer all
our prayers with smooth sailing and clear guidance, and on our timetable.

Even though we're Christians, life doesn't always work out the way
we want it to. No matter what spiritual maturity level we've achieved,
sometimes we still have to relearn and practice how to be patient. We
just have to wait and cling to God, trusting and obeying him until the
ordeals, in his timing, are over.

But while we're enduring, we can remember God's promise to us: he
will bless us when we patiently endure the trials. Patience doesn't come
from us; it's a gift of the Spirit.

So when the going gets tough, the tough Christian remembers God's
promise of an eventual crown of glory. It's worth waiting patiently for
such a great reward!

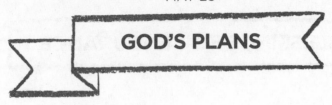

GOD'S PLANS

*"I know the plans I have for you," says the LORD. "They are plans
for good and not for disaster, to give you a future and a hope."*
JEREMIAH 29:11

HOW MANY TIMES have you seen this verse on a graduation card or encouragement plaque? It's a wonderful verse. However, most people don't know the story behind the Scripture.

God was giving instructions to the Israelites. They had been conquered by the Babylonians, had been carried away to be slaves, and were now living in exile. He told them that although they would have to live in Babylon for seventy years, he would bring them back to their homeland. He assured them that although things looked bleak, he hadn't forgotten about them and he still had good plans in store for them.

We, too, can take heart from this promise. God never guaranteed that our lives would be easy. But even when God allows difficulties to enter our lives, we can remember that he has a great future in mind for us. He has a plan that will bring good to us, not disaster.

Whether the road ahead is smooth or bumpy, remember that it leads to a positive future!

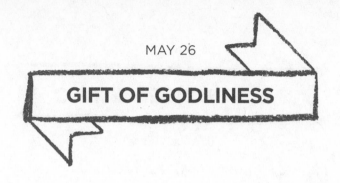

GIFT OF GODLINESS

By his divine power, God has given us everything we need for living
a godly life. We have received all of this by coming to know him, the one
who called us to himself by means of his marvelous glory and excellence.

2 PETER 1:3

HOW DO YOU measure godliness in your life? Justine has a list:

Serve at the soup kitchen—check.
Read my Bible—check.
Go to church—check.
Go to Bible study—check.
Give donation to the mission organization—check.

Justine feels that doing all these things is proof that she's godly.

All the things on Justine's list are great activities that help her grow closer to God and others. But do they really make her godly?

According to the Scripture verse above, godliness does not begin with what we do but with who we are. In this verse, God lets us know that he's taken care of everything we need to be godly people. We don't incorporate godliness on our own. We're godly because we belong to him. The better we know him, the more like God we become. It's a promise that depends on what he's done—not on what we do to try to please him.

In fact, when we stress and strive to achieve godliness, in a sense we're trying to work hard enough to earn what God has already given us. Devotion and good deeds will flow from the fact that in him we are already godly.

As we rest in our relationship with him, his grace empowers us to do the things that please him. He's promised that he's already provided what we need to be like him. As we trust that promise, the process will not be a duty or an ordeal but a privilege and a joy.

ALL YOU NEED IS TWO

[Jesus said,] "If two of you agree here on earth concerning anything you ask, my Father in heaven will do it for you. For where two or three gather together as my followers, I am there among them."
MATTHEW 18:19-20

THIS IS A great truth about prayer. What does it mean? Many times you have probably prayed in your home or while sitting in church, and you've received tremendous answers. But many times we, on our own, simply don't know how to pray or what to ask for.

That's where today's verses help. When we seek other Christians of like mind, whom we can trust and who offer us wise and thoughtful counsel, we can sharpen those prayers. We can hear the thoughts and ideas of our counselors in figuring out precisely what and how to pray.

The real beauty here is the promise: if all of you agree, whether it's two, four, or eighteen of you, you can be much more certain God has heard and will answer than when you simply shoot in the dark, not knowing what things to consider as you make your request. The Bible says that the Holy Spirit will pray for you, knowing what the real needs are (see Romans 8:26).

Friends are wonderful helps in this world. Fellowship can make life seem all the better. But when you get together with your Christian friends, let them know what's on your heart. God's promise is to be present in an even more powerful way and to answer your prayers.

NO LONGER SLAVES

We know that our old sinful selves were crucified with Christ so that
sin might lose its power in our lives. We are no longer slaves to sin.

ROMANS 6:6

SLAVERY WAS ONCE a big issue in the United States and Great Britain. Many people rose up to fight it, and eventually slavery as an institution was terminated in these countries. Today, trafficking in different forms is still practiced throughout the world.

Spiritual slavery is not talked about much, but it's a far more virulent brand of enslavement. It keeps people from being able to break the power of sin in their lives. They may have addictions, terrible habits, or numerous other ways sin has struck. But they seem powerless to overcome this slavery.

Though people sometimes do overcome the worst kinds of sinful addictions—drugs, alcohol, and sex—many others cannot. Until Jesus comes into their lives. Jesus came to destroy the power of sin. He did just that on the cross. Those who trust and love him will find in him not only a great friend and forgiver but also a source of power and support. God says he will not fail us. In Christ he will enable all of us to defeat sin in our lives now, and we will live without sin in heaven forever.

HELP THE DESTITUTE

He will listen to the prayers of the destitute. He will not reject their pleas.
PSALM 102:17

GOD HAS A special place in his heart for hurting, broken people. They often are the most likely to call on God for help because they really have nowhere else to turn.

A woman in India suffered from leprosy. Her family sent her away, and she lived in a colony where only lepers lived. Even the other lepers hated her because of her condition—they were afraid she might make them worse. With no friends anywhere, she wanted to die. But one day she heard about Jesus from a traveling preacher and decided to call on God because that preacher quoted the verse above.

God soon answered her prayer by having a church come out to the colony and offer food and help to the lepers. Several Christians befriended her, and soon she began to attend their services. One day, during testimony time, she stood up. "I have become a Christian, and I thank God for making me a leper because it was only then that I saw my real need. I know I'll always be a leper in this world. But in the next, I will be clean and perfect. And you people gave me that. Thank you, and thank God."

This kind of story is repeated over and over in the Christian world. It's when people get down low that they're most likely to call on God. His promise is that he hears the prayers of any needy person and will not turn away. Ever.

HE BORE THE PENALTY

I will give [my righteous servant] the honors of a victorious soldier,
because he exposed himself to death. He was counted among the
rebels. He bore the sins of many and interceded for rebels.

ISAIAH 53:12

OUR WORLD OFFERS many honors. The Pulitzer Prize is awarded for various types of journalistic and literary writing. Those who show excellence in television productions receive an Emmy. The Nobel Prize is given to those who achieve great success in the arts and sciences. Add to these the Oscar, the MacArthur "Genius" Grant Award, the Grammy, and numerous other awards. Victorious soldiers receive medals for their heroic actions. Even Christian organizations give awards to those who have excelled in different niches and skills.

What prize do you think Jesus deserves for what he did? Saving us. Dying for our sins. Destroying death once and for all. Giving us valuable and life-transforming teachings. Interceding for us now at the right hand of God. Performing miracles of help, healing, and power.

In Isaiah 53, the prophet paints a picture of Jesus as the suffering servant of God. But after all his pain and trouble, the passage comes to this final moment: revealing the honors God will give to him.

Jesus, however, isn't interested in medals, trophies, statues, or other awards. What he wants is our love, honor, and worship. When we give him these heartfelt offerings, he promises to shower us with awards and gifts too. He will give us a special calling to fulfill his work. Then, when we honor and follow his example, we, too, will share in his rewards.

UNFAILING LOVE

*His unfailing love toward those who fear him is as great as
the height of the heavens above the earth. He has removed
our sins as far from us as the east is from the west.*

PSALM 103:11-12

TIM LAY OUT on a hill, gazing up at the stars of the night. He had been reading his Bible and came upon this passage about how great God's love is. He wondered how the person of David's day would have perceived that, so he went out on the hill. In time, he realized how high above him the heavens were. Of course, he knew from science that the closest stars were more than four light-years away. The people of David's day didn't have such calculations. But what did it matter? To David and the people of his day, the stars appeared far away, more distant than even the sun itself.

Thinking about the analogy to God's love, Tim remembered a book he had read his daughter about a little rabbit who asked his father if he loved him as far as his little arms could reach. The father held out his own arms, much farther, saying, "But I love you this much." He remembered the connection with the cross as Jesus opened his arms on the cross and took our sins.

If Tim were to say to God, "Do you love me to the top of my head?"

"No," God would answer, "to the top of the mountains!"

If Tim asked, "But if I'm at the top there?"

God would say then, "As high as the clouds." Eventually, Tim would get to the stars. Seeing it that way made him realize that God's love for him and all others is greater than he could ever imagine, and it is a love that will never fail.

JUNE

FIGHTING THE CHAMP

*Put on every piece of God's armor so you will be able to resist the enemy
in the time of evil. Then after the battle you will still be standing firm.*

EPHESIANS 6:13

FROM THE MOMENT David heard Goliath's taunts and saw the Israelites cowering, he knew that this was a battle that had his name on it (see 1 Samuel 17). So on behalf of his people and God, David accepted the giant's challenge. The king tried to deck David out with the very best armor in the land.

But it didn't work. David wasn't used to armor, and it was so heavy he couldn't even move in it. Instead, he chose the simple weapons he was used to and trusted God to bring the victory, knowing it was the Lord's battle. And sure enough, the battle was won!

Many times in life we're called on to battle the enemy. But today's Scripture verse gives us the advice that David also had to learn: when we're fighting the Lord's battles, we can win them only as we use the weapons he's provided. Our own fleshly weapons will be ineffective in spiritual warfare. So we have to follow his directives. When we put on God's armor, the different parts of our lives are covered. With his armor we experience his protection, and we are able to overcome the enemies of our souls.

Have you been trying to use your own weapons to fight your spiritual battles? Make sure you're using the perfect weapons God has given you, not the heavy armor of the world.

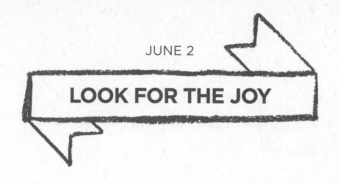

LOOK FOR THE JOY

*Be truly glad. There is wonderful joy ahead, even though you must
endure many trials for a little while. These trials will show that your faith
is genuine. It is being tested as fire tests and purifies gold—though your
faith is far more precious than mere gold. So when your faith remains
strong through many trials, it will bring you much praise and glory and
honor on the day when Jesus Christ is revealed to the whole world.*

1 PETER 1:6-7

A PASSAGE IN one of C. S. Lewis's Chronicles of Narnia novels, *The Horse
and His Boy,* pictures the lion Aslan, who represents Jesus in the stories,
and the boy riding through the night.

On the way to his destination, the boy has seen many trials, each one
strangely accompanied by chasing and growling lions. The voice of Aslan
reveals to the boy that each of those lions has been Aslan himself, giving
him courage to ride harder or to escape dangerous forces, and he even
appeared as a cat that slumbered next to him on a cold night. The boy is
amazed to realize that God has been there through his every trial.

You may wonder why trials have come into your life. Maybe it's a
relationship problem such as betrayal or divorce. Maybe you've lost a
job you loved. Maybe it's sickness or the loss of a loved one. It could be
anything and everything, from an expensive car accident to almost dying
under a surgeon's knife.

What God reveals here is that all these trials have a purpose in your
life: to build and purify your faith. He lets you know plainly that one
day your faith will receive "praise and glory and honor" when you are
rewarded for your consistent commitment.

IF YOU DO NOT . . .

If you fear and worship the LORD and listen to his voice, and if you do not rebel against the LORD's commands, then both you and your king will show that you recognize the LORD as your God. But if you rebel against the LORD's commands and refuse to listen to him, then his hand will be as heavy upon you as it was upon your ancestors.

1 SAMUEL 12:14-15

SAMUEL'S SPEECH TO the people of Israel as they received their new king, Saul, applies to any nation that seeks to honor God. Those in America and other nations where God is remembered and worshiped should take these things to heart.

First, fear and worship God, and listen to his voice. What is God telling you personally today? What does that "still small voice" deep in your heart counsel? Don't worry about everyone else. Many in your country may have no real beliefs or commitment to God. But God knows who you are and what you're doing. You keep doing what's right before God, and he will bless you.

Second, refuse the impulse to rebel. There will always be times when you don't like what God may want you to do. To witness to that nasty neighbor. To admit some wrongdoing at your place of work. To apologize to a spouse or relative about something you know is wrong. Hear God's voice in your heart and obey, even if it hurts. God will bless you for your commitment and trust.

Third, realize that a big reason entire nations get into turmoil and trouble is because so many of their people have rebelled against God and the truth. If where you live is experiencing some upheaval—even conflict, maybe war—look back to God. Get yourself right with him, and encourage others to follow. That is the only way to bring God's mercy and favor back to your land.

GOD HAS CHOSEN THE POOR

Listen to me, dear brothers and sisters. Hasn't God chosen the poor in this world to be rich in faith? Aren't they the ones who will inherit the Kingdom he promised to those who love him?

JAMES 2:5

OUR WORLD IS so judgmental. Sheila, a single mom and immigrant, feels it in the stares people sometimes give her when she makes a mistake speaking her new language. Nathan, a homeless man, spends most of his time hiding in alleys because of the way the world treats him when he ventures out. Poor people everywhere know what happens when they walk into a restaurant or a store wearing shabby clothing. At times they're even asked to leave. People who can't pay their bills get nasty calls from bill collectors.

But God sees people differently. The poor are often the people who are rich in faith. He chooses many of them to be his, and he often overlooks the self-satisfied, proud, arrogant, rich people. Why? Because poor people know their needs, and they often respond gladly to God's call. Rich people, though, often don't see any need of God.

When you're tempted to judge people by their looks, clothing, car, house, or other standards, remember they are as much God's chosen as you are. And God promises to treat you well when you treat them well.

FOR THE GENTILES

*God wanted them to know that the riches and glory of Christ
are for you Gentiles, too. And this is the secret: Christ lives
in you. This gives you assurance of sharing his glory.*
COLOSSIANS 1:27

IN OUR CULTURE, when a man loves a woman and she agrees to marry him, he usually puts an engagement ring on her finger. This shows the world that these two people have made a commitment. The two plan to get married and be together for the rest of their lives. When he gives her that ring, trust, security, and hope all ignite in one burst of joy and love.

In the same way, God has given us a sort of engagement ring to assure us of his love and commitment to us. What is it? Jesus in you, in your heart, there to be your helper, friend, and comfort all at once. Take a few moments to think of the meaning of that living reality. Christianity isn't a religion of rules and rituals. It's a relationship in which God promises to work in our lives, bring us to fulfillment, perfect us, and fill us with every spiritual blessing.

It might be easy to dismiss such promises, but God has sealed them with a powerful presence: Jesus inside us. That's a fail-safe way of making sure we understand and appreciate the depth of God's commitment to us.

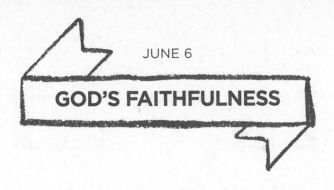

JUNE 6

GOD'S FAITHFULNESS

Your unfailing love will last forever. Your
faithfulness is as enduring as the heavens.

PSALM 89:2

SOME PEOPLE FEAR that God might change someday. He could cease to care about his people, get bored, and decide to start over with a whole new creation. Or his love might dry up and he'll suddenly go crazy and destroy everything because he is angry with this universe. None of this is possible. God's Word assures us over and over that God is eternal, that he is unfailingly loving and faithful, and that he can never change.

Nonetheless, why should we believe that? Just because he says it? How many of us have been promised things by people who seem honest on the surface but then turn out to be cheats? But when it comes to God, we have several things to assure us. First, his own testimony. He says he will never change, never desert us, always love us. Second, we have the stories of the Bible. In them we see God being faithful, ever and always. Next, there is the testimony of billions of Christians. Many attest to God's goodness. Finally, we have our own experience. Have we found him faithful in our own lives?

For many, such proofs are more than convincing. But if you need more, go to God. Ask him to show you his love and goodness. He promises to be faithful.

REFINING

I will bring that group through the fire and make them pure. I will refine them like silver and purify them like gold. They will call on my name, and I will answer them. I will say, "These are my people," and they will say, "The LORD is our God."

ZECHARIAH 13:9

GOD'S DISCIPLINE IS not fun. In fact, God says it's like being refined in fire. Have you ever watched a blacksmith or an artist refine some metal? Although the process doesn't look too bad at times, the reality is that the fire is very hot. The metal must melt. The impurities come to the surface, such as with silver or gold, and they must be scooped away. How does the fire work with Christians?

Troubles, disappointments, guilt, failure, anxiety, rejection—all kinds of things happen to us in this life, and God assures us that these are his means of refining us. Nothing ever happens to us by accident. It's all part of God's plan. God never causes evil or commits sinful acts against us, but he does allow difficulties and struggles to be a means of shaping us and changing us. He works around and through them to make us more like Christ.

Too many Christians think becoming a follower of Christ means having no more problems. But it's not that way at all. In fact, in some ways, following Christ means we may have even more problems because we choose not to go the way of the world. But God promises that he is refining us through the process and that one day we will emerge pure, beautiful, and perfect.

PRAY IN PRIVATE

*When you pray, go away by yourself, shut the door
behind you, and pray to your Father in private. Then
your Father, who sees everything, will reward you.*

MATTHEW 6:6

"THE ONLY CHANCE I have to steal a few minutes alone without my toddler is when I go into the bathroom," one mom moaned to her friend.

"You're fortunate," her friend replied. "Mine even follows me there."

Even if we're not at that stage of life when we have a little shadow, we all face interruptions and distractions that hinder us from truly concentrating on spending time with God.

In much of life, it's good to have an open-door policy—to be accessible to our family, friends, and work associates. But at times we just have to shut the door, figuratively or literally, for our own spiritual good.

For some people, shutting the door has meant just that—going into a room and shutting and locking the door while they commune with God. Others literally go into a prayer closet, where their family knows they are not to be disturbed. Some like to commune with God in a peaceful outdoor setting. Others may go to Starbucks to get away from the distractions of home. Susannah Wesley (1669–1742), "Mother of Methodism" and mom of nineteen children, reportedly was desperate enough to throw her apron over her head to get her private space with God.

When we're having a hard time maintaining a devotional time with God, perhaps we should put more emphasis on getting away from distractions. God is flexible; he'll meet us wherever we seek him.

THE MAN OF LAWLESSNESS

The man of lawlessness will be revealed, but the Lord
Jesus will kill him with the breath of his mouth and
destroy him by the splendor of his coming.

2 THESSALONIANS 2:8

UNDOUBTEDLY, THE MOST powerful human who will ever set foot on earth (apart from Jesus) will be this one: the man of lawlessness. Theologians identify him as the Antichrist, the one who will appear in the last days of the world. What will he be like, according to this passage?

He will be lawless. Isn't that enough? That doesn't necessarily mean that he will be a lawbreaker. Rather, he will be a law unto himself. Whatever he says to the world will be law, no matter how nasty, cruel, or crazy it might be. His wish will be the world's command.

Its people will kowtow to his every demand and will be mesmerized by his power. From other Scripture passages we know that this person will possess supernatural ability to do miracles, show signs in the heavens, and demonstrate all kinds of amazing power. Most of the people alive at the time will worship him as God.

Nonetheless, he is simply an imposter. And he will be destroyed with hardly a fight when Jesus returns. You can trust too, if you're around at that time, that God will rescue you from this imposter's deceptions and entrapments. Look to the Lord, and you will find him faithful and true.

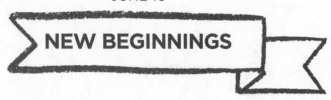

NEW BEGINNINGS

*You will be blessed if you obey the commands of the
LORD your God that I am giving you today.*
DEUTERONOMY 11:27

JESSI WAS BEGINNING a new way of life, and she was understandably a bit nervous about it. She was moving across the country to marry a man she'd been dating—primarily long distance—for a year.

With her move would come a new home, a new job, new friends, an unfamiliar church, and a whole new way of life. Even though Jessi's life was changing for a good reason—joining the man she loved—she wouldn't really know what was ahead for her until she jumped into the new world.

Jessi probably could understand a bit of what the Israelites were feeling at the time of today's Scripture verse. The Israelites were entering a new way of life in a new land, Canaan. There would be no more slavery like what they were used to in Egypt. But before they moved on, God led Moses to call them together and give them the instructions they would need for success in their new homeland.

We all go through new beginnings in life, whether a marriage, a new job, a new home, or a new social structure. But as we follow and obey the Lord, he promises to continue blessing us and being with us—even in the changes of life.

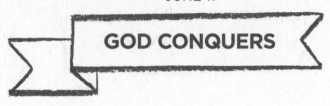

GOD CONQUERS

The LORD will conquer your enemies when they attack you. They will attack you from one direction, but they will scatter from you in seven!

DEUTERONOMY 28:7

BETTY AND TOM didn't like it when drugs and crime moved into their neighborhood. So they talked to God and felt called to do something about it. First of all, they began to work with their church, which was dying because long-term members were fleeing the area. Betty and Tom helped the church leadership adapt to the new circumstances to show the evolving neighborhood how Christ and the church could help them. Next, Betty joined the city council and helped plan ways to improve the neighborhood, such as planting flowers, cleaning up yards, and using her public relations skills to help the area get some positive press coverage.

Surprisingly, not everyone was happy about the changes. Before long some of the people at the church and a few on the city council began to attack Betty and Tom personally through hateful words and actions.

Though the word *enemy* seems a little extreme for individuals in our society, at times—especially when we're trying to serve the Lord—we'll encounter people who are intent on throwing roadblocks in our paths.

Just as the Israelites could count upon God to deal with their enemies, when we're following God's directions, we can count on God to take care of those who would keep us from answering his call in our lives. Just as God could take care of enemies then, he can send our enemies scooting today!

SUN AND SHIELD

The LORD God is our sun and our shield. He gives us grace and glory.
The LORD will withhold no good thing from those who do what is right.

PSALM 84:11

WHEN KEVIN HUNG up the phone after calming a vendor who was angry about an account problem, his boss stepped over to his desk. "I thought I told you we aren't paying the bill on that account until this customer fixes the problem on that machine we just bought."

Kevin took a deep breath. "This was for something else, not that machine. I don't think it's right to withhold the money for that when we owe it for the other thing that has worked out fine."

"Look, it's the only way to do business with these shysters," the boss seethed. "Call him back and tell him we aren't paying a cent till they get the machine fixed."

"It's not right!" Kevin fired back. "How do you feel when someone owes you money and cooks up some scheme not to pay for the wrong reasons?"

The boss looked away. "Fine. Take care of it. But I'm warning you: this attitude you have about always doing the right thing won't cut it in this business. Sometimes you have to play hardball."

Have you ever been in a situation like that? Ever been chewed out, demoted, even fired for doing the right thing? Take heart in the words of today's verse. God will bless you for your integrity. Just be patient while he takes care of the details.

SEEK FIRST

Seek the Kingdom of God above all else, and live
righteously, and he will give you everything you need.
MATTHEW 6:33

THIS VERSE IS Jesus' principle for overcoming worry. In the verses that precede this one, the Lord talks about the problem of anxiety and worry. Will I have enough food? Do I have a safe place to sleep tonight? Are there clothes in the closet?

For today's Christians, there are more things to worry about—finances, relationships, work problems, children, parents, other relatives, the world situation, nukes, terrorism, and the list goes on. It's very easy to become so paralyzed with worry that we might even refuse to venture out of our homes at all.

But Jesus gives us the antidote to worry. First, seek God's Kingdom. Do all you can to advance, build, spread, and nurture God's work on earth. Make that your priority. Second, live a godly life. Follow God's laws and principles. Treat your neighbors with dignity, love, and friendship. Give to the poor. Help people in need. Third, remember that God promises to give you all you need. What are you in need of? Food? Clothing? A place to live? A decent job? A drivable car? You can trust God to provide for your needs.

The principle is to go after God with all your heart, and in the end, you won't have anything to worry about.

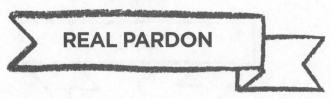

REAL PARDON

Where is another God like you, who pardons the guilt of the remnant,
overlooking the sins of his special people? You will not stay angry with
your people forever, because you delight in showing unfailing love.
Once again you will have compassion on us. You will trample our
sins under your feet and throw them into the depths of the ocean!

MICAH 7:18-19

HAVE YOU EVER thought about what forgiveness from God really means? Let's focus for a moment on what it *doesn't* mean.

It doesn't mean it didn't cost God anything to be able to forgive. No, it cost the blood and life of Jesus for God to forgive anyone, anywhere.

It also doesn't mean that you should take it lightly. One woman said, "God will forgive me. That's his job." She said it just as she was about to commit a sin. No, God's forgiveness comes only at the point of faith and repentance, nothing less.

But what *does* it mean? The Bible comes at this truth in many ways, but look at the last part of the verse above. It says God throws our sins into the depths of the ocean. While today we know just how great those depths are, to the people of Micah's day, the oceans seemed beyond penetration or comprehension. To throw our sins into those depths means that God utterly hides them from sight. No one will ever see them again.

Do you ever worry that someday God might bring up your sins in heaven? It can never happen. His promise is that he's cast them into the ocean, never to be seen again.

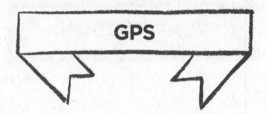

GPS

Your own ears will hear him. Right behind you a voice will say,
"This is the way you should go," whether to the right or to the left.

ISAIAH 30:21

GPS HAS REVOLUTIONIZED how people navigate. How handy it can be to have a voice and screen revealing exactly where to turn and how to easily get to your destinations. No pulling over and messing with maps! What a traveler's dream! It's amazing that a receiver in a car can somehow communicate with a satellite floating in space and that this can be translated into an interactive map that even gives verbal directions.

Of course, to use a GPS, we have to have the receiver activated and the machine turned on. And then, to get to our destination, we have to actually listen to that voice giving directions and follow them.

Today's Scripture verse tells us that we have a spiritual GPS—a God Positioning System. As we go through life, we don't have to wonder about which direction is the right way to go. When our spiritual receivers are connected and our prayer ears are turned on and we're listening for God's voice, we'll hear it.

Aren't you glad we don't have to travel alone!

KEEP DOING GOOD

Let's not get tired of doing what is good. At just the right time
we will reap a harvest of blessing if we don't give up.

GALATIANS 6:9

AN AUTHOR LISTENED to a bestselling and well-known novelist talk about her success and how God had led her. As he listened, he remembered his many failures as a writer and what he perceived as a total lack of success. He sat there and said, half to himself, "What have I ever done, God, that's worthy of mention?"

On his way out of the meeting, a young woman came up to him. "Are you _____, the author of _____?" The title was one of his early books, one that in his mind had been a huge failure, despite the fact that he believed God had led him to write it. She told him how that book had led her to Christ and changed her life.

The author walked away astonished. Then God seemed to whisper to him this very passage, reminding him that although he might not know in this world the results of his faithfulness, in the next he would. It's a remarkable promise: keep being faithful in doing good, serving me, and expanding my Kingdom, God says, and one day you will see a great harvest.

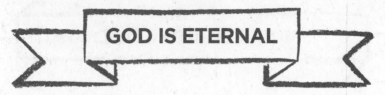

GOD IS ETERNAL

The eternal God is your refuge, and his everlasting arms are under you.
He drives out the enemy before you; he cries out, "Destroy them!"
DEUTERONOMY 33:27

NOTICE TWO WORDS in the above verse: *eternal* and *everlasting*. Have you ever thought much about the concept that God is eternal? There are several important truths attached to those words.

For one, God never grows old, will never die, will never cease to exist. He is always there. No matter what you face, where you are, or who attacks you, God can outlast all of it. He will be there when those who mistreated you are dead and gone, and he will still be there after you've worshiped him for one hundred thousand years.

Another element of God's eternity is that he cannot decay, break down, or deteriorate. There's no chance of his developing Alzheimer's disease. He will never slip into forgetfulness. He can't possibly get weary or tired of the battle, of you, of working in his beloved people.

A third aspect is that we can never go into a free fall. Just as God is above us, his arms are underneath us when we stumble and sin or are in danger from evil.

God will always be there, vigilant, caring, and forgiving. And his great promise is that he will keep us from slipping through the cracks of this world.

WHAT HAVE I DONE?

*Has not the LORD of Heaven's Armies promised that the
wealth of nations will turn to ashes? They work so hard,
but all in vain! For as the waters fill the sea, the earth will
be filled with an awareness of the glory of the.LORD.*

HABAKKUK 2:13-14

LOOK AROUND AT our world, and it's easy to think it's all about money, material possessions, love affairs, exotic adventures, and fame. Every day, Hollywood stars try to win notice in the press by doing something new and outrageous. Stockbrokers seek to manipulate numbers so they might gain another million for their millionaire clients. Nations build arsenals, great skyscrapers, and all manner of other physical structures to make themselves stand out and appear to be the "best and the brightest" in our world.

We might feel insignificant and wonder, *Who am I? What have I ever done worthy of notice?* One woman determined after her marriage to collect in a scrapbook every newsworthy thing that happened to her family. Fifty years later, she had only five pages of news clippings about their achievements.

It's Satan's lie, though, to make us think that what we do doesn't count compared to the grand things of presidents, nations, and the strong and powerful. But even for those people, it'll all disappear. It won't last. What you do for God and his people will.

RESCUE

The Lord knows how to rescue godly people from their trials, even while keeping the wicked under punishment until the day of final judgment.

2 PETER 2:9

CHERYL GLANCED UP and down the aisle. The old temptation had returned. The urge to shoplift something rose in her and was about to overpower her.

But something had changed a couple of months before: Cheryl had accepted Christ. For the first time, she had someone on her side, inside her, who could help. As the "push" to sneak a small item into her pocket grew, Cheryl stopped, closed her eyes, and prayed, "Lord, please help me."

A moment later she looked up and there was an attendant beside her. "Do you need some help, ma'am?"

Cheryl smiled. "You just gave it to me." Then she hurried up the aisle, paid for her items, and sped out of the store. Outside, she prayed, "Thank you, Jesus. Thank you. I couldn't have done it without her. Without you."

Are you struggling with some sin pattern in your life? God will help you escape the temptation each time it rises if you ask him. His promise is to rescue you, sometimes in rather colorful ways, from doing what you know you shouldn't. He cares about everything in your life, and he will always rise to the occasion.

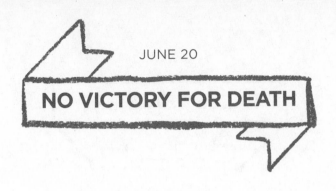

NO VICTORY FOR DEATH

"O death, where is your victory? O death, where is your
sting?" For sin is the sting that results in death, and the
law gives sin its power. But thank God! He gives us victory
over sin and death through our Lord Jesus Christ.

1 CORINTHIANS 15:55-57

THE REAL STING of death is not dying. It's what happens after. The Bible reveals there are two possible fates for all people. One is ending up in heavenly bliss with God by believing in Christ. The other is spending eternity in hell, forever separated from God.

God will live among the believers in heaven. The Bible tells us there will be no more pain or sorrow there (see Revelation 21:4). Neither the sun nor the moon will be necessary because the glory of God will provide light (see verse 23). "Nothing evil will be allowed to enter" (verse 27). Heaven will be a wonderful place for believers.

For those who do not believe, however, there is final judgment and then consignment to punishment in hell. That is called "the second death" in Revelation. People debate whether hell will be active punishment (the application of torture, pain, and fire) or passive punishment (deprivation, solitude, and all one's senses active but unable to be satisfied). Either way, it is not a happy place.

The promise is that God has eliminated the possibility of hell for all who believe in Christ. Because Jesus paid for our sin on the cross and because he rose from the dead, death has no power over the believer. Ever.

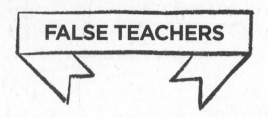

FALSE TEACHERS

*If someone claims to be a prophet and does not acknowledge the
truth about Jesus, that person is not from God. Such a person has
the spirit of the Antichrist, which you heard is coming into the world
and indeed is already here. But you belong to God, my dear children.
You have already won a victory over those people, because the Spirit
who lives in you is greater than the spirit who lives in the world.*

1 JOHN 4:3-4

OUR WORLD IS filled with so-called prophets. Some of them even appear
to teach God's Word. Many, if you look deeper, appear to be genuinely
interested in making the world a better place and helping believers grow
in grace.

But watch out. Find out what such people believe about Jesus. Do they
claim he is God incarnate, God in human flesh? Do they believe that he
died for the sins of the world and that by faith in him we receive eternal
life? Or do they say we have to do this and do that to get such a gift? Do
they say Jesus rose physically from the dead? Or do they say something
else—that Jesus was just a spirit or that he rose from the dead on some
spiritual plane but not in our world? Last, do they claim Jesus is coming
again? Do those claiming to be prophets believe these things, or are they
people we should be wary of?

False prophets are very subtle and devious. If ever you wonder if you
have met one, find out what he or she says about Jesus. That will be the
testing point. But make sure you get the exact words. They will deceive
you and sometimes even lie. God's promise is that he will not allow such
people to be victorious over you.

BE PATIENT WITH ME

[Paul said,] "I am certain that God, who began the good
work within you, will continue his work until it is finally
finished on the day when Christ Jesus returns."
PHILIPPIANS 1:6

PBPGINFWMY.

If you've been a Christian for many years, you may know right away what that string of letters means. And if you were a child of the 60s or 70s, you might remember this right along with "groovy" and "peace, man."

For the uninitiated, PBPGINFWMY means "Please be patient; God is not finished with me yet." Back in the 70s, this acronym graced all sorts of items—from clothing to plaques to spiral notebooks from Kmart.

The Scripture verse for today reminds us that, indeed, we are all still works in progress, and it gives us several good thoughts to ponder. First, it frees us from expecting ourselves to be perfect. God is continually shaping us into what he wants us to eventually be, so he's not expecting us to be perfect either.

Another thing to take to heart is that God loves us and thinks we are worth his time and effort. He's excited about the masterpieces we're becoming. Sometimes we may not like the fact that God keeps working, because it can feel like a fire that never ceases to cause pain. But little by little we see the results—in our attitudes and actions and in the positive responses we receive from others.

And since we're still in process ourselves, we can look at others and realize they're masterpieces in progress too. That can help us have patience and understanding and show grace to others.

God is not finished with any of us yet!

DON'T BE DISCOURAGED

Do not be afraid or discouraged, for the LORD will personally go ahead of you. He will be with you; he will neither fail you nor abandon you.

DEUTERONOMY 31:8

THIS IS ONE of those promises in the Bible that appears at first to apply only to the people of Israel. After all, it was spoken to them by Moses as they planned to conquer the land of Canaan.

Nonetheless, God rarely speaks to only one person or one group of people in his Word. His truth is to all people, in all ages. Some might make a case that this promise pertains to only one group of people in one place; the truth is that this is a verse we can all trust, because its truth is repeated throughout Scripture. God does promise to go ahead of us and behind us, around us and within us, at all times. It's not like he can be caught off guard or sleeping when something bad happens to you. He is still there, watching, ready to guide and help and protect no matter what.

Sometimes when you look to the future, you see only the logical culmination of the problems you have now, and it's not a pretty picture. Do you ever wonder if God will be there, if your future is secure? Take this promise and trust it. God is giving you his full attention. He knows what's ahead, how to bring you through every trial, and how to get you to his heaven intact, without blame, and full of joy. Practice the presence of Jesus in the now—it will make it easier to visualize by faith his going ahead of you into a bright future.

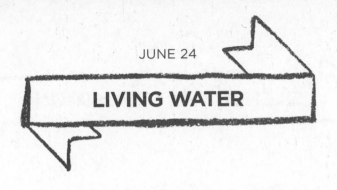

LIVING WATER

[Jesus said,] "Those who drink the water I give will never be thirsty again. It becomes a fresh, bubbling spring within them, giving them eternal life."

JOHN 4:14

LIVING WATER. JESUS spoke of it in various places in the Gospels. These words, spoken to a Samaritan woman at a well, must have intrigued her greatly. Every day, one of her chores involved walking to the local well and dipping her large jar into it to retrieve the needed refreshment for the day. This woman, because she was a social outcast, came at a time when the other women weren't present, perhaps during the hottest parts of the day. This made her chore even more complicated and, perhaps, hateful.

Thus, when Jesus engaged her in conversation and offered her living water, she leaped at the prospect, saying, "Give me this water!" (John 41:1-15). Jesus, though, wasn't speaking of physical water—unfortunately, she'd always have to contend with that issue. But the water he could give was spiritual. This water is the Holy Spirit, who dwells in every believer. Through him, a Christian receives comfort, encouragement, conviction, guidance, deep peace, and many other things so needed in today's world.

Do you find yourself thirsty for a spiritual drink at times? Avail yourself of God's promise—he has given the Spirit to all who believe.

SILENCE THE OPPOSITION

*It is God's will that your honorable lives should silence those
ignorant people who make foolish accusations against you.*

1 PETER 2:15

MARTHA, A CHRISTIAN, worked as an office assistant. Some of her coworkers ridiculed her for her beliefs. In time, jealousy raged through the department because Martha, a solid and consistent worker, got various promotions and pay raises for her faithfulness. Soon, accusations were floated that claimed Martha fudged on certain reports, stole from the supply closet, and took overlong breaks.

Her boss, taking the accusations seriously, decided to do an investigation without Martha's knowing it. Several people watched her, timed her, and calculated every little thing she did. In time, they had quite a record—showing that Martha was not only highly honest but never did any of the things she was accused of. She proved herself faithful both to her job and to her Lord.

In the same way, others may accuse you of wrongdoing. How will you overcome it? By always doing right. By conducting yourself righteously before God and before others.

Today's Scripture verse is a promise that the truth will eventually come out, and if you have been trustworthy, you will be rewarded with respect and God's support.

NEVER ABANDON YOU

Even if my father and mother abandon me, the LORD will hold me close.
PSALM 27:10

THE FEAR OF abandonment is strong in many people, especially children. For a little boy named Braxten, who'd spent the first months of his life in an orphanage in another country, the fear and worry were nearly unbearable. Whenever his mother and father tried to get away for a few days and leave Braxten and his sister with relatives, Braxten went ballistic. He threw fits, refused to sleep, and kept everyone awake all night. The parents could never take time for even a date because of it.

After some counseling, though, the parents began to teach Braxten to pray to the Lord about his fears. He learned to talk to God about what worried him, and he seemed to find a listening ear every time.

Though it was slow going, when he turned five, he began to show signs of improvement. One night he told his mom about a dream he had in which he was in a tunnel. But in the dark, he could see a light ahead. He told her that God said that he, Braxten, was moving into the light of joy and peace.

Today, Braxten rarely suffers nightmares and can let his parents go away for a trip without "losing it." Even as a little boy, he claimed the promise of God that no matter what happens in this life, he will always have the Lord there with him.

God makes the same promise to you.

SECRETS

*Ask me and I will tell you remarkable secrets you
do not know about things to come.*

JEREMIAH 33:3

HAVE YOU EVER asked God a heavy question like, Why did such and such happen to me? It might have been a terrible accident or a loss you've never come to terms with. Or perhaps it's something in the Bible: Why did you order King Saul to kill all those people? It seems like genocide.

Did you get an answer? You probably did. And perhaps it was quite amazing. For instance, one young man puzzled over God's order to exterminate the Amalekites in 1 Samuel 15:1-3. On the surface, it simply looked like revenge. But when he studied it more, he found out how truly evil these people were and how they had vowed to wipe Israel off the face of the earth. It was simply a matter of survival for the Jews. Thus, God was not ordering the punishment of a people for no reason but because the Amalekites were wicked.

When you pray, when you come up against a hard question, don't hesitate to ask God about it. His promise is to answer and also to tell you some "remarkable secrets." These insights will expand and enhance your love for God and your understanding of him. So go for it!

JUNE 28

LOVE MAKES IT UP

Hatred stirs up quarrels, but love makes up for all offenses.
PROVERBS 10:12

WE HAVE CERTAINLY seen much of the results of hatred and malice in our world. From petty family quarrels to the acts of terrorists, we find that bigotry, evil, and hatred reign in our world as the number one killer of people.

What causes quarrels and problems like these? Hatred! Without hatred, people wouldn't be inclined to hurt or kill one another. It's hatred that makes evil go 'round. We may not literally kill someone, but we may kill their reputation or relationships.

What is the antidote? Love. The Bible constantly preaches a message of love. We are to love God with all our hearts, souls, minds, and strength. God tells us to love our neighbors as ourselves. Jesus said we should love our enemies (see Luke 6:27). And Paul spoke of how "love will last forever" (1 Corinthians 13:8).

While love can't make anyone love in return, the truth is that the more love there is in the world, the less hatred will have its say. What do you do, then, when you see hatred in your world? Step in and show love. The promise is that hatred is overcome and love "makes up for" whatever offense has been committed.

SPIRITUALLY PARCHED

*I will pour out water to quench your thirst and to irrigate
your parched fields. And I will pour out my Spirit on your
descendants, and my blessing on your children.*

ISAIAH 44:3

HOW WOULD YOU feel if the roof and walls of your house suddenly started showing cracks?

For several years, areas of Texas went through a drought. As the ground went months without moisture, it cracked. And the cracks affected the foundations of even well-built homes, causing cracks in the walls and ceilings. With low moisture for years, the ground was totally parched.

Have you ever felt parched spiritually? Thirst can happen quickly—one or two days of not taking time with God can make us thirsty. But if we keep going without spending time with God, our souls become parched.

When we're parched spiritually, we may not find renewal in just one watering. For instance, if you forget to water a potted plant for a couple of weeks and then suddenly pour water into it, sometimes the water runs out of the pot and overflows the water dish instead of being absorbed by the plant—it is just too parched to be able to handle much water. You might have to add water slowly, consistently, several days in a row to get your plant healthy again.

Are you feeling spiritually parched? Spend time with the Lord until you're sated—whether you're facing simple thirst or are completely parched. Then he'll pour out blessings not only on you but also on those you love.

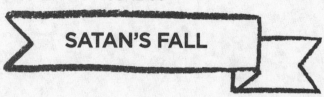

SATAN'S FALL

"Yes," [Jesus] told them, "I saw Satan fall from heaven
like lightning! Look, I have given you authority over all the
power of the enemy, and you can walk among snakes and
scorpions and crush them. Nothing will injure you."

LUKE 10:18-19

TO MANY CHRISTIANS, Satan seems amazingly powerful. Missionaries attest to the darkness he brings upon tribes and families in Africa, India, and other places. Sometimes a demon-possessed or Satan-controlled person will wreak great havoc in a village. And in the rest of the world, people who act as mediums, spirit channelers, and prophets can deceive many with their charms and predictions.

One young man felt he was being attacked so fiercely by the devil that he slept with a Bible under his pillow every night. He believed that would ward off future attacks.

For the Christian, though, there is no need ever to fear Satan. Jesus defeated him at the Cross. By paying for the sins of the world, Jesus blocked Satan's power to induce guilt and hold people under his accusations. By rising from the dead, Jesus broke Satan's other bastion of power: death. Christians do not need to fear either guilt or death.

God gives his solemn word that he will protect you and help defeat Satan in your life. No matter what part of your life you may think Satan has power over, trust God. He will defeat him in that area too.

JULY

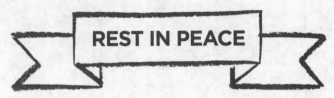

REST IN PEACE

*In peace I will lie down and sleep, for you
alone, O LORD, will keep me safe.*

PSALM 4:8

CARMEN KNEW SHE was being ridiculous, but she couldn't help it. Ever since she'd read about increased nighttime burglaries in her city, she was having a hard time sleeping. She reminded herself that she and her husband not only had good locks on all their doors but also had two big dogs roaming the house at night who would bark at anything unusual.

But Carmen still stirred at every noise. She often either couldn't get to sleep or woke in the middle of the night and stayed awake. She felt an almost compulsive need to be a sentry for her family, while her husband and kids slept peacefully. Often she was up until past four in the morning, the time she'd read most burglaries happened. Then, when the danger hour was over, she was finally able to sleep. Not surprisingly, her sleep schedule began wreaking havoc on Carmen's days and on her work quality.

Fortunately, about that time, Carmen ran across the Scripture verse we're focusing on today. She realized that, in a sense, her sleeplessness was related to a trust factor. Since she'd done the practical things to protect her home, she needed to leave the rest of her concerns in the Lord's keeping. It took a while, but as she meditated on this verse and repeatedly committed her family's nights and home to the Lord, she eventually began to enjoy that nighttime peace.

Have you ever had concerns that kept you up at night? God wants you to enjoy peace and rest. Turn your concerns over to him. His rest will fill your quiet hours.

HEADED FOR HEAVEN

*God himself has prepared us for this, and as a guarantee he has given us
his Holy Spirit. So we are always confident, even though we know that
as long as we live in these bodies we are not at home with the Lord.*

2 CORINTHIANS 5:5-6

HOW CAN CHRISTIANS be sure they are headed for heaven? How can they know without question that they will never face hell, judgment, or pain and suffering after departing this world?

There are many assurances God has given us in his Word. The testimony of other believers bolsters us. Preaching and teaching also help. But ultimately, the real guarantee God has given us is the Holy Spirit. He comes to reside in our hearts, and through him, we receive assurances, comfort, guidance, conviction of sin, and many other things. Why does God give us his Spirit? Because it's the way God becomes personal to us. Without the Spirit, God would remain distant, and he would appear not to care much about us because of that distance.

How do you know you have the Spirit in your heart? This passage reveals one way: confidence. That's an internal sense of assurance and the ability to "see" beyond this world. Through the Spirit, you sense that God is there, watching, protecting, loving. His promise is to go through every circumstance of life with you.

CARE FOR THE ELDERLY

*Those who won't care for their relatives, especially
those in their own household, have denied the true
faith. Such people are worse than unbelievers.*

1 TIMOTHY 5:8

MILLIE'S MOM, WHO lived in a nursing home, wore Millie down. Every time she visited, her mom begged Millie to take her home. Millie tried to explain about medical procedures and procedures she simply couldn't do, but her mom refused to listen to any of it. Because of her mom's actions, Millie always felt miserable and guilty.

Then one day, a friend mentioned the verse above to her, saying that her faithfulness to her mother would be rewarded by God. Millie took it seriously. She kept visiting her mother, no matter how difficult her mother made it, and she brought her presents, pictures, magazines, and all the things her mother loved. People noticed Millie's faithfulness, and several mentioned it to her, saying, "Not many people are as dependable as you are. It's heartbreaking to see some of these people who never get a visit a year."

Nursing care and all the problems that come with aging can cost bigtime. But the promise is that those who take it seriously will find God's blessing and pleasure in their lives. No one, not even God, says it will be easy. But he always honors those who take his Word seriously.

A CHRISTIAN NATION

*I will cleanse them of their sins against me and forgive all their
sins of rebellion. Then this city will bring me joy, glory, and
honor before all the nations of the earth! The people of the world
will see all the good I do for my people, and they will tremble
with awe at the peace and prosperity I provide for them.*

JEREMIAH 33:8-9

A COMMON ARGUMENT among American Christians is whether or not
the United States is a Christian nation. Most of the founding fathers were
not evangelicals. In fact, several were deists, who most believers would
not consider Christians at all. Our nation has put a premium on such
things as freedom of religion and separation of church and state. In some
cases, the latter idea has been taken to such an extreme that arguments
rage about allowing the words *in God we trust* on our money, removing all
religious plaques and references to God from public places, and so on.

Whether the United States is truly a Christian nation will probably be
argued till Jesus comes. We do know that this is less and less the case, as
other worldviews make advances. However, the truth is that because a lot of
its founding principles were based on Christian values, America has been
blessed by God in numerous ways. One of the means God uses is to give
us prosperity, peace, and other elements that point to his helping hand.

Just as God promised the Israelites in today's verses, he promises to
honor those who honor him. If you honor God in your life, regardless
of what the government does, God will honor you.

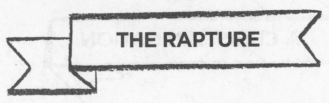

THE RAPTURE

The Lord himself will come down from heaven with a commanding
shout, with the voice of the archangel, and with the trumpet call of
God. First, the believers who have died will rise from their graves.
Then, together with them, we who are still alive and remain on the
earth will be caught up in the clouds to meet the Lord in the air.

1 THESSALONIANS 4:16-17

THE TIMING OF the return of Jesus for his church is sometimes a controversial issue in Christian circles today. What is that timing? How will it affect us?

There are many different answers. But if you deal with simply the words of this passage, you will find some rather direct statements about what will happen. First, Jesus will come out of heaven with a shout that the whole world will hear. Second, Christians who have died will be raised up alive. This presumably includes every believer from every age, even those who lived before Jesus was born, although Paul does not say that here.

Third, if we're still alive at this time, we also will be pulled up into the clouds to meet Jesus in the air. From that moment on, we will be with Jesus forever, see his face, and know him in a way we never did in this world.

This is often called the "blessed hope" of the church. While some of the details about it are not clear, the great promise to all of us is that Jesus will rescue us from sin and eternal death and make a new world for us to live in. In our lives today, just as in the end times, Jesus has the last word, the "commanding shout" that may sound faint to us at times but is nonetheless real and decisive. He is still in control.

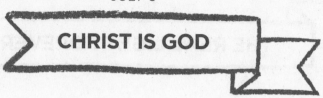

CHRIST IS GOD

In Christ lives all the fullness of God in a human body.
So you also are complete through your union with Christ,
who is the head over every ruler and authority.

COLOSSIANS 2:9-10

"YOU COMPLETE ME" was a theme in one movie a few years ago. The plot revolved around the hero's realization that he did need the heroine in order to be a complete person.

It's a lovely romantic thought. But this theory isn't very practical in real life, and if we want to be sticklers, it's actually theologically inaccurate!

Perhaps that's one of the problems with our relationships. We expect others—a friend, a spouse, or even a church—to make us feel fulfilled. While all these relationships can bring great blessing, joy, and wisdom into our lives, none of them can give us ultimate fulfillment.

You might say our lives are like jigsaw puzzles with a "God-shaped" piece missing. God has created us to have fellowship with him and depend upon him. We have a space or void in our lives that only he can fill. We may look around trying to find another human, an organization, or possessions to complete us, but they're only short-term fixes—and it's not even fair to expect someone else to complete us. In fact, this passage states that Jesus is the head of all these things and supersedes them. Only he can bring that sense of fullness and satisfaction.

Are you looking for completeness in all the wrong places? Let's look to Jesus to fill all our voids.

THE REAL LIGHT FOREVER

*I saw no temple in the city, for the Lord God Almighty and the
Lamb are its temple. And the city has no need of sun or moon, for
the glory of God illuminates the city, and the Lamb is its light.*

REVELATION 21:22-23

HAVE YOU EVER heard a report in the news that our sun will start to run out of fuel in a hundred million years? Or that the solar system will collapse in a billion years?

Every now and then, we get those kinds of reports. Sometimes it's funny the way people will breathlessly report that news with a tinge of horror in their voices. Like they'll be around when it happens!

But more serious is the truth the Bible gives us: yes, one day heaven *will* disappear, earth *will* be burned up, and everything *will* be made new. But the next time, God won't give us a sun to illuminate our planet. Instead, God himself, who is called "light" in I John 1:5, will be our light. We will literally be standing in God's light, and he will be our temple. We can't imagine what that will involve, but it's a great truth. Why?

Because the details in today's verses mean that God—who is eternal and everlasting and can never die—will be our sustainer, source of power, and energy provider forever. We needn't worry about the universe powering down or about ever having a problem where we might disappear forever. No, God plans to keep us around for all eternity. He wants us to be so close to him that we'll be one with him.

SPREADING THE MESSAGE

[God said,] "I have singled [Abraham] out so that he will direct his sons and their families to keep the way of the LORD by doing what is right and just. Then I will do for Abraham all that I have promised."

GENESIS 18:19

FROM THE BEGINNING, God's plan has been to spread the message of his love, goodness, and forgiveness to the people he created. The characters in the Bible have played different roles in this plan. Adam and Eve sinned in the Garden of Eden, introducing the need for God's forgiveness. Noah's Flood and God's having to start over with Noah's family demonstrated God's justice when it destroyed the world, but it also demonstrated God's love in saving Noah and his family so humankind could continue to live on the earth.

One day, though, God began the next step in his great plan that would transform the world. He called Abraham out of Ur of the Chaldees and guided him to a new country. God's intent was not just to bless Abraham with a new place to live. No, his ultimate purpose was to use Abraham and his descendants to bring into the world the greatest resource that would lead to world redemption: Jesus, the Messiah.

God wanted Abraham and his descendants to pass on all they learned about God. He directed that they "keep the way of the LORD" as a means of showing the other nations that God was good, loving, and willing to help.

His promise, if we do what is right and keep God's way, is to bless us and protect us, just as he did Abraham.

REVEALING HIMSELF

[Jesus said,] "Those who accept my commandments and obey them are the ones who love me. And because they love me, my Father will love them. And I will love them and reveal myself to each of them."

JOHN 14:21

SOMETIMES THIS FAITH thing required of the Christian is so difficult. You can't see Jesus. You can't touch him. He's not on the evening news. We feel as if we've heard the stories in the Bible a million times. In some ways, they can get old. We yearn for something different, something new.

Actually, every religion out there has stories, words of wisdom, promises. But not one of them has something like the last line of the verse above. Jesus says, I will "reveal myself to each of them." What is this? Something to do with mystical apparitions?

No, it's nothing like that. Every Christian receives a personal visitation from Jesus in his or her heart. There probably won't be an actual voice. You probably won't see him. But what this means is that Jesus will make himself *real* to you. If you believe in him, follow him, love him, his promise is that he won't leave you in the dark. He won't hang you out to dry on some "faith line" and expect you to believe without any inner assurance. No, if you trust him, he will reveal himself to you.

Jesus' revelation will be different for each of us. But the promise is it will happen to those who love him.

HIDING IN HIM

He will rescue you from every trap and protect you from deadly disease.
He will cover you with his feathers. He will shelter you with his wings.
His faithful promises are your armor and protection. Do not be afraid
of the terrors of the night, nor the arrow that flies in the day.

PSALM 91:3-5

HAVE YOU EVER watched a flock of hens and their little chicks as they pecked corn? What happens when some barking mongrel shows up and threatens them? The little chicks run. But not for the chicken coop. Not for a hole to hide in. Not for a barn to protect them.

No, those chicks run for Mom, and they nestle under her wings. Then they stick out their little tongues at the oppressor and cry, "Hah! Now come near! Our mom will peck your eyes out!"

Well, maybe that is a little far out, but that's a picture God gave us so we can understand his care and concern for us. And what wings! What a giant that God of ours is! Ever wonder what Satan must think when we scurry under God's wings in prayer and trust? Ever picture him shaking his fist at you, and God just staring back at him, daring him to come closer?

How many other times have you experienced God's protection—such as being rescued from temptation or being protected from a drunk driver? Once in a while God does let us stand and face a monster, but there are many, many times he pulls us under his wings and stares down the monsters till they finally run away, their tails between their legs.

CONFESS WITH YOUR MOUTH

If you openly declare that Jesus is Lord and believe in your heart
that God raised him from the dead, you will be saved. For it is
by believing in your heart that you are made right with God,
and it is by openly declaring your faith that you are saved.

ROMANS 10:9-10

SOMETIMES SEEKERS ASK, "What are the critical steps I need to take to become a Christian?" Here, Paul capsulizes the whole process in two very strong statements.

First, we need to believe in Jesus. Believe what? That he's God incarnate. That he rules the universe. That he died on the cross for our sins and extends to us all the rights and privileges of belonging to him. That he rose from the dead physically and can never die again. That he reigns now from heaven at God's right hand. And that he will come again and take us back to his home forever.

New believers do not need to understand the lengths and depths of all those statements. In fact, all they may really comprehend is that Jesus died for their sins. But that's the starting point of belief.

The second step is to confess Jesus as Lord. This is the public part of the private act of believing. The truth is that it's not enough to believe silently while sitting by your fireplace or reading in bed or even when attending church. No, God wants you to confess your faith in Jesus in a public way, whether it's to a small group of friends, in a church service, or before a stadium-packed rally led by a famous evangelist. Even to one other person is fine. But you should and must let the world know: "I'm new inside"; I believe in Jesus"; "I'm going to follow him."

That seals it forever as far as God is concerned.

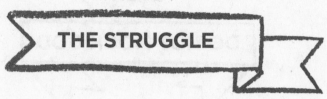

THE STRUGGLE

Because you belong to [Christ], the power of the life-giving Spirit
has freed you from the power of sin that leads to death.

ROMANS 8:2

PEOPLE THE WORLD over struggle with addictions, bigotry, sinful attitudes, and every kind of dysfunction imaginable. Many cry out for help, for someone to step in and show them the way. When they don't find it, they turn to mediums, other religions, self-help books by unbelievers, and any other kind of falsehood out there. It's only when they look to Christ, though, that they will find true help.

Notice what this verse says happens when we belong to Christ: God gives us the Spirit, who in turn frees us from sin. Many Christians will testify to how Christ enabled them to overcome their struggles with sinful attitudes and habits. It doesn't happen overnight. Many times, we're in for a battle when we try to change the habits of the old life.

God's promise is that the "life-giving Spirit" will give us the life we crave—the life of joy and peace, the life of freedom and hope, the life of love and kindness. You can tap into that power at any moment, for the Spirit lives in us and is always ready to begin the work that will truly set us free.

DO NOT MOCK GOD

Don't be misled—you cannot mock the justice of God. You will always harvest what you plant. Those who live only to satisfy their own sinful nature will harvest decay and death from that sinful nature. But those who live to please the Spirit will harvest everlasting life from the Spirit.

GALATIANS 6:7-8

WHEN YOU DRIVE through the Midwest, you'll find lots of different crops growing in the fields. In some areas, you'll drive by miles of cornfields or fields planted with soybeans or wheat. In the South, you might drive by miles of cotton or tobacco or peanuts or soybeans.

No matter what part of the country you drive through and what crops you see growing, you can be sure of one thing: whatever is growing in that field is what the farmer planted months earlier. That's the law of nature: what you plant is what you'll reap.

This is a spiritual law as well. Whatever seeds of priorities, habits, attitudes, and spiritual focus we plant in our lives will eventually become what we harvest. If we are bitter, dishonest, lazy, unbelieving—anything related to our old nature—we will reap a bad harvest.

But when we plant godly habits, positive actions, a spirit of praise, and love for God and others, eventually those seeds will grow. For a while we may not see the evidence of the seeds we plant, but when they start growing, they'll fill proverbial fields. And the seeds we've planted in our lives will become a harvest that will feed us—and others!

Keep planting the good seeds, and look for the great harvest God has promised.

HUMBLE YOURSELF BEFORE GOD

Humble yourselves before the Lord, and he will lift you up in honor.
JAMES 4:10

MANY CHRISTIANS LOOK at their lives and wonder whether anything they have done has counted in God's eyes. *I'm just a church janitor.* Or, *I'm not a Billy Graham. I try to share my faith, but no one ever believes.* Or, *I'm just not very good at anything like some of those big, important pastors.*

Kenny had that attitude. An assistant to a class of elementary children at his church, he wasn't a great teacher, and whenever it was his turn to lead, the children often groaned. But he turned to the Lord and said, "Help me get better at this. I'll learn if you'll lead."

Kenny decided to join Toastmasters and to take every class the church offered on teaching; he even attended several children's ministry conferences. He learned a lot, applied it, and soon became a very effective teacher. Once, the students he worked with selected him as the best teacher they ever had.

God uses people in all situations of life. If all of us were Billy Grahams, who would clean up the stadium after the preaching? If everyone were a pastor or an important Christian politician or a doctor or a lawyer, who would grow Christmas trees, plant the fields, or watch over us from their police cruisers as they patrol the streets?

God wanted Kenny to see himself differently. When Kenny humbled himself before God and did his will quietly and rightly, God raised him up and used him in great but simple ways to build his Kingdom. God promises to do the same with all who follow the promise.

FORGIVEN FOR EVERYTHING

[Jesus said,] "I tell you, her sins—and they are many—
have been forgiven, so she has shown me much love. But
a person who is forgiven little shows only little love." Then
Jesus said to the woman, "Your sins are forgiven."

LUKE 7:47-48

HOW MANY SINS do you think you've committed in your lifetime? How about this past year? How about recently?

The woman who came to Jesus was a known prostitute, and presumably she had committed many sexual sins. Perhaps she had also sinned in other ways—stealing, lying, cheating, or cursing. As a result, when she came to Jesus, she knew how badly she needed his love and forgiveness.

Simon the Pharisee, on the other hand, probably thought he was pretty good compared to her. In fact, he felt a little outraged that Jesus submitted to this woman's ministrations. But was he really that different from her? Hadn't he committed many sins too, perhaps more than she had, if the truth were told? How about pride, hypocrisy, and greed?

In reality, all of us have committed sins, any of which means we deserve death. It's just our faulty perception that makes us think we're better than others. We're not. When we realize that, we can claim the great promise of God's total forgiveness. And also rejoice in it like that woman so long ago.

TAKE ACTION

Trust in the LORD and do good. Then you will
live safely in the land and prosper.

PSALM 37:3

MANY CHRISTIANS TALK about trusting the Lord. Trusting him to meet their needs. Trusting him with their finances. Trusting him with their relationships.

"Trust in the LORD." That's the "spiritual" part. Too many, though, forget the other part of the verse: "Do good." That's the action part. Shelley looked at this verse and realized that she was missing this component. She trusted God and told him so. But she didn't take much action. Thus, when she felt worried, she learned to take her situation to the Lord and put it in his hands, and then refused to listen to the worrisome thoughts that came into her mind.

When her neighbors rebuffed her for inviting them to church, saying they had no interest in it, she trusted the Lord to lead her. And he did, helping her apply the second part of the command. Over time, she gave help to them when a storm blew off their roof. She took them some meals when they suffered a death in the family. And when one of their kids got into trouble, she, an attorney, offered to help with the defense at a special rate. In time, Shelley's neighbors realized that she backed up her talk with her walk; they came to her church and eventually became Christians.

God wants you to do good everywhere you go. You can't blithely say, "I trust God" but *do* nothing else. God wants you to be his hands and feet and go out into the world doing good deeds everywhere you go. A nice tip for that waitress. A kind word for a coworker. A prayer for your pastor. God promises to work in all these situations and more, but first you must act.

GOD LIKES YOU

The LORD your God is living among you. He is a mighty savior.
He will take delight in you with gladness. With his love, he will
calm all your fears. He will rejoice over you with joyful songs.

ZEPHANIAH 3:17

IF THERE'S ONE thing the Scriptures make abundantly clear, it's that God loves us. God created us, after all. He became one of us and died on a Roman cross in order to save us from our sins. He gave us the Bible to help us learn about him and about important truths such as salvation and eternal life. He's proved himself in so many ways in order to make it crystal clear that he has given us everything he cherishes, especially his Son.

Yet, deep down, we as Christians often struggle with a secret fear that God doesn't *like* us. We fear that he disapproves of us and our stubborn commitment to sin—that he puts up with us only because he loves us in the same way that a frustrated parent still loves a wild and wayward child. We fear that God associates with us only out of a sense of duty or obligation.

Thank goodness we have verses like Zephaniah 3:17 that help us put such fears to rest. The reality is that God has promised to "take delight in you with gladness." Remember how you light up inside when one of your favorite people walks into a room? That's how God feels when he interacts with you. He delights in you.

God likes you so much that he's promised to calm your fears—even the fear that he disapproves of who you are and what you do. God has even promised to rejoice over you with "joyful songs." In the same way that children become so full of mirth that they can't help but break into song, so God dances with joy at the thought of spending eternity with you.

In short, God not only loves you but also likes you very much, and he's excited about spending eternity with you.

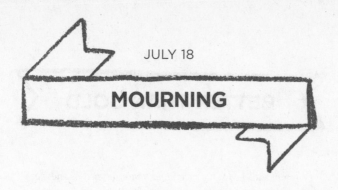

MOURNING

God blesses those who mourn, for they will be comforted.
MATTHEW 5:4

IS JESUS TALKING about people who have suffered great losses here? Or is there something deeper?

Surely, Jesus spoke to the hurting hearts of so many who have lost possessions, homes, and loved ones. But another possible meaning of the verse above might refer to those who look at their lives and mourn over their failures, mistakes, and sins, then repent before God, asking for forgiveness and redemption.

When Josie looked at her life one day, she realized how full of mistakes and sins it was. She had wronged so many people, including her husband and children. She mourned deeply, thinking of all she had done. But it was with joy that she found God's forgiveness. As she went to each of those she'd wronged, she found they forgave her, too, and offered her words of encouragement. In the process, she found the promise above to be true: she was comforted as a result of her mourning over her sin.

To those who repent and mourn over sin, God promises to give real comfort. Think about the last time you sinned and felt so guilty, wishing you hadn't sinned at all. That's mourning when you go to God, admit those sins, and ask for his forgiveness and help. God will not only wipe away the sin but give you comfort and strength that will help you not to commit the same sins again.

BETTER THAN GOLD

*[Wisdom said,] "I have riches and honor, as well as enduring
wealth and justice. My gifts are better than gold, even the
purest gold, my wages better than sterling silver!"*

PROVERBS 8:18-19

IN THIS PASSAGE, wisdom is personified and speaks of the power of wisdom in a person's life. When you have wisdom, you learn to solve your problems effectively and honestly. When you develop wisdom, you discover that you conduct the affairs of your life better than most, and often you succeed, not only spiritually but financially and emotionally as well. As you grow in wisdom, God often blesses you with the joy of family, hope in faith, and love from friends and others. Wisdom is one of the most powerful things you can gain in life.

Where do you get it? From God's Word. While some may disdain the concept, people who have committed its words to memory, applied them in their lives, and obeyed them find that it's powerful, life changing, and enriching.

An example is Will. He found himself with prodigal children, a failing marriage, and a losing business situation. He went to his pastor, who taught him to memorize God's Word, and he spent much time reading and studying its wisdom. He began with simple principles about walking with God, being honest, and giving to the church. He followed through on lessons about being a good father and nurturing his wife. In time, it seemed every problem in his life was turned around. The process wasn't easy, but it was worth the effort.

God's wisdom is a gift that you, too, have readily available in your Bible. Read it. Digest it. Apply it. And God will fill your heart with the wisdom that brings all other good gifts.

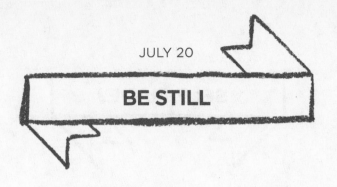

BE STILL

Be still in the presence of the LORD, and wait patiently
for him to act. Don't worry about evil people who
prosper or fret about their wicked schemes.

PSALM 37:7

DO YOU EVER have a tough time waiting?

Abraham did. In Genesis 15, God promised Abraham a son. We don't know how old Abraham was then, but apparently he grew tired of waiting for God's timing and impregnated his wife's servant when Abraham was around eighty-six years old. What a mess that turned out to be—especially when his promised son was born fourteen years later! The descendants of Abraham's two sons are still at war today, at the heart of what we know as the Middle East conflicts.

Anytime we get tired of waiting on God and try to force his hand or make his promises come true in our own timing, we bring trouble on ourselves!

Trouble was nothing new to the writer of today's verse, King David. He was used to conflict—running for his life from King Saul, battling against enemy countries, even fighting in combat against his own son.

Somewhere along the way, David learned that his life was the smoothest and most successful when he refused to worry and waited patiently for God to act.

Waiting on God and refusing to fret are tough practices to follow. I'm sure David didn't always find it easy to do so. But we'll reap God's blessings when we wait for his timing.

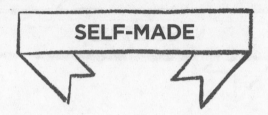

SELF-MADE

Remember the LORD your God. He is the one who gives
you power to be successful, in order to fulfill the covenant
he confirmed to your ancestors with an oath.

DEUTERONOMY 8:18

HAVE YOU EVER heard a celebrity, relative, or friend proclaim, "I'm a self-made man"? Or "woman"? Even if some people don't actually utter the words out loud, they think it in their hearts. *I worked for this. I earned it. I deserve every reward, accolade, and paycheck I have! No one did it for me, so I'm going to take credit. Why shouldn't I?*

This Scripture puts the nix on that whole line of thinking. It's God who gives any and all of us the "power to be successful." Think about it. Where did your brain and body come from? How did you gain the talents and abilities you have? Do you have more determination, more gumption, better ideas, and a stronger plan than others? Where do you think they came from?

Many of us like to think we developed such things ourselves. But the truth is, they're all from God, everything from a singer-songwriter's talent for penning compelling lyrics, to the woman who has an eye for decorating her home to make it a cozy, inviting place for friends and family. It's all from God. Why not stop right now and give thanks for the gifts God has showered on you?

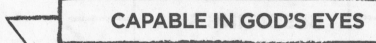

CAPABLE IN GOD'S EYES

Who can find a virtuous and capable wife?
She is more precious than rubies.

PROVERBS 31:10

TO KNOW WHAT it means to be virtuous, all you need to do is review the myriad character qualities found in the inspired writings of the New Testament. To have a spouse who exhibits these behaviors is in itself more valuable and satisfying than possessing any amount of material wealth.

But what does it mean to be capable? The whole of Proverbs 31 fits well with today's cultural gains for married women. The woman described in this chapter not only manages her husband and children well but also takes advantage of newly won opportunities in the marketplace and has a successful career.

Unfortunately, this brings condemnation for some women who measure themselves by this standard of perfection. They strive to be the very best lover, friend, worker, mother, and charitable giver. They compare themselves with other Christian women who appear better, and they feel they fail at being "capable" in every area; sometimes they burn out. That's the wrong approach.

First, God promises to equip you for the tasks he is calling you to at various life stages, and he says his burden is light. He's not calling you to do everything, maybe only a few things well. Second, your spouse hopefully loves you as you are, and though you're on the road to perfection in Christ, enjoy the journey together through grace.

BESETTING SINS

The godly may trip seven times, but they will get up again.
But one disaster is enough to overthrow the wicked.

PROVERBS 24:16

HAVE YOU EVER struggled with a "besetting sin"? That's the kind of sin people commit over and over and over. They simply fall into it repeatedly. No matter how many times they confess it, no matter how often they vow to stop doing it or to resist it, they end up giving in. It can be a smoking habit, a sexual addiction, abuse of drugs, anger, jealousy, greed, or any of a multitude of other things.

A sin like that can wreak havoc on your life. You feel constantly guilty, like a failure, a loser, and a sneak. You try hard not to let anyone else know about this problem in your life. And when you keep stumbling, even after you've confessed it to others, you're often too ashamed to admit the truth again.

What does God say to those who have such problems, who have trusted him for their salvation but still struggle with sins they can't seem to overcome? Keep facing it. Keep trying. Don't give up. You belong to God, and though you may not find victory quickly or all at once, he promises to be with you, to help you, to show you the path to victory. Peter was told he had to forgive his enemy seven times seventy; in the same way, we might fall that many times, instead of the seven times found in this verse.

God doesn't fix everything in a Christian's life at once. We all struggle. But we can trust his promise that he will not give up on us—he will enable us to keep getting up and getting back into the fight.

POPPING THE PROUD

The LORD detests the proud; they will surely be punished.
PROVERBS 16:5

DO YOU REMEMBER what it's like to blow up a balloon? You huff and puff with all the wind you can muster, forcing more and more air into the colorful rubber. After a while you pinch the neck of the balloon to check your progress, noting how much larger and rounder the balloon has become. If the size of the balloon doesn't match your expectations, you pull in another gasp of air and get ready to blow again.

Of course, eventually you'll get to a point where the balloon doesn't have room for any more air; it's full. If you keep blowing, the balloon will start to swell dangerously. It will become hard and thin—and eventually it will pop right in front of your face.

The same is true of the proud.

So many people in our culture become overinflated with their own sense of self-worth. They huff and puff about their virtues and achievements and accolades. They gulp in flatteries and shallow praise, reveling in their own importance.

Sooner or later, however, they pop. When people stretch beyond the limits of reality, they always experience the consequences of their vanity and prideful actions.

When this happens, we must remember that God—not karma, not the universe, not society or any kind of cultural standard—is the source of their punishment. God has promised to punish the proud, and he will always do so.

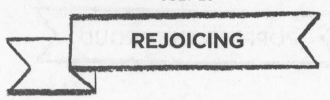

REJOICING

We can rejoice . . . when we run into problems and trials, for we know
that they help us develop endurance. And endurance develops strength
of character, and character strengthens our confident hope of salvation.

ROMANS 5:3-4

LOOK AT THE progression in these verses. First, we rejoice in our problems and trials because we know they develop our ability to endure. As we grow in that area, God builds strength of character in our lives. That is, enduring through tough situations is what leads to our growing in love for the unlovely, patience in trying circumstances, and joy in the midst of trouble.

As we grow in character, another quality develops too: we grow in confidence and in our hope of salvation. The more we draw near to God through the problems of life, the more we learn to trust him and have confidence in his love and his goodness.

God is working with you right now to build these kinds of qualities in your life. Thus, the question is, Are you rejoicing in "problems and trials"? Are you letting God hone you, guide you, empower you? Are you trusting him and turning to him for help and hope? As you learn to do those things, you will become a more confident and joyful Christian. His promise is that he will use your character to impress others with the hope of his salvation.

GOD BE PRAISED

*In the west, people will respect the name of the LORD;
in the east, they will glorify him. For he will come like a
raging flood tide driven by the breath of the LORD.*

ISAIAH 59:19

IN MANY PLACES in the world today, God's name is little more than a curse word. God is vilified, hated, rejected, and spit upon. People the world over think of him as the "white man's God," "namby-pamby Christian God," and so on. Unfortunately, they have no idea whom they're really blaspheming. Satan has lied to them about who God is and what he is like, and they have bought into those lies.

One day, though, according to this passage, every person will know the truth. God will be glorified, and his Son, Jesus, will stand at his right hand to be worshiped and exalted by every person.

Do you ever wish that Jesus got a better "rap" in this world? Unfortunately, that won't happen except as, one by one, people come to believe in him and know him. All the rest will continue to cast insults at him. But God's day is coming. He promises to deal with all the blasphemers, and then the Lover of your soul will be known, seen, and worshiped. Trust God's Word. Look forward to his exaltation, and to yours, too.

GOING THROUGH DEEP TROUBLE

*When you go through deep waters, I will be with you. When
you go through rivers of difficulty, you will not drown.
When you walk through the fire of oppression, you will
not be burned up; the flames will not consume you.*

ISAIAH 43:2

SURELY ONE OF the most relaxing moments in life is being buoyed by a soft inner tube in a swimming pool or river—with the sun warming you from above and the water keeping your body cool from beneath.

When we're floating in a pool or river, it doesn't matter how deep the water is beneath us or what's going on under the surface. We're usually oblivious to all of that as we just relax on the tube and let the water carry us along.

Have you ever gone through deep waters in your own life? Perhaps you've faced the running rapids of illness or discouragement or some other tough or traumatic situation. At such times, the waters threaten to overwhelm you, to drown you.

At such times we should take the words of this verse to heart. Our waters may be deep, but God will not let us drown. In fact, he pulls us through those challenges, much like the water carries our tubes along. If we relax and let him carry us, we don't have to struggle.

When the challenges of life seem too deep to handle, let's relax and realize who's carrying us and will protect us in the floods and fires of life.

JULY 28

THOUGHTS

We use God's mighty weapons, not worldly weapons, to knock down
the strongholds of human reasoning and to destroy false arguments.
We destroy every proud obstacle that keeps people from knowing God.
We capture their rebellious thoughts and teach them to obey Christ.

2 CORINTHIANS 10:4-5

AS OF THIS writing, a great battle is surging in the theological arena. A number of atheists have published books that attack God, the Bible, Christianity, and God's people. These atheists claim that the Bible is full of problems, that God himself is a nasty and ridiculous caricature, and that Jesus is a fraud.

One might be tempted to respond with reasonable arguments to these people. We might come up with statistics and so-called proofs from science or history or other sources. But what is the best weapon against these scorners? God's Word.

Paul tells us in the Scripture verses above that he fights these kinds of lies with God's weapon. What is it? His Word. While these people will knock down our closely reasoned treatises, what they cannot destroy is the power of God's Word. It can penetrate their hearts in ways no amount of philosophy and legal proof can.

Trust God's Word to speak to the hearts of even the most atheistic people. God promises you that his Word will achieve his purpose.

HOUSE IN HEAVEN

We know that when this earthly tent we live in is taken
down (that is, when we die and leave this earthly body),
we will have a house in heaven, an eternal body made
for us by God himself and not by human hands.

2 CORINTHIANS 5:1

MANY PEOPLE WONDER how it's possible for us to have recognizable bodies in heaven. Take a look at what happens to dead bodies in this world, and you see the problem. A dead body deteriorates. It ends up returning to dust. If a body is cremated, there is virtually nothing left. An old gambit in Sunday school for many young skeptics was to ask the teacher how a person who fell overboard in the ocean, drowned, was eaten by sharks, caught by a fisherman, carved up and turned into food, etc., etc., etc., could end up with a whole new body in heaven.

The answer is that God is not starting with that old, broken, sinful body. Instead, he begins with the seed from that body, the spirit that is most truly you. On earth, God clothed that spirit with your physical body. In heaven, though, you will receive a spiritual body that will be recognizable, will never age, will last forever, and will be perfect from day one.

We don't know all the details, but we know God's promise is that one day it will happen. You can look forward to it as you gaze in the mirror and notice the new wrinkles, bags under the eyes, and so on that your present body is unable to prevent.

GOD'S BLESSING

God blesses those who are persecuted for doing
right, for the Kingdom of Heaven is theirs.
MATTHEW 5:10

THE BIBLE OFTEN tells us that if we strive to live for God in this world, obey his truth, and love him above all else, we will be persecuted. The world—as led and controlled by the enemy of God, Satan—hates everything about God and what he stands for. Thus, anyone allied with God will face malice, evil, and sometimes even destruction at the hands of such people.

Then why don't many of us Christians experience such persecution? Perhaps because we're not really living like Christians. We're "stealth Christians," the kind who never speak up for God, the Bible, Jesus, the church, or others.

Some Christians believe their lives alone should be evidence of their beliefs. But too often their lives just aren't that noticeable. Exceptions would be those who speak for strict biblical truth on sexual mores, or in totalitarian countries, those who suffer and even die because they call themselves Christians.

If you really want to get out there and shake up your world, there is one way: do right everywhere you go, every chance you get. Help the downtrodden. Give liberally of your time and treasure to good causes. Love others unconditionally. Even if others stand against you, you can know that God will bless you with his Kingdom.

FINDING REAL PEACE

*Since we have been made right in God's sight by faith, we have peace
with God because of what Jesus Christ our Lord has done for us.*

ROMANS 5:1

OFTEN PEOPLE WILL do anything for peace. Divorcing her husband, Maria gave up her home and the right to see her children every day so she could find "peace." Josh crumpled before his boss's demand that he put in sixty-hour weeks just so he didn't have to listen to his boss's complaints about his lousy work habits. And Connie won a peace with her son simply by giving him the money he demanded every time he called. But that's all peace at a price.

God's peace comes at a price too: that of faith and repentance. When we confess we've broken his rules, rejected his leadership, and led our own lives, God brings us back into fellowship with him. Suddenly, we experience spiritual, supernatural peace, something the world cannot give and does not know. We find that God suddenly becomes a friend, not a foe. And we discover that he is the best friend we could ever ask for.

Have you found peace with God? All you need do is believe in his Son, ask him to forgive your sins, ask him for his peace, and stop fighting him. His promise is you will gain the peace that passes all understanding and is so real and beautiful you'll never get over having found it.

AUGUST

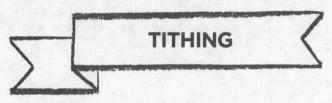

TITHING

*Remember this—a farmer who plants only a few seeds will
get a small crop. But the one who plants generously will get
a generous crop. You must each decide in your heart how
much to give. And don't give reluctantly or in response to
pressure. "For God loves a person who gives cheerfully."*

2 CORINTHIANS 9:6-7

MANY CHRISTIAN LEADERS preach that tithing—giving a tenth of all you
earn to the work of God—is a command. However, this verse points
out that you should decide in your heart what to give. You should not
give under coercion or because the preacher told a sad story or because
someone pressured you into it. Instead, go to God. Talk to him about
your situation and *what* is appropriate for you to give.

Next is the test of *how* you should give: will you give cheerfully, or will
you give reluctantly? Will you trust God's promise to bless you for giving?
Or will you become bitter and focus on what you couldn't buy because
you gave that portion to the church or a ministry?

Funny thing . . . when you give cheerfully and see God's blessing,
you get even more cheerful and want to give even more. God's promise
is never to hold back a blessing from those who truly sacrifice to meet
another's need. He will bless you not only by meeting your needs but also
by giving you a joy that is incomparable.

BAD THINGS

The people will proclaim, "This is our God! We trusted
in him, and he saved us! This is the LORD, in whom we
trusted. Let us rejoice in the salvation he brings!"

ISAIAH 25:9

WHY DO BAD things happen to Christian people?

Years ago, a book by Rabbi Harold Kushner tried to answer a similar question. His conclusion, though, was that we live in an evil world, and though God is powerful and he cares about us, he is not *that* powerful. Is that very encouraging?

Not really. So why do those bad things in life happen to all of us? This verse reveals one reason: so that when God delivers us, we can proclaim to the world how we trusted God and he came through. We can shout from the mountaintops, "This is what God did for us! Take a look! He is a God of love and salvation!"

Have you ever experienced the joy that comes when you escape from some horrid situation or when some problem is fixed for good? That's how God often works. He lets us go through hard times so that, in the end, we will see his glory. That's his promise and his fervent desire for all of us.

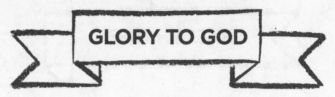

GLORY TO GOD

*All glory to God, who is able, through his mighty power
at work within us, to accomplish infinitely more than we
might ask or think. Glory to him in the church and in Christ
Jesus through all generations forever and ever! Amen.*

EPHESIANS 3:20-21

AL METSKER WAS a country boy entering a thriving career in the city when God got hold of his life. Almost immediately, Al wanted to lead teenagers to Christ. These were the days before most churches had youth programs, so Al began reaching teens through small Bible clubs.

Al soon quit his business career to work with teenagers full time. What started as a few school Bible clubs eventually turned into a youth ministry that had weekly youth rallies for fifteen hundred teens, weekly Bible clubs in two hundred schools, two youth camps that ran all summer, a Christian television station, a home for pregnant teens, and other outreaches. The ministry was huge.

When he was asked if he'd ever envisioned Kansas City Youth for Christ, now Youthfront, becoming so large, Al laughed.

"No, I would have told God I couldn't do it," he replied. "I would have been like Moses, asking God to pick someone else. I think that's why God doesn't show us everything that's ahead of us—his plans for us are so great that we'd be scared and run the other way."

We may not be called to lead a large ministry, but God still has plans for each of us—plans to work through us in ways that are better than we can even imagine. The key is to walk step by step with him, willing to be whatever he calls us to be.

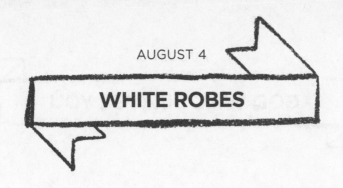

WHITE ROBES

Blessed are those who wash their robes. They will be permitted to enter through the gates of the city and eat the fruit from the tree of life.
REVELATION 22:14

NO ONE CAN enter heaven in an unclean, tainted, sinful state. If God ever allowed us to come into that blessed place with wrong attitudes, thoughts, words, or deeds on our slates, we would soon have the whole place messed up and polluted. Thus, God requires that only those who "wash their robes" can enter. What does that mean?

In other places in Scripture, God speaks of Christians washing their garments in the blood of the Lamb. It's a spiritual idea, not a physical one. It pictures those who have gone to Christ, confessed their sins, and asked for forgiveness. They have also committed themselves to Christ's care and will work together with him to grow in grace and learn to walk in the power of the Spirit. Those are the people who are fit for heaven.

A multitude of blessings comes to those who have trusted Christ and become clean inside through his blood. This verse speaks of being allowed to enter the heavenly gates and eat from the tree of life. Have you ever gone to a city such as New York, Chicago, Los Angeles, or other major metropolis and eaten at some marvelous place? That experience is nothing compared to what the experience above will be like.

Get ready for it. God's promise is firm. We will be righteous saints who will eat the food of God. You can trust that he will fulfill his promise beyond your wildest dreams.

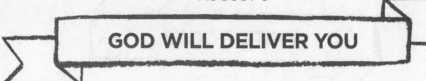

GOD WILL DELIVER YOU

Your sun will never set; your moon will not go down. For the LORD will be your everlasting light. Your days of mourning will come to an end.
ISAIAH 60:20

ISRAEL WAS ON the ropes. Jerusalem had been sacked and destroyed, the nation had been conquered, the youth and great men of Israel had been taken into slavery, and the people certainly had little hope of a great future. It looked as if the end had come. All the great promises of God in the Scriptures appeared to be grim jokes.

The worst part was that the people knew they had brought it on themselves. God had warned them over and over that desolation and doom were coming if they did not repent and get their "houses" in order. The book of Habakkuk was written as a prophet's appeal to God about the rank sin in Israel's midst. So God finally took action, disciplining Israel severely with defeat and destruction.

God never leaves people he's disciplined without hope, though, and he gave Israel the words above to assure them that their punishment wasn't the end. God would later restore Israel to a right relationship with him and then send Jesus to accomplish complete forgiveness and redemption.

Have you thought your own sins and errors might have brought down God's hand of discipline on your life? Take heart. God disciplines only to correct bad behavior, not to crush you entirely and destroy your life. Look to him. Repent. Ask for his forgiveness and help. He will restore you. He will once again shine as "your everlasting light."

THE HEAVENS

Your unfailing love, O LORD, is as vast as the heavens;
your faithfulness reaches beyond the clouds.

PSALM 36:5

ONE EVENING GERALD took his kids out to study the heavens. Having a longtime interest in the constellations and the stories about them, he pointed out the Big and Little Dippers, Cassiopeia, Orion, and other easy-to-see pictures in the sky.

But one day, he came upon this verse and realized all those stories were insignificant next to this truth. He took the kids out again and said, "Look at how big and wide and long and high the heavens are. But they're just a little bit of space compared to God's perfect, unfailing love."

He explained how he had seen God come through for him in his life over and over, from meeting and marrying their mom to finding a job he loved and working in a church where he could build up others.

Tears came to his eyes as he looked back on his life and saw all the small and great and intricate ways God had blessed him. It was a turning point in his life as the leader of his family. In time, all his kids came to Christ as he taught them about God's "unfailing love."

When you entrust yourself to God's love and care, you have signed on with someone who possesses "unfailing love" and unending "faithfulness." That means God will never fail you. All his promises hold at all times, even though sometimes you have to wait patiently for his timing in carrying them out. Just as he manages the stars and the entire universe, so he can manage your life and follow through with his great plans for you. He is eternally faithful.

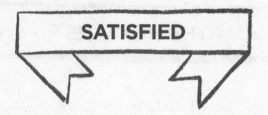

SATISFIED

He satisfies the thirsty and fills the hungry with good things.
PSALM 107:9

IN HIS REPORT to a church that supported him, a missionary spoke of his experiences in a country that had war, famine, and destruction. Someone asked, "How are the Christians there faring?"

The missionary was understandably quiet. Then he said, "It's kind of remarkable. Though some of them are badly persecuted and some have been killed, the rest are always strong and made stronger by the testimony of those who have died. God takes care of them in amazing ways. Food seems to come out of nowhere sometimes. When we need water, the well is suddenly full. I've never seen a Christian starving or forgotten. God really does take care of his people."

That kind of testimony is found over and over throughout the world. God does take care of his people. Even if he ultimately takes some of them home through terrible death, people report that somehow those tortured individuals didn't waver, and many even appeared to welcome a chance to speak for Jesus.

His promise is to meet our needs in this world, and the truth is that he does. It might not be the way we wish. But it will be done. Don't let Satan tell you otherwise.

OVERWHELMING VICTORY

Overwhelming victory is ours through Christ, who loved us.

ROMANS 8:37

HAVE YOU EVER seen an "overwhelming victory" against all odds? In our world, it is rare. How many people totally beat terminal cancer? Small countries don't crush superpowers in war. The ravages of the forces of nature can only be deflected, not stopped. And even our personality deficiencies and bad habits can rarely be eliminated 100 percent.

Other battles may come to your mind, but in today's verse, Paul refers to the overwhelming victory of all time, when Christ defeated Satan at the cross. For millennia, Satan had roamed the earth, disparaging God to his face and destroying the lives of his people, with what seemed to be no consequences. But then Jesus came along and dealt Satan a serious blow. In the end, Jesus so completely defeated Satan by dying on the cross and rising again that Satan's best weapons—lies, accusations, and the specter of death over every person—were finished in one fell swoop.

Jesus' victory was overwhelming because of how great the enemy was. No other man could ever have stood against Satan. But Jesus did. And his promise is that when we stand with him, the victory is ours, too.

NO CONDEMNATION

There is no condemnation for those who belong to Christ Jesus.
ROMANS 8:1

TOO MANY CHRISTIANS suffer from fear and guilt before God. It's not necessarily because they've done anything horrible but perhaps that they've done things they're ashamed of. Or maybe they have made mistakes they regret. But somehow, something in their minds keeps reminding them of their guilt, making them feel worthless and undone.

This Scripture from Paul's writings helps greatly. Paul tells us that when we became Christians, God put up a big sign over our lives: "Forgiven, free, and guiltless. No condemnation."

Some people in Christians' lives may continue to accuse and berate them for past sins. Satan himself, known as the accuser, will come and spew every memory of wrongdoing into their minds and try to make them feel terrible.

But there is actually only one who can judge: God. And he has written "No condemnation" on your life. Don't worry if some attack, accuse, or even abuse you. God's promise is that you are free from their accusations and that one day when you stand before him, he won't bring up a single sin. Ever.

GOD IS PATIENT

The Lord isn't really being slow about his promise, as some people think. No, he is being patient for your sake. He does not want anyone to be destroyed, but wants everyone to repent.

2 PETER 3:9

KIDS NEVER FORGET anything an adult promises them. Whether it's a day at the zoo, a trip to McDonald's, or even a gift, they like promises and want all promises fulfilled *now*! They don't seem to know the meaning of conditional promises or "We'll go to the zoo *after* . . ."

It doesn't matter what good reasons an adult has for not fulfilling a promise at that moment; kids don't understand. They want whatever they want *now*.

In today's Scripture, Peter was writing to Christians who were excited that Jesus was going to return. In fact, they were becoming impatient. Perhaps the faith of some of them was even wavering—wondering if Jesus was really going to come through on his promise to return.

Peter reassured them that God was not fulfilling the promise right away for a reason—because the more time that passed before Christ's return, the more opportunity people would have to give their lives to him.

God gives us many promises in his Word. At times we may be like those early believers—we grow impatient and perhaps even begin to doubt.

No matter what the promise, like the early believers we can keep holding on to our faith in the Lord, believing he has a reason for what seems like a delay, and he'll fulfill his promises in his perfect timing!

STRONG TO THE END

He will keep you strong to the end so that you will be free from
all blame on the day when our Lord Jesus Christ returns.

1 CORINTHIANS 1:8

SOME TIME AGO, as Ruth Graham, the late wife of Billy Graham, was dying, her family gathered around her with words of love and encouragement. They all looked back on her life and reminded her of the many great deeds she had done that influenced the world for good and for God. Do you wonder what kind of reception she had in heaven? Undoubtedly, quite a grand one.

Yet such accolades are not only for great people like Mrs. Graham. All Christians who have served God well will be rewarded in the next world for their faithfulness, but God often gives them glimpses of what they've done in this one. They might receive a note from a former student, a gift from a friend thanking them for their influence in his or her life, or even an accolade from their church.

However God does it, we can be sure we will arrive in heaven without blame, safe, whole, and full of joy. Paul tells us that God's promise is to keep us "strong to the end" so that when we stand before him at the judgment seat of Christ, we will be "free from all blame." When you made your commitment to Christ, God made a commitment to you: to see you through to the end, blameless and whole. That's a powerful promise you should thank God for every day.

FORGIVE THOSE WHO HURT YOU

*If you forgive those who sin against you, your
heavenly Father will forgive you.*

MATTHEW 6:14

WHILE JESUS OFFERS us all total forgiveness for past, present, and future sins if we trust his death on the cross, the practical matters of living in this world—making mistakes, sinning against others, and our sinning against them—are issues that have to be dealt with day by day. In this passage from the Sermon on the Mount, does Jesus mean that God's forgiveness is contingent on our forgiving others? Does he mean that when we stand before him, he will bring up grudges, hatreds, and other things we may not have dealt with?

It's a tricky question, but the thrust of Jesus' sermon is how his Kingdom operates in the real, "today" world. Thus, he is not referring to our eternal and full forgiveness that comes at salvation, but he speaks specifically of our failing to forgive people who have sinned against us. Holding a grudge, breaking a relationship, condemning others, and refusing to grant forgiveness and reconciliation are serious sins. While God will not take away our salvation, he will not let us experience the joy and hope of our salvation when we refuse to forgive.

It's really a simple matter. Are there people in your life whom you need to forgive? To extend a peacemaking hand to? To reconcile with? If so, get the problem fixed and over with today. God will not give you the joy of salvation without it.

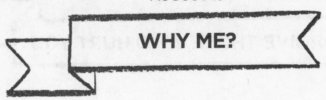

WHY ME?

*In his kindness God called you to share in his eternal glory by means of
Christ Jesus. So after you have suffered a little while, he will restore,
support, and strengthen you, and he will place you on a firm foundation.*

1 PETER 5:10

SERRO WAS A young immigrant who came to America seeking religious
freedom, having suffered greatly in his home country. He found that
freedom soon after he arrived. He joined a church, began to speak about
the problems in his home country, and eventually began to support missionaries who went there to spread the gospel. In time, he even returned.

When Christians face terrible suffering, they sometimes ask, "Why
me?" "What did I do wrong?" "When will this end?" "Why is God letting
this happen to me?" It's natural and normal to ask such questions. Often,
God does not answer until they actually emerge from the trial, perhaps
years later, free and whole. But, like Serro, they find God faithful.

As you learn, grow, and see God work in your life, you will understand too what God means by "a little while." Some might think that
could be a very long time. But when you see God use you and you grow
in grace, you realize your sufferings were minor compared to the glory
you have seen as God did marvelous things through you and in you. We
can trust that the end of all suffering eventually comes, and then God will
restore you and put you back on that foundation that will never crumble.

GET CONTROL!

*Stop being angry! Turn from your rage! Do not lose your
temper—it only leads to harm. For the wicked will be destroyed,
but those who trust in the LORD will possess the land.*

PSALM 37:8-9

THERE ARE SO many things to get angry about in this world. Sam cursed at his next-door neighbors because so many of their leaves blew onto his lawn. Janetta was furious with her mother for telling some of her friends about Janetta's problems with her children. Lawrence quit his job because his boss made so many demands on him. And Mary was oversensitive and spent most of her time being angry at someone about something, usually some comment someone else made or a suspicion that someone had talked about her behind her back.

Unhealthy anger destroys many relationships. All kinds of bad things happen because so-and-so gets angry at a friend, a relative, or a coworker and doesn't deal properly with it.

If improper anger is the wrong response, what is the proper response? According to this passage, trusting the Lord about a situation is how to handle it. Trust him to help you work it through and be forgiving. Trust him to lead you in efforts at reconciliation. Trust him to deal with the person who has sinned against you.

God wants you to trust him about such things and to act in faith. His promise is he will make it right.

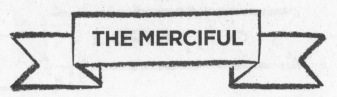

THE MERCIFUL

God blesses those who are merciful, for they will be shown mercy.
MATTHEW 5:7

"WHAT GOES AROUND comes around" is a famed maxim of our world. Many glorify revenge stories. We love to see some nasty guy get his come-uppance. Those who get payback, who destroy those who have hurt them, are the ones we watch movies about, the ones we hear about in the news. Often, the stories many tell around the dinner table are how they got back at so-and-so for wronging them.

That is not the way of Christ. When he stood before his enemies and oppressors, he could have called twelve legions of angels to deal with them. But he never took revenge on them. He submitted to their terrors, and in the end, he accomplished the greatest deed in all of human history—the redemption of humankind.

God does not want us to seek revenge. If you want to impress him, give mercy to those you have power over. Offer forgiveness and kindness to those who have hurt you or your loved ones. Show grace and goodness to those who have been hurt and victimized by the nasty, cruel people who roam our world.

God's promise is simple: if you are a person of mercy, he will grant you mercy when you make a mistake that may hurt others. He will offer you forgiveness and hope because you have done the same for others.

THE WORLD

[Jesus said,] "I'm not asking you to take them out of the world, but to keep them safe from the evil one."
JOHN 17:15

HAVE YOU EVER heard the expression "We are to be in the world, but not of it"? The idea is that we as Christians will not subscribe to the temptations, lies, and tricks of the world. Rather, we listen to God and follow his directives, even when the world may laugh at us and scorn us for our obedience.

At the same time, God does not want to take us out of the world, as Jesus prays above. He needs us to remain here to pass along the Good News and to communicate about him to those we know and care about. What we do need while we're here, though, is precisely what Jesus prays: that God would "keep [us] safe from the evil one."

Peter wrote that the devil prowls about like a lion looking for people to devour (see 1 Peter 5:8). Clearly, he's out for blood. If we didn't have some protection in this world, he would tear us all to pieces. But Jesus prayed precisely that nothing of that sort would happen. And you can bet that what Jesus prays for, he gets.

This world can get you down at times. But Jesus is watching and protecting each of us. His promise is that we will be kept safe from the evil one.

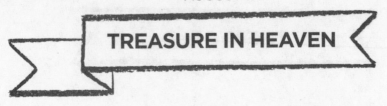

TREASURE IN HEAVEN

*Store your treasures in heaven, where moths and rust
cannot destroy, and thieves do not break in and steal.*

MATTHEW 6:20

AS WILDFIRES JUMPED the highway in San Diego, one family was awakened by pounding at the door. It was their neighbor, warning them to get out. Seconds later, as the family fled, the blaze nipped at their heels, even singeing the woman's housecoat.

Wildfires, floods, tornadoes—it seems as if we've had more than our share of natural disasters the past few years. For many years, people have used this conversation starter at parties: "If you had only two minutes to get what you valued out of your house, what would you take?" And now more people than ever are not just contemplating that question but living it.

In our consumer society, it's easy for all of us to get caught up with acquiring more and more possessions. This Scripture reminds us of the simple truth: possessions—no matter how cool—are temporary. A sudden twist of nature, and all the treasures we inherited or spent our precious money on are gone.

But the spiritual things we've stockpiled in heaven will remain forever, and they will never wear out or need to be fixed. Where's your treasure?

GETTING RIGHTEOUSNESS

*The LORD took Abram outside and said to him, "Look up
into the sky and count the stars if you can. That's how many
descendants you will have!" And Abram believed the LORD, and
the LORD counted him as righteous because of his faith.*

GENESIS 15:5-6

HOW DOES A person gain righteousness in the eyes of God?

Many people throughout the world believe it's by reciting certain prayers, following rituals, and earning merits by doing, doing, doing.

The problem is, how does all this offset the wrong things many people do? It seems that one terrible sin could cross out a whole lifetime of grand deeds.

Actually, no one can gain real, lasting righteousness in God's eyes by doing anything. Righteousness is attained only by faith.

How does that work? Jesus accomplished two basic things regarding sin when he came to earth. First, he lived a perfectly righteous life while he was here. Second, because he was righteous, he was qualified to pay the price for all the sins of the world.

If you trust Christ, you gain two things: one, your sins have been paid for at the cross, and two, Jesus' perfection and righteousness are transferred to you because of your faith.

Simply believing God, accepting his Word and truth, grants you forgiveness and righteousness. Forever. A promise worth claiming.

WHITE AS SNOW

"Come now, let's settle this," says the LORD. "Though your sins
are like scarlet, I will make them as white as snow. Though they
are red like crimson, I will make them as white as wool."

ISAIAH 1:18

IF YOU SPEND a lot of time doing laundry, you know that some substances are especially difficult to wash out of clothes—particularly from white or lightly colored clothes. For example, the juice of fruits such as pomegranates, cherries, and strawberries is difficult to clean. The same is true for grease stains and marks caused by certain kinds of ink.

But few stains are more difficult to wash away than those caused by blood. For most launderers, white fabric stained with blood is a nightmare not even worth tackling.

Of course, a few secret tips and tricks have been handed down throughout the generations. Some people recommend washing the clothes in cold water. Others rely on different combinations of salt, ammonia, and baking soda. Still others use meat tenderizers to break down the proteins in blood and allow for easier cleaning.

Our all-powerful God doesn't need special techniques when it comes to cleaning. The Creator of the universe can make something look new just as easily as he made it in the first place. Fortunately for us, God is more interested in cleaning our souls than washing our fabrics. He works to clean away the stains of our sins rather than our more mundane stains.

Ironically, God's own blood is the agent through which our sins can be cleansed. Jesus' death on the cross opened the way for our forgiveness. His blood removes the stain of our rebellion against him and makes us clean.

THE RESURRECTION AND THE LIFE

Jesus told [Martha], "I am the resurrection and the life. Anyone who believes in me will live, even after dying. Everyone who lives in me and believes in me will never ever die. Do you believe this, Martha?"

JOHN 11:25-26

ONE OF JESUS' primary missions in coming to our planet was to defeat death permanently. The hold the prospect of death has on all of us is a tremendous cause of anxiety in our world. Many people live in terror of what happens when we die. They have an intrinsic sense that death is not the end, that they will face God and answer for all their sins, mistakes, and errors.

Jesus, though, vanquished death once and for all. When Jesus rose from the dead, Satan's trump card ended up on the ash heap. No longer would Christians need to fear standing up for the truth and living it out. Never again should we quake when threatened with death for being believers. Satan had nothing with which to force us to do his will any longer.

Do you have a fear of death? If you are a believer, there is no reason to fear. To be sure, many people fear the *process* of dying. That's normal. But what comes after that should never scare any of us. Jesus gives us a guarantee that we will live with him in heaven, where death will never touch anyone, ever again.

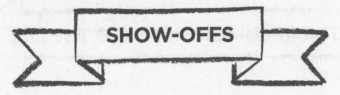

SHOW-OFFS

When you fast, comb your hair and wash your face. Then no one will notice that you are fasting, except your Father, who knows what you do in private. And your Father, who sees everything, will reward you.

MATTHEW 6:17-18

WE ALL KNOW people who like to show off—those who take an inordinate amount of pleasure in the attention of others. Show-offs usually don't care whether the attention they receive is positive or negative; they just want to be noticed. Indeed, this desire is so strong that huge numbers of people are willing to degrade themselves on reality TV shows simply to be seen and heard.

Thankfully, most Christians try to avoid making public spectacles of themselves. But there are still a number of "acceptable" techniques we often use in order to be noticed. For example, sometimes we memorize and quote large passages of Scripture. Sometimes we offer long, elaborate prayers. Sometimes we make major sacrifices for the sake of God—and make sure everyone around us knows we've done so.

Such displays are not as publicly embarrassing as reality TV, but they are still spiritually destructive. They still reek of a desire to be noticed. Worse, they reveal that we're more concerned about the approval of other people than we are about the approval of God.

Fasting and other spiritual disciplines are wonderful practices. The same is true of prayer, memorizing Scripture, and making sacrifices for God—Christians certainly should engage in such activities. But only by offering these practices to God alone can we receive the blessings and rewards he's promised.

GOD'S DISCIPLINE

Come, let us return to the LORD. He has torn us to pieces; now he will heal us. He has injured us; now he will bandage our wounds.

HOSEA 6:1

WHAT HAPPENS WHEN God's people sin by committing wrongs and engaging in ungodly practices? The Bible clearly shows us that God does something: he disciplines us. He will not let us continue in our sin indefinitely.

Hosea wrote to a sinful, rebellious people. Their lives were full of wrongdoing, evil, cheating, lying, stealing, and murder. God could not let that continue, so he stepped in and began a disciplinary process that involved famines, attacks from various enemies, and powerful judgments that left the people in deeper and deeper trouble. In time, their sin became so blatant and so rampant that God judged them by allowing the nation to be conquered and its people carried off into slavery.

God has a purpose, though, in such actions. When we sin, he disciplines. But when we repent and return to him, he heals us and bandages our wounds. He comforts us.

God has promised that he will never make us suffer endlessly or discipline us without the hope of redemption and forgiveness. With God there are more than second chances; he gives many chances to those who need them.

TOO MANY WORRIES?

Can all your worries add a single moment to your life? And why worry about your clothing? Look at the lilies of the field and how they grow. They don't work or make their clothing.

MATTHEW 6:27-28

SO MANY WORRIES. Your spouse's success at work. Your child's achievement in school. Your own needs for food, clothing, and shelter. We worry about everything from whether we can lose ten pounds after the holidays to whether we will die in a flaming car accident this afternoon. Many people become paralyzed by fear and worry, some even refusing to go out of their homes because of a phobia that keeps them terrorized and quaking indoors.

God does not want us to worry. In this passage in the middle of the Sermon on the Mount, Jesus confronts the age-old problem of anxiety. What does he say? That worry not only doesn't help us but can't add anything to our lives. We may worry and fret about death, but it will come when God is ready, and not until. We cannot stave it off by sitting around biting our nails.

What does Jesus tell us to do about worry? He says to look at how God works in nature. He says to look at the lilies. They do nothing but sit there and grow. They don't work or spend hours gathering material for the winter. No, they let God handle their needs. That doesn't mean we shouldn't work, but we should trust God and not worry about our needs. He promises to meet them. You can put that one in the bank!

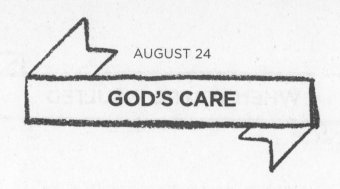

AUGUST 24

GOD'S CARE

The LORD cares deeply when his loved ones die.
PSALM 116:15

EMILY SANK INTO her favorite chair in a stupor. Slightly more than a year earlier, her husband had been diagnosed with colon cancer. Months of treatment didn't tame the ugly disease. She watched her big, strong man with his football-player build shrink before her eyes. Her days became more and more wrapped around caregiving for her husband. Finally he couldn't even get out of bed. By the time hospice was called in, he was nearly gone.

Now, on the day of the funeral, Emily woke up early as usual, dressed, and put on coffee. As she sat down, she picked up her daily devotional book by habit. The devotional that day was about Jesus weeping when his friend Lazarus died. The editor who assigned the devotion to that date, more than a year earlier, had no idea that Emily would face a funeral and need encouragement that day, but God did.

"I realized how much God cares for us when someone we love dies," Emily said. "I had felt his strength while I cared for my husband. But I never stopped to think that God didn't just joyfully receive my husband into heaven but also understood and cared about me still on earth."

Perhaps you're going through the pain and suffering of life without someone you've loved. Whether you agonized over deteriorating health for weeks or are still recovering from the shock of a sudden death, God cares. He cared for the person you loved, and he cares for you. When you're going through grief, lean on his eternally strong arms.

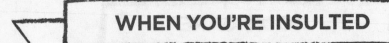

WHEN YOU'RE INSULTED

If you are insulted because you bear the name of Christ, you will
be blessed, for the glorious Spirit of God rests upon you.

1 PETER 4:14

INSULTS COME IN many forms. They can be subtle, like the grousing a coworker may do about you behind your back. Or at times, someone insults you to your face because of something you did badly: "You are such a loser." "I think you are the lowest of the low." "You are the epitome of stupidity. Get a life!"

Sometimes we have to deal with these kinds of confrontations. But what about insults you receive simply for being a Christian? "Oh, so you're one of them? I suppose you think you're perfect too?" "You're a hypocrite just like the rest of them." Or "Why don't you take your Jesus and your Bible and throw them in the lake?"

But it can get worse. Some people will attack you where you're most vulnerable. Say you're a little sensitive about criticism; you take things personally—a harsh word or insult might send you into a depression, make you feel guilty, or cause you to feel incompetent.

How should you handle such insults? Peter offers us a great promise: when it happens to you, remember that it's a moment when God's glorious Spirit rests on you in a special way.

GOD TOOK YOU OUT

*He has rescued us from the kingdom of darkness and
transferred us into the Kingdom of his dear Son.*

COLOSSIANS 1:13

THINK ABOUT THOSE words, the *kingdom of darkness*. What picture do they
form in your mind? An impenetrable blackness all around that would
keep you from seeing where to go? An enveloping darkness like a fog that
would make you fear something will dart out and hurt you? A reeking
swamp of despair that would keep you feeling terrified?

The kingdom of darkness is Satan's domain. The main thing he does
is keep people in the dark so they can't see the light that would lead them
out of it to a place of hope, joy, and peace. How does Satan's kingdom
work? Through dark lies, Satan keeps people afraid, unable to move
in any direction. Through accusations and guilt-inducing deceptions,
people become further immobilized. By keeping people chained to their
sins, bad habits, and addictions, Satan immerses them in despair.

But there is a way out. How? By the light of Christ's Kingdom. Jesus
is the Light of the World (see John 8:12), and when his light shines on
people, he enables them to escape from this darkness. Do you ever feel
guilt, fear, and despair? Look to the light of Christ. His promise is to
lead you into his Kingdom.

NEVER DISGRACED

The Scriptures tell us, "Anyone who trusts in
[God] will never be disgraced."
ROMANS 10:11

JOSH FACED THE police with terror. His wife, separated from him, had accused him of abusing their children. He would not be allowed to see them until the problem was resolved.

Josh, a strong believer, could not understand how this could have happened. His wife had serious mental problems, but even so, he knew she could be very believable to the authorities. Nonetheless, after the police left, he stopped and prayed for God's help, asking that he not be disgraced.

Throughout the investigation by several officers, a social worker, and a psychologist, Josh remained calm and hopeful. When his case went to trial, he had all the nonpartisan authorities on his side. In the end, he won custody of his children.

Many times Josh looks back on this Scripture verse as his turning point. "I trusted God not to let me be disgraced, and he came through."

There may be many occasions in your life when you face failure, abandonment, scorn, or humiliation. God will come through for you, too. Trust him. God will bring out the truth, and you will be amazed.

DISUNITY

[Jesus said,] "I have given [the believers] the glory you gave me, so they may be one as we are one. I am in them and you are in me. May they experience such perfect unity that the world will know that you sent me and that you love them as much as you love me. Father, I want these whom you have given me to be with me where I am. Then they can see all the glory you gave me because you loved me even before the world began!"

JOHN 17:22-24

GRACE AND JENNA had a problem. Grace felt Jenna had tricked her about a new program she wanted to bring to the church. Jenna believed she'd just given Grace her best advice, and unfortunately it all went wrong. Each began enlisting the ears and thoughts of others in their quest to prove that the other was the bigger idiot. Soon, people took sides, and factions developed in the church. The church boiled over with accusations, recriminations, finger pointing, and even hatred.

Have you ever been in a church situation like this? Probably any of us who have been members of a church for even a few years have been witnesses to turmoil, disunity, and arguments. Christians can get loud and unpleasant when something they hold to might be removed, changed, or even simply disparaged.

Against such eventualities, Jesus specifically prayed that his church would be unified. It was his primary concern when it came to his people. Why? Because it's through unity and a unified front that Christians most clearly show the world that they worship and love and follow Jesus.

If Jesus is as concerned about unity as the passage indicates, shouldn't we also be? Is there an element of disunity in your church right now that you can help to change, fix, and bring to reconciliation? Pray that God will be glorified through your humble efforts.

GOD KEEPS YOU

*All glory to God, who is able to keep you from falling away and will
bring you with great joy into his glorious presence without a single
fault. All glory to him who alone is God, our Savior through Jesus
Christ our Lord. All glory, majesty, power, and authority are his
before all time, and in the present, and beyond all time! Amen.*

JUDE 1:24-25

AN OLDER MAN slipped into the seat in the pastor's office, his face drawn
and despondent. The pastor asked immediately, "You look worried.
What's up?"

"I'm so afraid," the man said. "I've been a Christian for years. But
I've messed my life up so many ways. I went through a divorce that was
really my fault. I fight against drinking continually, but sometimes I give
in and get drunk. I'm lonely. Sometimes I don't even know if I have a
relationship with the Lord anymore."

The pastor opened to the above passage and read it. Then he said,
"Have you confessed your part in these things? Have you admitted to the
Lord you flubbed up, and you want to do better?"

"Yes, but . . ." The old man shook his head. "I'm just afraid I'll die
and get up there and Jesus will simply chew me out for about a thousand
years."

The pastor smiled. "That's the good news from Jude, my friend. Jesus
intends to get you to heaven blameless, without fault, and without falling
away. That's his plan and part of his job description."

"He would do that for me?"

"Absolutely."

Have you ever felt that way? Read Jude 1:24-25 again and memorize
it. Jesus has no intention of erasing your name from his list or excori-
ating you in heaven. He wants to get you there whole, complete, and
blameless.

LOOKING FORWARD

If we look forward to something we don't yet have,
we must wait patiently and confidently.

ROMANS 8:25

REMEMBER WHEN YOU were a kid and you so looked forward to a birthday or Christmas? Why do we look forward to such events? Because we believe something good will happen. Our parents will give us a new bike or that new game we hoped for or that dollhouse we so wanted when we saw it on television.

One of the best things in life is looking forward to something. Whether it's a present or a visit from an old friend or a big event like the Super Bowl or the Golden Globes, we can be on tenterhooks until it comes to pass.

Christians look forward to many things, a number of which are beyond this world. Heaven. Eternal life. Jesus himself. Seeing the Father. Having everyone see the little things we did for him. Hearing his "Well done, good and faithful servant."

It's that looking forward that helps us patiently trust and hang in there through even the most difficult times. Some of God's greatest promises are yet to be fulfilled. But one day, be quite confident, they will be.

GETTING THE KINGDOM

*Don't be afraid, little flock. For it gives your Father
great happiness to give you the Kingdom.*

LUKE 12:32

THE LITTLE BOY was unbelievably quiet and timid. While the snacks were being passed out, he watched with big eyes but didn't eagerly call out for them like the other children did. Finally, when everyone else had been served and he was asked if he wanted a treat, he quietly nodded.

One of the saddest things in life is to watch children whose spirits are broken act as if they don't expect or deserve anything good out of life and almost seem afraid that everyone is going to yell at them for merely breathing!

Almost as sad is to watch adults who act this way—adults who act as if there is nothing lovable about them and that no one could care, even God. Adults who seem to believe that someone will inevitably find fault with them.

How many times do we act this way with God—afraid to enter his presence?

When it comes to approaching God, no matter what our personalities, we do not have to be timid, shy, or afraid. God is not only willing to meet our needs and wants but finds joy in caring for us and revealing more of himself to us.

Let's boldly come to God, knowing that he's a loving parent—delighted to give us good things!

SEPTEMBER

NO LONGER GRIEVING

[Jesus said,] "I tell you the truth, you will weep and mourn over what is going to happen to me, but the world will rejoice. You will grieve, but your grief will suddenly turn to wonderful joy."

JOHN 16:20

AFTER WITNESSING JESUS' capture, trial, and walk to Golgotha, all the disciples but John deserted Jesus. Some of them feared capture themselves. Others, like Thomas, were too grief stricken to watch what they knew would happen. None of them really understood at that point what the Crucifixion was all about. Above all, they clearly did not see the coming Resurrection, although Jesus had explained it to them several times.

When Jesus appeared to them afterward—alive, whole, and perfect—they rejoiced like never before and rushed out to tell the world all that had happened.

Similarly, Christians who lose loved ones—especially children and others who have had a huge impact on their lives—mourn their deaths. But God's promise is that one day all those horrors will be reversed. If they were Christians, we will rejoice to see our loved ones in heaven, alive and glorified and perfectly reflecting the image of Jesus.

But even now we don't have to mourn like those who have no hope. Our grief will turn to joy when we reunite with our loved ones in heaven.

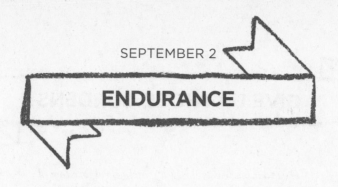

ENDURANCE

You know that when your faith is tested, your endurance has a chance to grow. So let it grow, for when your endurance is fully developed, you will be perfect and complete, needing nothing.

JAMES 1:3-4

HOW DOES A person develop the important quality of endurance? Sticking with the biblical program? Staying in the game? Hanging in there despite setbacks, reversals, and the underhanded actions of others?

The way it happens is by being tested and going through difficult circumstances. No one ever developed perseverance by having a happy, no-conflict kind of life. Such pampered people become spoiled, and when bad times come, they throw tantrums instead of dealing with the real problems.

God sends such tests to all Christians so that they will develop this all-important quality. What kinds of tests? The kind that will push your patience to the limits. The kind that might send you into a fury if you were another kind of person. The kind that push your buttons, nail you to the wall, and feel like pains in the neck.

Are you experiencing a trial or two these days? Remember, God may be testing you to develop your endurance. He wants to bring you to the place where you lack nothing in terms of character. His promise is that as you learn it, you will emerge one day, "perfect and complete."

GIVE UP THOSE BURDENS

*Give your burdens to the LORD, and he will take care of
you. He will not permit the godly to slip and fall.*

PSALM 55:22

ON THE PHONE, Beth poured out her feelings to her best friend, Lana.
A new believer, Beth struggled to keep her faith intact in the midst of
mounting difficulties. "I just don't know if I can take any more. One
huge problem is my brother, Ryan, who has simply gone off the deep
end. First, he dropped out of high school. Now he's living with this girl.
I fear that we'll lose him completely or that God will judge him in some
way and really leave him hurting."

Lana thought about it before answering, then she turned to this passage in today's reading. "Beth, listen to these words. You have to give all
this to the Lord. Just tell him."

"But I have. And it all just keeps coming back."

Lana smiled wryly. "That means you keep on giving the problems to
him. Over and over till the words stick. His promise is he will take care
of you. And Ryan. And that girl. And everyone. He loved you enough
to die for you. Do you think if he went that far, he'll hold back any of the
daily things you need?"

"I know. I'm just afraid I'm doing everything wrong."

"That's the final promise here: he won't let you slip and fall. Sure, you
feel like you're making mistake after mistake. But God is working behind
the scenes. Just trust him about it. He'll get you through."

Beth, with tears in her eyes, nodded.

Are you struggling with a heavy burden? Use this verse to still your
soul and your fears. It's powerful comfort, and it's also great truth.

BEING PUT DOWN

*God blesses you when people mock you and persecute you
and lie about you and say all sorts of evil things against you
because you are my followers. Be happy about it! Be very
glad! For a great reward awaits you in heaven. And remember,
the ancient prophets were persecuted in the same way.*

MATTHEW 5:11-12

"HE'S ONE OF those super-Christian morons."

"She thinks she is just so perfect."

"I'd like to slap the guy every which way but loose. He's one of those snooty Christians who think they know everything."

Ever heard such comments around the watercooler at work, in the line at Walmart, or in the doctor's office? Many people dismiss Christians on the most ludicrous grounds. One young man converted after college. When he stopped drinking beer, carousing, and raising the devil everywhere he went, his friends were incensed. The funny thing was that he never said one judgmental word about their behavior and antics. He simply ordered a Coke instead of a beer, went home early, and bowed out when some mad caper was in the air.

Many times, the Spirit of God convicts the ungodly of their evil ways by the simple faith and actions of Christians who sincerely go about doing good, being pure, and staying away from sinful practices. How should Christians regard put-downs, animosity from former friends, and even rejection and ridicule? Remember Jesus' words from the Sermon on the Mount: "A great reward awaits you in heaven."

It might be tough out there at times. But God will deal with your persecutors in time. And a great reward awaits you in heaven for your faithfulness.

A NEW SPIRIT WITHIN

*[God said,] "I will give them singleness of heart and put a new spirit
within them. I will take away their stony, stubborn heart and give
them a tender, responsive heart, so they will obey my decrees and
regulations. Then they will truly be my people, and I will be their God."*

EZEKIEL 11:19-20

WHERE DOES A loving, tender Christian heart come from? Look around
you. While you might not see that many compassionate, caring people
out there in our world, that may be because the bad ones stand out so
terribly. But those in the church, those Christians who seek to live out
God's truth in their lives, have had their stony, uncaring hearts removed.
In their place God has put tender, responsive hearts.

That defines a person such as May, who always seems to have an ear
for those who need counsel, are in trouble, or just need a kind word. Or
like so many who serve in the church, will "give away the shirt off their
backs" when someone has a real need. Many of those people, if you ask
them, will tell you they weren't always that way. But one day they met Jesus
and were forever changed. God took out their hard, cold hearts and put
in new and compassionate hearts so that they were able to serve, do good,
and spend their lives helping others.

A miracle of Christianity is, first, that God even cares, and second,
that he makes the effort to change us. But the great truth is that he does.
God works in his people not only by encouraging us, teaching us, and
leading us, but by actually giving us new spirits and hearts. When we
become Christians, a transformation takes place, according to the above
verses. God does a miracle in us—he makes us new inside.

His promise is that that's only the beginning. He gives you that new
heart, and then he enables you to live as you should live.

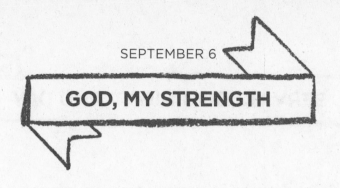

GOD, MY STRENGTH

The Sovereign LORD is my strength! He makes me as
surefooted as a deer, able to tread upon the heights.

HABAKKUK 3:19

HABAKKUK STRUGGLED WITH a basic question all of us ask sooner or later when we look around at the sinful world about us: Why don't you do something about it, God? He saw murder and rebellion, but the murderers and rebels not only seemed to slip away but also boasted of their sins to their friends. Habakkuk looked around and spotted thieves robbing good people right on the street, prostitutes standing on the corners and beckoning young men and old, and merchants who cheated those who bought their goods. Sound a little like what we often see in the world today?

God answers Habakkuk that he will send the Babylonians to discipline Israel by defeating them in war and taking them into slavery. The Babylonians were merciless, torturous, bloodthirsty people. Habakkuk is horrified. He cries out, "How can you do such a thing?"

God answers again, this time saying that all who rebel against him—Israelite, Babylonian, or whoever—will be judged. It's then that Habakkuk realizes a grand truth: God truly is in charge of all things in human life. For that reason, Habakkuk can trust that no matter what happens, God will be there and will give him the strength he needs to triumph. God gives you the same promise.

SERVING GOD NIGHT AND DAY

They stand in front of God's throne and serve him day and night in his Temple. And he who sits on the throne will give them shelter. They will never again be hungry or thirsty; they will never be scorched by the heat of the sun. For the Lamb on the throne will be their Shepherd. He will lead them to springs of life-giving water. And God will wipe every tear from their eyes.

REVELATION 7:15-17

"WHAT DO YOU think about a presidential candidate who is a draft dodger?" the reporter asked the World War II vet. She knew he was proud of his time in the service, and she expected him to denounce anyone who would avoid serving his or her country.

But the old man's answer surprised her.

"I can't say I entirely blame anyone not wanting to be in a war," he said. "Sometimes it's necessary, and I'd serve again if I needed to. But the horrors of war stay with you your whole life."

In this Scripture passage John describes his vision of the future. The pronoun in this Scripture refers to those who endured the horrors of the Great Tribulation and died for their faith. But John also learned that no matter what horrors they experienced, God would wipe the tears from their eyes.

This is not just a promise for the future or for martyrs. The compassionate God we will see face-to-face in Christ has the same compassion for us as we walk on earth. No matter what horrors, pain, or disappointment we encounter, his caring is unlimited. As we turn to him, he will wipe away the tears from our eyes—not just in our heavenly future but in the here and now.

PEACE AFTER THE STORM

*To all who mourn in Israel, he will give a crown of beauty
for ashes, a joyous blessing instead of mourning, festive praise
instead of despair. In their righteousness, they will be like
great oaks that the LORD has planted for his own glory.*

ISAIAH 61:3

"AFTER THE STORM, peace." Isn't that something many people say about the storms of life? We all know that storms won't last forever, even devastating hurricanes. Afterward, we all climb out of our shelters and start to rebuild. Sometimes the blessings that follow in the quiet of new life are overwhelming.

One man reported how he worked with a family that had lost their house in New Orleans to Hurricane Katrina. These Christians, though devastated, spoke of how God had blessed them through it. "It brought me and Joe closer together," the wife said. "We feel like a team again." "We saw how much Mom and Dad loved each other," one of their daughters said. And their son shared, "I lost my football, but now I have a better one, signed by one of the New Orleans Saints."

God promises to bring that peace after the storms in our lives. It might not come the moment the storm ends. The storms might leave us a little bewildered for a time. But as we get back in touch with God, he promises to restore it all.

YOU'LL NEVER BE SHAKEN

This is what the Sovereign LORD says: "Look! I am placing a foundation stone in Jerusalem, a firm and tested stone. It is a precious cornerstone that is safe to build on. Whoever believes need never be shaken."

ISAIAH 28:16

THIS IS A passage predicting the coming of Jesus. He was the "foundation stone" in Jerusalem. Today, a cornerstone—or "foundation stone"—is almost meaningless. It's mostly decorative. But in that time, a cornerstone was laid first to ensure that the rest of the building would be upright and not easily broken or knocked down. That's why Isaiah says that this stone is "firm and tested." What does this mean?

First, it's "firm." That makes it hard to be dislodged, destroyed, blown over by weather conditions, or anything of the sort. With Christ as the foundation stone, the one that holds the building together and makes it strong and unbreakable, the building—his church, including the saints of all ages—would never be moved or obliterated. God founded his church on a rock, Jesus himself, who could never be moved or toppled.

Second, it's "tested." Our cornerstone, Jesus himself, was put through the fire. His enemies tried hard to destroy him. But he held. He proved himself. That's the reason we can trust him. We can be sure no one can ever turn him against us or tempt him to do something wrong or evil. He will always do the right thing and can never be overcome by any force.

When we trust him, we're promised a firm and tested Savior. When we believe in him, we will never be shaken.

SEPTEMBER 10

SENDING THE RAINS

*[God] will send the rains in their proper seasons—the early
and late rains—so you can bring in your harvests of grain, new
wine, and olive oil. He will give you lush pastureland for your
livestock, and you yourselves will have all you want to eat.*

DEUTERONOMY 11:14-15

THIS PASSAGE REPRESENTS an extension of the covenant God initiated
and maintained with the people of Israel. Because Abraham acted in
faith, God promised to bless him and his descendants for as long as they
remained faithful to him (see Genesis 15).

The details of God's covenant were spelled out clearly for his people.
If the Israelites obeyed God's commands, they would receive his blessings. God promised to reward their obedience, faithfulness, and goodness with land, pastures, and harvests—all of which were vital ingredients
in an agrarian society. If the Israelites disobeyed, however, God promised
to dry up the rains and remove them from their land.

As Christians today, we don't have a part in that original covenant
between God and Abraham—but that's not a bad thing. Instead, we've
been offered a new covenant through the blood of Jesus Christ. By
accepting his sacrifice on the cross as atonement for our sins, we can live
as God's children. As heirs with Christ, we can look forward to countless
blessings both now and throughout eternity.

As in the original covenant, however, many of those blessings are tied
to our obedience. When we submit to Christ and do what he's called us
to do, we will be rewarded. This reward probably won't include cattle
or rain; in fact, it may not include any form of material blessing in this
life. But we can rest assured that we will receive all the joy and satisfaction
God created us to crave.

HUMBLE YOURSELVES

*If my people who are called by my name will humble themselves and
pray and seek my face and turn from their wicked ways, I will hear
from heaven and will forgive their sins and restore their land.*

2 CHRONICLES 7:14

KATIE LISTENED RAPTLY to the speaker at the prayer breakfast as she
spoke on this verse, calling the attendees to prayer and commitment to
having an impact on the culture. On the way home, she kept thinking
about it. While the call to prayer was important, it occurred to her that
other things the verse said were also powerful.

She thought about humbling herself and told the Lord, "Show me
all the ways in which I'm proud." The verse spoke of seeking God's face,
and she prayed, "Help me to have a closer relationship with you, Lord."
And last, she determined to repent of any evil in her life. For the first
time, she decided to work hard on being a better employee, refusing to
gossip, and seeking opportunities to speak up for God.

Not much happened at first. But gradually she began to see things happen around her. She did become a more humble person by learning to be
a listener, and a doer when action was required. Her fellowship with God
took off as she committed more and more to seeking him daily. And when
her coworkers noted that she refused to gossip in the lunchroom, they asked
her what had happened. When she explained, they wanted to know more.

While many quote this verse as referring to our whole nation, change
always starts with one person—the whole of one's inner life and actions.
God promises that if you take this route, you will be forgiven, and he will
restore what you have lost in walking apart from him.

GOD NEVER FORSAKES HIS PEOPLE

*Once I was young, and now I am old. Yet I have never seen
the godly abandoned or their children begging for bread.*

PSALM 37:25

SOMETIMES IT'S WISE to take an assessment of how God blesses Christians in this world. Missionaries often report that even in the worst areas of the world—where war, injustice, tyranny, and slavery are rampant—the Christians often find their needs met in unusual and even miraculous ways. While persecution is rife and many have died for the faith, those who remain firm find that God is there through it all and that their trust yields great dividends as they see him work in their lives and answer their prayers.

One couple shared in a prayer meeting how their financial needs were met one night when a person they didn't know arrived at their door with a cashier's check to cover their pressing bills. The giver said only that it was "from the church." Amazed, they came to prayer the next Wednesday with the story and new praise for God. Others began to follow their lead and trust God for their needs instead of only praying about them. They kept a running list and soon had a whole notebook full of answers that God had given them, proving the truth of these verses.

God works through his people, and the testimony of many is that God gives us just what we need to see us through. Do you trust him for that? With this great promise, you know that he will not leave you lost, bereft, without what you need.

THE THIRST FOR JUSTICE

*God blesses those who hunger and thirst for
justice, for they will be satisfied.*

MATTHEW 5:6

A CHRISTIAN READ in the newspaper about a judge who had let off a child molester with only three months' probation. The judge, saying that he didn't believe the prison system worked, let this man go on to commit other crimes, all because he had reservations about the system's ability to rehabilitate that offender.

The Christian didn't just sit on his hands about it. He sent a letter to the editor of his local newspaper. That began a debate in the news about the judge and his actions. Soon, pastors in churches began preaching about the problem. Residents in the state heard about the case and listened to new arguments, and soon that judge was voted out of office.

As Christians, we might be tempted to despair at the realities we find in our world. But we have a better and greater hope. While God promises to deal with all the evil that has ever been perpetrated—on us, our friends, our churches, and our nations—we also often see God work for justice in our world through individual Christians. William Wilberforce helped end slavery in the British Empire through his persistent crusade against it. Through the ages, others have done much to bring about justice, often in the name of God.

Refuse to simply despair in the face of the harsh problems of our world. You can have an impact on your community through all kinds of means. Pray, and listen for God's leading. He may use your thirst for justice and satisfy it with the changes you seek.

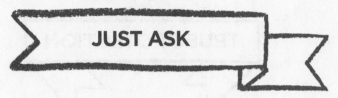

JUST ASK

If you need wisdom, ask our generous God, and he will
give it to you. He will not rebuke you for asking.

JAMES 1:5

"I JUST DON'T understand what the teacher is trying to tell us," the fourth grader explained with panic in his voice when his mom studied his report card and asked about his low grades.

"Well, have you told your teacher when you don't understand what she's saying?"

"No," the boy replied. "I'm afraid she'll think I'm talking back to her. I don't want to get into trouble."

The next day, the boy, his mom, and the teacher sat down together, and the teacher explained that she welcomed questions—that he would never get in trouble for requesting help.

Have you ever faced a situation that was over your head and made you feel a little panicky? Maybe today you have too much month or mortgage at the end of your money. Maybe you're facing difficult health issues. Perhaps you're going through a relationship problem.

Like any good teacher, God delights in helping us, his pupils, learn. He loves to reveal his wisdom to us. He doesn't expect us to know everything on our own; he welcomes our questions and promises to give us the answers we need.

TRUE PROTECTION

The LORD protects all those who love him, but he destroys the wicked.

PSALM 145:20

THERE ARE LOTS of people in the world today who need to be protected. Children need to be protected because they lack the ability to care for themselves. The poor need to be protected because they lack the financial resources to deal head-on with the usual problems of life. Those who are marginalized need to be protected because they lack a voice with which to speak on their own behalf.

Here's someone else who needs to be protected: you. There are wicked people in the world who would tear you apart simply because they have the means and the opportunity. There are forces in this world that can truly be called evil—forces that are especially hostile to those of us who choose to follow Christ.

For those reasons and more, all of us have a deep-seated desire to be protected. At our core, we all crave security and comfort and a bulwark against everything that would cause us harm.

That's what's so amazing about Psalm 145:20. It's a promise that speaks directly to our hearts, calming our fears and soothing us with the knowledge that God is on our side. He will destroy the wicked (which means we don't have to), and he will watch over us for all time. In fact, because we love him, we're protected daily in ways we cannot even see. We can trust that even when he allows some trials, he protects us from many others that would do us serious harm.

GOD'S LOVE NEVER ENDS

The faithful love of the LORD never ends! His mercies never cease.
Great is his faithfulness; his mercies begin afresh each morning.
LAMENTATIONS 3:22-23

DO YOU CONSIDER yourself a morning person? Some people like waking up from a good rest, grabbing some breakfast and a cup of coffee, and preparing for the excitement of a new day. Others prefer to hit the snooze button three or four times before stumbling into the shower.

Regardless of your personal preferences, one of the best things about mornings is the certainty of their coming. No matter how dark the night may be, we know that sooner or later the sun will appear—light will come to chase away the darkness. Mornings are something on which we can count. We can find comfort in the reliability of each new day.

In these verses, the prophet Jeremiah reminds us that God's love, mercy, and faithfulness are as reliable as the dawn. They are new every morning. Nothing can stop them, and nothing can stop us from experiencing them if we're willing to seek God and follow him each day.

What's especially remarkable about this promise from Jeremiah is that it comes from the book of Lamentations—a book written during one of the darkest moments in Israel's history. Jeremiah and his people had experienced calamity after calamity. They were suffering, and yet they still found comfort and hope in the certainty of God's continued mercy, faithfulness, and love. God has promised that same mercy, faithfulness, and love to you in your darkest moments.

REVEALED

*We look forward with hope to that wonderful day when the glory of
our great God and Savior, Jesus Christ, will be revealed. He gave
his life to free us from every kind of sin, to cleanse us, and to make
us his very own people, totally committed to doing good deeds.*

TITUS 2:13-14

LYDIA WAS ALWAYS struck by the hope she found in the Bible. One of the
things she most looked forward to was the day when Jesus would reveal
himself to the world. She prayed about this constantly.

What she never expected was that God would use her now to reveal
himself to others. Lydia helped rake leaves on her elderly neighbors'
lawn, and when they came over to thank her, she had a chance to tell them
about her hope and why she did that good deed. When new people moved
in across the street, she sent them a box of chocolates, a casserole, and a
note inviting them to church. Although they didn't come immediately,
through her witness they began to change some of their negative images
of Christians.

When a coworker was stricken with cancer and ended up in the hospital, Lydia was one of the few who kept coming by with gifts, kind words,
and occasional affirmations from the Bible. In time, her friend told her
that she saw God reflected in Lydia.

While the day is coming when the glory of Christ will be revealed, we
can also be sure that he promises to reveal himself through our witness
and good deeds as well.

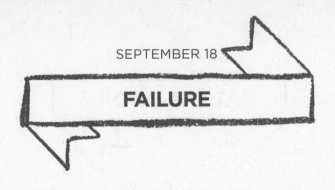

FAILURE

If you fail under pressure, your strength is too small.
PROVERBS 24:10

MANY HAVE SAID that failure is not giving in but rather giving up entirely. Every person who ever faced a difficult task had to work through problems, setbacks, even complete reversals.

There's a story about a missionary who created a dictionary for people who needed the Bible translated into their language. His work compiling the meanings of all those words had taken him decades. Over the years, his wife grew more and more resentful and jealous of the many hours he spent on this project. Finally one night she took the pages of the only copy of his book and cast them into the fire while he slept.

The next morning, discovering the evil of her actions, he stared into the fireplace. A man of less faith might have simply gone back to his home country and said, "I'm done."

Instead, that missionary turned to his glaring wife and said, "You have given me a world of trouble." He sighed, and then started over. In time, he did reproduce that dictionary and completed a translation; many were converted as a result.

If your strength is too small for a task, cry out to God. He will empower you. He doesn't want you to "fail under pressure" but instead to allow the pressure to push you on to great success.

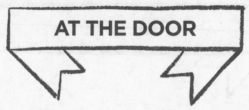

AT THE DOOR

Look! I stand at the door and knock. If you hear my voice and
open the door, I will come in, and we will share a meal together
as friends. Those who are victorious will sit with me on my throne,
just as I was victorious and sat with my Father on his throne.

REVELATION 3:20-21

HAVE YOU EVER gone to a museum or castle and seen the thrones kings or queens once sat upon as they delivered their pronouncements?

The shah of Iran once sat on a "peacock throne." This throne was a 6-by-4-foot platform supported by four golden feet. The name came from the shape of two peacocks behind the throne, their tails encrusted with sapphires, rubies, emeralds, pearls, and other precious jewels.

The kings of England sat on a chair made almost entirely of gold. Other thrones have featured encrusted jewels and intricately carved wood.

If earthly thrones can be so grand, just imagine what God's throne must be like! The Bible speaks of the "great white throne" in Revelation 20. When Isaiah stood before God's throne in Isaiah 6:1, it was "high and lifted up" (NKJV). Seraphim, an elite hierarchy of angels, gathered around it. God's train was so huge it filled the Temple.

But as amazing as God's throne is, this verse promises us that those who overcome sin and shallow commitment to become totally sold out for Jesus will actually sit on his throne with him.

Savor that for a minute. What a remarkable time that will be! But one day it will happen. That's God's guarantee.

SPECIAL GIFTS

*To everyone who is victorious I will give some of the manna that
has been hidden away in heaven. And I will give to each one
a white stone, and on the stone will be engraved a new name
that no one understands except the one who receives it.*

REVELATION 2:17

EVERYONE LIKES RECEIVING gifts, but there's something extra special about receiving gifts that are personal—gifts that were purchased or created with a specific person in mind. That's why these two promises from the book of Revelation are so exciting.

Manna is a symbol of God's provision. It was originally given to Moses and the Israelites as they wandered through the wilderness, unable to find food for themselves. It was one of the ways God provided for their physical survival. In this passage, however, those who are victorious in following God are promised "manna that has been hidden away in heaven." This is a spiritual provision rather than a short-term physical sustenance. It represents God's promise to care for and sustain us throughout eternity.

In the same way, God has promised his followers a white stone. Many scholars believe this refers to the ancient practice of presenting a stone to someone on trial. A black stone meant guilt and punishment, while a white stone represented innocence and freedom.

Even better, God has promised to engrave our white stones with new names—names so special that they will be known only to the recipient and to him, like a pet nickname given to you by your friend or spouse—a term of endearment. This is the gift of an intimate relationship. It's the blessing of being truly understood for who we are and truly loved by the one who created us and knows us better than we know ourselves.

FRIENDS

*The LORD is good, a strong refuge when trouble
comes. He is close to those who trust in him.*

NAHUM 1:7

WHAT MAKES PEOPLE remain friends? What makes them continue to
feel close even though they may not see each other for years? What makes
them "pick up right where they left off"?

George was pondering these questions after he'd been with a group
of people he served with in ministry nearly two decades earlier—many of
whom he hadn't seen for years.

"I think it's the fact that when you go through the same experiences;
a bond is formed," George speculated. "When we were all serving in
that ministry together, we spent hours not only working with teenagers
but also doing all the behind-the-scenes things that go with the terri-
tory . . . serving together at banquets for donors, praying together, plan-
ning events together. Sharing all those experiences, I believe, bonded
us tightly."

If sharing good experiences can knit people together, how much
more do we feel bonded to someone who walks through "the valley of
the shadow of death" with us? And how much more do we feel bonded
with God when he's seen us through tough times!

The bad news is that sometimes troubles will come into our lives. The
good news, though, is that the Lord will go through each experience with
us. Even better than a good friend, he can stay with us 24/7 through the
whole ordeal. And each experience will strengthen that bond between
God and us.

GOD STOOD WITH ME

*The Lord stood with me and gave me strength so that I might
preach the Good News in its entirety for all the Gentiles to hear.
And he rescued me from certain death. Yes, and the Lord will
deliver me from every evil attack and will bring me safely into
his heavenly Kingdom. All glory to God forever and ever!*

2 TIMOTHY 4:17-18

ABOUT THE TIME Paul wrote this letter, he stood before courts that could
soon sentence him to death. But even in the face of that, Paul had great
confidence in God. He knew that the God he believed in would deliver
him, either through life or death; that God would give him the grace
necessary to endure it; and that the end result would bring glory to God.

Paul speaks words of promise that should kindle hope in every heart:
God will bring you "safely into his heavenly Kingdom." This means not
only through death but also through all the difficulties of life. God will
bring us through in a way that allows us to triumph. Paul went through
troubles that we will probably never face and saw God help him every step
of the way. He also witnessed many great victories in the name of Christ.
Paul had turned the world upside down with his preaching about Jesus,
amid the opposition of Jews and Gentiles alike. The gospel he preached
is a gospel of hope and of redemption. And Paul himself was able to
experience that hope and redemption as he lived and preached.

God watches, he works, and he uses us to change our world. Paul
said that happened in his life, and so it will in yours. His promise is
to rescue us not only from "some" evil attacks but from "every" attack
from Satan. And his continual deliverances lead to a hope that good
things will always come, some in this world and some in the next.

GOD SENDS THE RAIN

Ask the LORD for rain in the spring, for he makes the storm clouds. And he will send showers of rain so every field becomes a lush pasture.

ZECHARIAH 10:1

IN A FARMING society, rain is essential. Thus, the Bible is filled with images of God promising rain for the people's crops. When the Israelites sinned against him and followed idols, God punished them with droughts and famines. His purpose was to draw them back to himself and make them realize that only faithfulness would be rewarded.

The principle still works. Though physical famine may not be a problem in Western society, God sometimes disciplines sinning Christians by sending them hard times and difficulties meant to make them turn back to him. Usually, one of two responses follows: either to be angry and hate God and curse his name or to repent and admit their wrongdoing and cry out to him for forgiveness and renewed blessing.

It's all a matter of attitude. What approach are you taking these days—fighting him and being angry? Or seeking him and asking for mercy and understanding? If you turn to God, he will shower his blessings on you and make the pastures of your life rich and green.

FILLED UP

He fills my life with good things. My youth is renewed like the eagle's!

PSALM 103:5

SOMETIMES IT'S GOOD to take inventory of all the great blessings God has brought into your life. One young couple, on the brink of divorce and wondering what ever made them want to marry in the first place, were counseled to think of every blessing their partner had been to them over the time they had known each other.

As they compiled their lists, they soon discovered that God had showered them with blessings from each other that they'd forgotten about in the face of petty disputes that nearly destroyed them.

In the same way, when you feel God is simply not coming through on his promises to help and support you, make a list of his blessings in your life in the past—perhaps even write it up and frame it for reference every now and then when circumstances look bleak. You will undoubtedly find that God has indeed filled your life with good things.

Instead of feeling like a turkey on the ground, you will soar like an eagle, rising above your problems into the stratosphere, where God dwells in peace and safety.

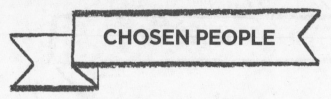

CHOSEN PEOPLE

*You are not like that, for you are a chosen people. You are
royal priests, a holy nation, God's very own possession. As
a result, you can show others the goodness of God, for he
called you out of the darkness into his wonderful light.*

1 PETER 2:9

MONA LED A sad life as a single woman. She had never met the love of her life. She worked at a tiring, unfulfilling job. She had few friends. She also struggled with poor self-esteem and felt like a loser. Finally, one day she went to a pastor she'd heard about for some counseling.

Naturally, he shared the truth about Christ with her. It seemed interesting, but to her it didn't sound like much of an answer. Then the pastor showed her this passage and explained how becoming a Christian would make her part of a distinguished, holy nation. He spoke of how God chooses believers, and how they are royalty, priests meant to go to God on behalf of others and help them out. Above all, she would belong to God.

That idea clicked with her, and she prayed that God would forgive her and come into her life. Changes did not come quickly. But as Mona immersed herself in church life, built some good friendships, and learned more about God, she began to pray for things she'd always dreamed about but could never attain. In time, she met a widower with children. He fell in love with her. She found a job she enjoyed too. And her sense of self-worth vastly improved.

When God takes you on, he commits to everything in your life. His promise is that you will never regret becoming part of his family.

HELP IN WEAKNESS

*The Holy Spirit helps us in our weakness. For example, we don't
know what God wants us to pray for. But the Holy Spirit prays
for us with groanings that cannot be expressed in words. And the
Father who knows all hearts knows what the Spirit is saying, for the
Spirit pleads for us believers in harmony with God's own will.*

ROMANS 8:26-27

AS JOYCE FELL to her knees in her bedroom and began to pray through
her tears about her father's health situation, she seemed too bereft to
find the words to say. She had run out of words. She had prayed so many
times about this horrible circumstance that she no longer knew what to
say. As she tried unsuccessfully to speak, only a long, steady groan came
out. She laid her head on the bed and moaned.

Have you ever prayed about some situation, about a friend, about
a need, about some trouble in your life that literally left you without
words? You simply didn't know what to say? In those times have you
ever simply "groaned," feeling desolate and broken and without hope?

From this passage we see the way God operates in such times to inter-
pret our true needs. The Spirit begins interceding for us through such
groans. He articulates our pain and anguish to our Father, and the Father
understands the multiple needs beyond our comprehension and what
divine action should be taken to make our lives right again.

Even when all seems lost or we're off track in our prayers, God promises
that the Spirit will translate our yearnings and even our fears, and he knows
precisely how to make those prayers better than we can imagine. If all you
can do is moan and groan, that's fine. Sometimes that may be the Spirit
working in you to let God know just how deeply you feel about the situation.

LOVE ONE ANOTHER

[Jesus said,] "Your love for one another will prove
to the world that you are my disciples."

JOHN 13:35

THERE ARE DIFFERENT ways to prove something in today's society—different standards that can be used to make judgments and decisions. During a criminal trial, for example, prosecutors must prove that a defendant is guilty beyond a shadow of a doubt. Proof must be absolute. In a civil trial, however, defendants can be proclaimed guilty if there is a preponderance of the evidence—in other words, if the evidence for guilt merely outweighs the evidence for innocence. Proof is more flexible in that circumstance.

The New Testament offers several ways for us to evaluate whether we are truly following Jesus. Disciples of Jesus should feel his guidance in their lives, for example (see John 10:27). They should demonstrate spiritual fruit for his Kingdom (see Matthew 7:16-20). They should experience God's discipline when they go astray (see Hebrews 12:6-8).

But this verse offers one of the clearest evidences of salvation directly from the mouth of Jesus. Namely, true Christians demonstrate self-sacrificial love. Genuine followers of Jesus display love for one another through their actions. They also express love for the rest of the world—for those who don't yet know Christ.

Interestingly, this evidence of salvation is a key principle from John 13:35—but it's not the promise contained in that verse. The promise is that when we demonstrate self-sacrificial love for one another, the world will take notice. They will see our actions, and they will recognize us for what we are: disciples of the one who sacrificed himself on the cross in order to save all of us from our sins.

DELIVER ME FROM EVIL

A time is coming when people will no longer listen to sound and wholesome teaching. They will follow their own desires and will look for teachers who will tell them whatever their itching ears want to hear. They will reject the truth and chase after myths. But you should keep a clear mind in every situation. Don't be afraid of suffering for the Lord.

2 TIMOTHY 4:3-5

HAVE YOU EVER had a "suicide"?

That's a fountain drink that's just what you make it. You might start with a bit of Coke and then add orange soda, maybe a bit of Sprite, a portion of root beer, and perhaps a splash of cherry syrup. The concoction is never the same twice and is limited only by the drinker's imagination—and the ability to tolerate something that could be a really disgusting drink.

That kind of illustrates some religions in our society today. The person wanting to be spiritual may develop beliefs that include some Protestant heritage, some cultish works, some Buddhist tenets, some Eastern practices, and some Muslim teachings. He or she might even throw in a splash of paganism or humanism.

The society Paul walked in mirrored ours. In this passage, Paul pointed out to the believers that a time was coming when people would no longer listen to sound spiritual teaching. They would depend on their own man-made teachings. At times, Paul's life was even in danger because he spoke of Christ as the only way to God.

If we're living for Jesus in a "make your own religion" society, we *will* face evil attacks at times. When they come, we can look at Paul's life and turn to these verses for encouragement.

ALL OUR NEEDS

*[Paul said,] "This same God who takes care of me
will supply all your needs from his glorious riches,
which have been given to us in Christ Jesus."*

PHILIPPIANS 4:19

IF YOU'VE OPENED a bank account any time in recent decades, chances are good that account is insured by the FDIC—the Federal Deposit Insurance Corporation. Like most insurance plans, the FDIC is essentially a safety net. If your bank fails or is the victim of fraud, your accounts will be covered and reimbursed by the federal government, up to a certain limit on each account.

In this way, the FDIC provides a critical service for both the banking industry and individual account holders. Banks can remain focused on serving customers because of the protections offered by the FDIC. Individual account holders can feel secure when they entrust their hard-earned money to a bank because they know that bank is supported by another corporation with a huge supply of resources.

In today's verse, we're promised that God will supply all our needs—and that's a wonderful guarantee. That's cause for us to feel joy and contentment and satisfaction in our journey through this life. We don't have to struggle on our own! We don't have to depend on ourselves to provide what we need—what our families need. We're covered.

Best of all, we have far greater insurance available to us than any government entity could offer. Instead of the FDIC, we're insured by God's "glorious riches." We're covered by the Creator of the universe, and we've been given access to his wondrous resources because of what Christ did for us on the cross.

GOD WILL ANSWER

*The LORD is my light and my salvation—so why should I be
afraid? The LORD is my fortress, protecting me from danger, so
why should I tremble? When evil people come to devour me, when
my enemies and foes attack me, they will stumble and fall.*

PSALM 27:1-2

WRITTEN BY DAVID—a man who saw his share of conflicts—Psalm 27
paints a picture of a man relying on God in the midst of trouble. David
had many enemies throughout his life. He was pursued by relentless
forces far beyond his own powers. He faced an implacable enemy who
wouldn't let up: King Saul. David's own followers tended to write him
off, and even some of his family members turned against him.

It's hard to imagine how we would deal with such circumstances. We
know from Scripture that David ran from his enemies (particularly Saul)
for a long time, but he didn't run because of cowardice—he understood
that a confrontation would cost him and his pursuer greatly. Yet even in
that conflict, David leaned on God and did not use unrighteous tactics.
He trusted that God would take care of him if he maintained his integrity.

That's the way we should face difficult circumstances as well—by being
brave and courageous. Not giving up. Pushing through the difficult
obstacles. Refusing to surrender. And sometimes, waiting, not acting
hastily out of fear. David could afford to wait; he was safe in a fortress not
made of rock or steel but built on God's character and covenant promises. In time God blessed David and dealt with the murderous King Saul.
He allowed David to unite the whole kingdom of Israel and become one
of the nation's greatest kings.

Sometimes God doesn't bring deliverance on our schedule, which
can be tough. Our enemies don't always stumble and fall when or how
we'd like. But God's promise in this psalm and throughout Scripture is
that they will not overcome us. In his plan, God will come through at a
time best suited for us.

OCTOBER

GOD BUILDS THE HOUSE

*Unless the LORD builds a house, the work of the builders is
wasted. Unless the LORD protects a city, guarding it with
sentries will do no good. It is useless for you to work so hard
from early morning until late at night, anxiously working
for food to eat; for God gives rest to his loved ones.*

PSALM 127:1-2

OUR WORLD HAS many building projects, many bustling cities. Technology allows everything—computers, smartphones, tablets—to move faster and everyone to be connected and to communicate through the Internet. Everywhere you look, you see what seems to be growth and progress.

Yet this race toward progress has caused much calamity as well. As we become more connected to cyberspace, we find it more difficult to unplug and take part in "real" life. The more opportunities we have to work, the harder it is to stop working and rest. As our technology improves, so do our weapons—people find new ways to attack and enslave other people, while nations invent new ways to strike against other nations.

This should remind us that progress and advancement are good—but only when seen in the light of God's ultimate provision. Human striving can provide temporary benefits, but it can also produce long-term destruction. Only by conforming our efforts to God's will and God's plan will our frantic efforts construct anything worthwhile. That's one of God's promises in this passage: that he can prevent our work from being wasted.

But there's another promise that we should find even sweeter—that "God gives rest to his loved ones." God didn't wire us to be 24/7 automatons. And in the midst of others' constantly spinning and analyzing and producing in their own strength, he has promised to give us rest and balance, because we can trust him with the results.

STAND FIRM

By standing firm, you will win your souls.

LUKE 21:19

ONE OF THE best testimonies to unbelievers is how believers stand firm in troubling times. For instance, Merrilee faced a terrible fight against breast cancer. All her friends and coworkers visited her in the hospital to encourage and comfort her. But funny thing: because Merrilee was a Christian, she had more encouraging and comforting words for them than they did for her.

As she testified of her love for God and her confidence in him no matter what happened, many of those visitors were astounded. Some wanted to know more about this Jesus she believed in and served.

In the end, Merrilee lost her struggle with breast cancer. But she didn't lose the struggle in her friends' minds. At her funeral, many spoke of how her serene spirit and encouraging words had led them to faith and made them long to be as strong and sincere as she was in her life.

At some point you will be called to stand firm in tough times. God wants you to use such times to win the hearts of your friends and others who see what happened. His promise is that through your witness some souls will be won.

JESUS KNOWS

Since [Jesus] himself has gone through suffering and testing,
he is able to help us when we are being tested.

HEBREWS 2:18

HERE'S SOMETHING THAT may surprise you: Jesus knows what it's like to face the problems you've been facing in your life. He may not have faced the exact same problems as you, of course, but the underlying principles and conflicts are more than similar.

Jesus never went to high school, for example, but he was a boy who played and lived and learned among other children. Jesus never had to worry about corporate advancement, but he was part of a successful carpentry business alongside his earthly father, Joseph. Jesus never struggled with the consequences of sin—lust, greed, selfishness, laziness, and so on—but he was tempted with opportunities to commit those sins.

And Jesus suffered. Though his life on earth was relatively short compared to what we hope for today, he suffered more than we can imagine. He was rejected by his people and ostracized by many who should have loved him—including members of his own family. He was betrayed by his friends. He was abandoned and tortured and ultimately murdered on a Roman cross.

All those experiences form the basis of the promise given in Hebrews 2:18: that Jesus is able to help us when we come against difficult situations and hard-to-resist temptations. Not just because he's God but because he overcame the power not only of sin but also of temptation. Whether we're being tempted or actually suffering, he overcame both in his flesh and can now, by his power, do the same in us.

GREAT NEWS FOR EVANGELISM

[Jesus said,] "When I am lifted up from the
earth, I will draw everyone to myself."
JOHN 12:32

THERE ARE A lot of people (not just kids) who view vegetables as a necessary evil. They understand that vegetables are good for them. They agree that vegetables are part of a healthy diet, and they willingly eat vegetables several times a week—but they wish they didn't have to. They could go the rest of their lives without tasting another stalk of broccoli or lettuce leaf.

In a similar way, most Christians understand that evangelism is a good and healthy part of following Jesus. We know that sharing our faith with others is important for God's Kingdom, and we willingly go on missions trips or talk to our neighbors—but deep down, some of us wish we didn't have to. Deep down, we'd be happier if someone else could do it for us.

Here's the great news: someone else *can* do it for us! Jesus has already done the heavy lifting when it comes to evangelism—he shed his blood on the cross to open the door of salvation to all people. We don't have to drag people toward Jesus, because he's promised to draw all people to himself.

In the same vein, we don't have to convince people that they're sinners or get them to change their behavior—that's not our job. The Holy Spirit is the one who convicts people of their sins and works to make them born again. All we need to do is share the good news of our experiences as we follow the one who was lifted up on the cross.

THE WINNING TEAM

*[The Son of Man] was given authority, honor, and sovereignty
over all the nations of the world, so that people of every race
and nation and language would obey him. His rule is eternal—
it will never end. His kingdom will never be destroyed.*

DANIEL 7:14

IF YOU'RE A sports fan, you're not alone. Athletic competition is one of the most popular forms of entertainment in the world today among both men and women. People from all cultures and nations regularly invest their time and energy in rooting for team sports such as football, soccer, baseball, basketball, gymnastics, and more.

But the sad side of following sports is that the vast majority of fans are disappointed at the end of the season. That's because most athletes and teams don't win a championship or a coveted prize in a given year.

Take football, for example. The National Football League has thirty-two teams, and each team has millions of devoted fans. Yet only one of those teams will win the Super Bowl each year—which means only one set of fans won't feel the sting of disappointment and loss. Even worse, some professional sports teams can go decades without winning a championship. In fact, in baseball, the Chicago Cubs haven't won the World Series in more than one hundred years!

As disciples of Christ, we have a different experience than most sports fans do. That's because we have a guarantee that our team will emerge victorious at the end of all things. Who and what will be defeated? Satan, sin, and death, to name a few. God's promise in Daniel 7:14 (and in many other places throughout his Word) is that his Kingdom will never end but those in opposition will. Therefore, those who choose to follow him can do so with complete commitment, trust, and confidence in the final outcome.

NO FLOOD EVER AGAIN

*[God said,] "I swore in the time of Noah that I would
never again let a flood cover the earth."*

ISAIAH 54:9

AT ONE TIME, God became so angry with humanity's sin and rebellion
against him that he decided to start over. He conscripted Noah, a righteous man and a believer, to be part of the greatest disciplinary action
ever. Over the next hundred years, Noah preached of the coming judgment. No one believed, though, and the flood that followed wiped out
all humanity except Noah and his family.

But God is not a God who exhibits anger meaninglessly. He sent
Noah a sign in the sky that would be a reminder of his promise: a rainbow. It was meant to assure the world that another worldwide flood
would never occur.

Why did God use the rainbow? How many times have you seen one?
While most people today don't connect it to the truth of God's commitment never to flood the world again, it was a powerful reminder to those
who lived shortly after the Flood. Imagine the fear and worry they must
have felt whenever it started to rain. God gave them that promise not only
to assure them of his love but also to move them to have true faith in him.

We can recognize God's love in the rainbow too. While we're not so
afraid of another flood, it's one more reminder that God is here and
is still ruling in the world of men. We can trust him about everything,
even when it rains and we worry about the possibility of flooding. It's
still a promise that he will not harm us but will exercise his mercy and
patience—and that's lasted thousands of years beyond the rainbow!

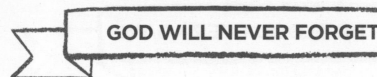

GOD WILL NEVER FORGET

*God is not unjust. He will not forget how hard you have
worked for him and how you have shown your love to
him by caring for other believers, as you still do.*

HEBREWS 6:10

IN TODAY'S CULTURE, one of the lessons we learn early as children is that good work should be recognized. As babies, we receive praise every time we say a new word or take a new step. In school we're regularly rewarded with good grades whenever we put in the effort required to earn them. As teenagers, our demonstrations of newfound responsibility are often matched by new privileges—such as driving the family car.

Sadly, this pattern often comes to a grinding halt when we reach adulthood and enter the "real world." Most jobs come with a high standard of effort, and it seems like the only reward we get for meeting that standard is the privilege of keeping those jobs. Parents work diligently to love and support their children day in and day out—usually with little or no thanks.

Life can be a grind. Life can be tough. It can be an endless repetition of daily routines, and there are times when we just wish someone would *notice* how hard we're working. Yes, there are days when even the smallest hint of praise or appreciation can lift us up and carry us smiling into tomorrow—but those are often few and far between.

Thankfully, mercifully, this will not always be so. God sees what we do. He sees the ways we love our neighbors and help those in need. He will reward us for the smallest of sacrifices. He greatly approves when we put aside our jitters and proclaim the good news of Jesus Christ. And God has promised he will never forget.

SAVED FROM CONDEMNATION

Since we have been made right in God's sight by the blood of
Christ, he will certainly save us from God's condemnation.

ROMANS 5:9

HAVE YOU SEEN any good courtroom shows recently? Whether cameras are catching the action of "real" court cases or filming fictional scenarios, the entertainment industry (and our culture at large) seems to become more fascinated with the judicial system every day.

But have you ever actually been in a courtroom? Have you sat in the jury box and listened to the evidence and arguments for yourself? That's an intimidating experience for most people. Serving as a prosecutor or a defense attorney and delivering those arguments would be an overwhelming experience for most people. But being the focus of a court case, put on trial and forced to defend your actions under the threat of being declared guilty, would be the most terrifying experience of all.

Think about sitting across from a judge as he or she receives the verdict—your verdict—from the jury foreman. Imagine the helplessness you would feel in that situation. Your immediate and long-term future would be spelled out on that small slip of paper, but you would have no control over what happens next. Your very freedom would be in the hands of strangers.

Thankfully, Romans 5:9 reminds us that followers of Jesus will never have to feel that kind of helplessness when it comes to our eternal destiny. Even though we're guilty of sin, we will not be condemned. Our prosecutor, Satan, won't even win a hearing because we've already been saved by the blood of Christ.

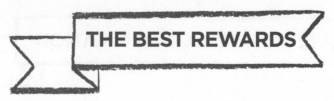

THE BEST REWARDS

When you give to someone in need, don't let your left hand
know what your right hand is doing. Give your gifts in private,
and your Father, who sees everything, will reward you.

MATTHEW 6:3-4

THERE'S NO QUESTION that helping people in need is a wonderful thing. Giving of our time and resources in order to bless others who are hurting is the essence of godliness. It's something we're commanded to do many times throughout the Bible. All followers of Jesus should give to those in need.

And yet, strangely, this act of loving our neighbors through giving can also be a dangerous undertaking. We may become tempted to start wishing that other people could see what we're doing—that they were around to see how good and merciful and generous we are.

It's natural for us to desire recognition and approval when we do something good. It's human nature for us to crave a reward for our positive behavior—which is why it's so easy for us to slip into the habit of making sure others hear about it whenever we donate to charity or buy a hamburger for a homeless person on the street. But the approval of others isn't of much value in the long run.

We need to remember that the best rewards come from God. We don't have to settle for the temporary admiration of other people when we know that God takes note of our actions—and that he's promised to reward us for good deeds done in private.

THE BREAD FROM HEAVEN

*[Jesus said,] "I am the true bread that came down from heaven.
Anyone who eats this bread will not die as your ancestors did
(even though they ate the manna) but will live forever."*

JOHN 6:58

THERE'S A LOT to like about food. In a very real and practical way, food is deeply connected with life for all human beings. It nourishes us and enables us to grow and perform. It provides the energy we need to keep our hearts pumping, brains thinking, and muscles flexing.

Food is also fun. We enjoy the variety of flavors that can be encountered from different kinds of meals from different places prepared in different ways. There are few things we enjoy more than gathering together around a table to eat, drink, and be merry. Food is a catalyst for enjoyment.

But food is temporary. When we eat a meal, we enjoy ourselves and become nourished—for a time. But soon the nourishment fades and we become hungry. We must eat again. And again. That's what Moses and the Israelites experienced when they ate manna day after day in the wilderness. They always needed more or they would die.

In John 6:58, Jesus used the concept of earthly food as a contrast to the spiritual nourishment we can find through him. Eating normal food is a temporary experience with superficial satisfaction, but when we encounter Jesus as the Bread of heaven—when he becomes a part of us and changes us from the inside out—something permanent happens. The promise of this verse is that when we partake of Jesus, we will be totally satisfied, live forever, and be spiritually nourished for all time.

NO MORE SELF-DECEPTION

> *If we claim we have no sin, we are only fooling ourselves and not
> living in the truth. But if we confess our sins to him, he is faithful and
> just to forgive us our sins and to cleanse us from all wickedness.*
>
> 1 JOHN 1:8-9

IF THERE'S ONE activity at which all human beings are especially gifted, that activity would be self-deception. No matter how much evidence we may observe regarding the truth about something, we have the capacity to fool ourselves into believing the exact opposite to be the case.

When we see all the sweets and treats around the holidays, for example, it's so easy for us to convince ourselves that feasting on them won't affect us. Then, when we gain a few pounds after overindulging, it's easy to tell ourselves, *It's just water weight.* This kind of self-deception is often harmless and sometimes humorous—it's a kind of joke we play on ourselves whenever we don't want to face a certain reality.

But there's nothing funny about self-deception when it comes to sin. There's nothing to joke about when we fool ourselves into believing that God's wrath and judgment are reserved for rapists and murderers, not for "good people" like us. The Bible is clear that "everyone has sinned" (Romans 3:23) and that "the wages of sin is [eternal] death" (Romans 6:23).

That's the bad news, but the great news comes in this promise from 1 John 1:9. If we choose to be honest about our sin and confess our struggles to God, he promises to forgive us. He has the ability to separate us from all our past wickedness. We only need to take him at his Word.

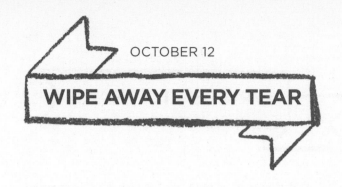

OCTOBER 12

WIPE AWAY EVERY TEAR

[God] will wipe every tear from their eyes, and there will be no more death or sorrow or crying or pain. All these things are gone forever.
REVELATION 21:4

CAN YOU IMAGINE a world without "death or sorrow or crying or pain"? Most of us can't. Those problems are such daily realities in most of our lives that to imagine a world without such things seems a stretch.

Yet that's what God promises. One day, we will enter heaven, where we will find true completion and unity with God. Jesus will personally wipe our tears away, whether we've cried many or few during our time on earth. He will lead us into a place where unhappiness, hatred, rejection, failure, and fear will never reign again.

Can you imagine it? Perhaps not, but you can keep your mind and heart focused on the truth of the above verse and those like it. God's promise is that this place we live in, this "vale of tears," will not be like that forever. The situations that cause us to weep and wail and hurt now can also cause us to turn to God for the real hope, the kind of hope that lasts and will ultimately come true.

Trust him about all those troubles you may be facing right now. You may be weeping, feeling there is no way you'll ever be happy again, but you can trust the promise that one day all of that will be behind you. What is ahead can't be anything less than a marvel.

WRITTEN TO TEACH

Such things were written in the Scriptures long ago to teach us. And the Scriptures give us hope and encouragement as we wait patiently for God's promises to be fulfilled.

ROMANS 15:4

WHY DOES THE Bible have so many stories? Especially stories of failure, lust, deceit, and violence? One reason may be to teach us, to give us hope and encouragement when we fail or are tempted to sin.

Maybe God wants us to read and study the Bible because those stories will dig deep into our hearts and show us how to triumph in difficult times. Job, Samuel, Abraham, and King David all went through tough circumstances, but we can take comfort and strength from their experiences.

What story in the Bible most encourages you? Which one do you consider precious because it has helped you so many times? Everyone has different favorites. God gave you those stories to keep you stoked, make you believe things can work in your life, and motivate you not to give up.

Through stories God teaches us the great principle that he is with us and works in a mighty way. His promise is to use those stories to build us up.

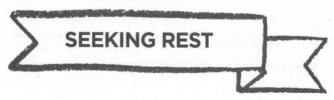

SEEKING REST

Jesus said, "Come to me, all of you who are weary and carry heavy burdens, and I will give you rest."
MATTHEW 11:28

WHAT'S THE VALUE of a good night's sleep? That seems like an unanswerable question at first. But when we really think about it, there are ways to go about connecting a monetary figure to a night of unbroken rest.

We could look in a local pharmacy, for example. Several companies make over-the-counter sleeping aids for a relatively low price—anywhere from five to twenty dollars a bottle. There are also a number of prescription sleep medicines that can be purchased, but things get a little more expensive behind the counter, and such medicine requires a doctor's visit.

Speaking of a doctor, we could answer the question another way by finding a psychiatrist. Many people seek counseling to deal with insomnia, nightmares, and other disorders, often stemming from anxiety, that regularly disrupt their sleep. These visits are not cheap either—anywhere from fifty to more than two hundred dollars an hour.

We could also assess the value of a good night's sleep by finding a quality mattress store. Some people spend several thousand dollars for a quality bed on which to rest.

With that in mind, let's not forget the incredible value of what Jesus promised in Matthew 11:28. In a world where people desperately seek something as simple as a good night's sleep, imagine how wonderful it is to receive the gift of rest from our Creator—and not just rest for our physical bodies but also for our souls. It's a rest that can remove all anxiety, conflict, and guilt from our lives and give us perfect peace.

BLESSED ARE THE MERCIFUL

There will be no mercy for those who have not shown mercy to others.
But if you have been merciful, God will be merciful when he judges you.

JAMES 2:13

THERE ARE SOME verses in the Bible that always seem to surprise us when we come across them. James 2:13 is a good example of such a verse. Is it true that the mercy God will show us in eternity is somehow connected to the mercy we have shown others here on earth? Can that be right?

The answer is yes, of course. That's what James clearly wrote in his epistle. That's also what Jesus himself proclaimed in the Sermon on the Mount: "God blesses those who are merciful, for they will be shown mercy" (Matthew 5:7). And just two chapters later, Jesus made it clear that he meant what he said: "You will be treated as you treat others. The standard you use in judging is the standard by which you will be judged" (Matthew 7:2).

Theologians have wrestled for centuries over the exact meaning of these passages and how they correspond to Jesus' additional message of salvation through faith. But one thing is clear: one of the evidences that a person has genuinely been transformed by Jesus is that he or she demonstrates the same kind of mercy he demonstrated.

If we refuse to show mercy to others, we will be hard pressed to find mercy ourselves from God. That seems like cause for concern, at first. But this verse contains a second promise that is much more cheerful: if we commit to demonstrating mercy in this life, we also will receive mercy in the life to come.

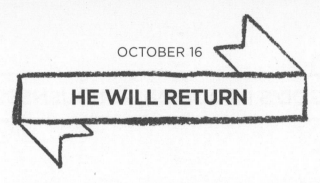

HE WILL RETURN

"Men of Galilee," [two white-robed men] said, "why are you standing here staring into heaven? Jesus has been taken from you into heaven, but someday he will return from heaven in the same way you saw him go!"

ACTS 1:11

"I'LL BE BACK soon." How often have you heard promises like that when you said good-bye to a friend or family member? "See you tomorrow." "Catch ya later." "I'll be home at ten."

We hear such phrases all the time. We say them all the time too. They roll easily off our tongues without a second thought. And yet, deep down, these kinds of words can spark a tiny flame of fear whenever we hear or say them—whenever we're forced to admit the reality of being physically separated from someone we care about.

That's because the risk of permanent separation is always present. There's always a chance that the person we care about won't be back soon. There's always a chance our loved one won't come home by ten—that he or she won't come home at all. We live in a world troubled by sin and separated from God, which means we never know when that casual good-bye will end up being a final farewell.

After Jesus ascended to heaven, the disciples were probably standing there with their mouths agape. *Why did he leave us, and in such an awesome way? Will he come back one day? Can we be sure he'll return to gather us up and bring us to his heavenly Kingdom?* These fears are understandable, and we may sometimes share them, but we must not give in to such doubts. Though we don't know when it will happen, the words of Scripture ring clear: "He will return from heaven."

GOD'S PROOF OF SERIOUSNESS

*The Spirit is God's guarantee that he will give us the inheritance
he promised and that he has purchased us to be his own
people. He did this so we would praise and glorify him.*

EPHESIANS 1:14

ARE YOU FAMILIAR with the concept of earnest money? If you've ever purchased a house, your answer to that question is almost certainly yes.

Earnest money is a type of insurance. When people make an offer on a house they wish to buy, they're typically asked to include a sum of money as part of that offer—anywhere from five hundred to several thousand dollars—which is held in an escrow account. If the homeowners accept the offer and the purchase goes smoothly, the earnest money is rolled into the down payment and nothing is lost for either side. However, if the prospective buyers back out of the purchase after a contract has been signed, they lose their earnest money. It's given to the homeowner as compensation for wasted time and effort.

In its basic form, then, earnest money is proof of seriousness. It's a way for would-be homeowners to prove their sincerity when they make a promise to purchase.

As Christians, we've been promised a divine inheritance. We've been promised God's "glorious riches" through Jesus Christ (Philippians 4:19). We've been promised a crown of life (see James 1:12). Most important, we've been promised salvation, forgiveness of our sins, and eternal life as members of God's Kingdom.

According to Ephesians 1:14, the Holy Spirit is a kind of earnest money in relation to those promises—he lives in us and works through us as proof of God's full blessings to come. This is wonderful news! Therefore, the proper response to such a gift (and such a promise) is for us to praise and glorify God and let the Holy Spirit shape us in the image of Christ so we will be fully ready for this glorious inheritance.

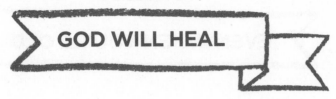

GOD WILL HEAL

*"I will give you back your health and heal your wounds," says the LORD.
"For you are called an outcast—Jerusalem for whom no one cares."'*

JEREMIAH 30:17

THE WORDS ABOVE were spoken to the Israelites as they languished as
slaves in Babylon. After years of rebellion, Jerusalem had been destroyed,
many Israelites had been killed, and the Temple had been sacked and
plundered. The young Israelite men with the most potential were taken
to an idol-worshiping nation, where the priests of that religion would
try to indoctrinate them into adopting their religion. After so much suffering, the Israelites had little hope.

But God spoke his words of hope into this desolation through the
prophet Jeremiah. Jeremiah had been reviled and hated for his prophe-
cies against the sins of God's people. But now the children of God sat
up and took notice.

Too many leaders teach today that with God, it's more like three
strikes and you're out. But the promise given in today's verse is the truth.
God calls us back to himself, even when we've messed up terribly, and
promises to heal our wounds, bind up the "broken bones," and bring us
back to wholeness. That's the great message of the Bible: it doesn't matter
how much of a mess you've made of your life. God still loves you and
invites you to come back and start over.

EVEN WHEN YOU'RE OLD

Even in old age they will still produce fruit;
they will remain vital and green.

PSALM 92:14

AS DOROTHY BEGAN to age and her health gradually deteriorated, she couldn't get around much. Her husband pastored a church, as he had for many years, but Dorothy could no longer even go to church with him.

Still, Dorothy had a vital ministry from home. She cheerfully talked of the Lord with her children, her grandchildren, and their friends. She ministered to many from her husband's congregation over the phone. She sent notes of encouragement and cards to mark special events in people's lives. And she prayed for others.

When this diminutive woman died after more than a decade of being mostly homebound, people stood in line for hours to tell her family how much she had ministered to them, and her funeral was packed.

You've probably known people like Dorothy. People who may not be able to do what they could in their younger years, but as they age, even increase their ministry. Whether it's taking their RV and ministering at mission sites around the country, volunteering to help in the church office, or being a hospice counselor, they realize their age and physical limitations aren't going to give them an excuse not to serve the Lord.

Whether we're old or young, God has a job for us to do—and a blessing to pour on our lives for doing it.

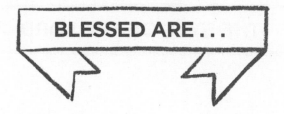

BLESSED ARE . . .

Blessed are those who trust in the LORD and have made the LORD their hope and confidence. They are like trees planted along a riverbank, with roots that reach deep into the water. Such trees are not bothered by the heat or worried by long months of drought. Their leaves stay green, and they never stop producing fruit.

JEREMIAH 17:7-8

THESE VERSES GIVE a picture of people at rest in Christ. These are Christians who walk closely with God, seek him daily, and put him first on the list of priorities. What exactly does God do for such people?

When things get tough, they don't wilt. Like trees whose roots go deep, the heat of life doesn't dry them up. They have resources that go far below the surface, and there they find calm and peace.

They don't worry about bad times. Drought can kill crops and trees. But people rooted in Jesus will not fear bad times in this world—financially, physically, or emotionally. They will always know that God is with them, no matter what has gone wrong in the world around them.

They keep producing fruit, in good times and in bad. This kind of Christian is resilient, flexible, and always ready for action. He or she doesn't give up on bad people and is not riled by the supposedly "good" people.

God wants your life to be like this. He promises that if you walk with him, he will make you strong, resilient, and persevering.

THE EYES OF THE LORD

The eyes of the LORD watch over those who do right, and his ears are open to their prayers. But the LORD turns his face against those who do evil.

1 PETER 3:12

WHY DO BAD *things happen to good people?* Chances are good you've pondered that question once or twice in recent years. Most Christians wrestle with the reality of pain and suffering in the world. We struggle to understand why those who try to help others and do the right thing so often find themselves in difficult times—and we especially struggle to understand when the same thing happens to us.

There's another question that bugs us from time to time, isn't there? *Why do good things happen to bad people?* At some level we can understand that the trials of life produce character in those who suffer through them (see James 1:2-4), but what about those times when wicked people prosper? What good can come from cheaters and liars who seem to rise higher and higher each day on the wings of their own greed?

Peter's words in this verse offer comfort in the face of such big questions. "The eyes of the LORD watch over those who do right" and "the LORD turns his face against those who do evil." That's a promise from God's Word. We may not always understand how that promise works itself out, but we can have confidence that God's open ears mean he wants to hear from us. We don't have to strain to get God's attention.

We can rest assured that God works against those who do evil, even if they appear to be "getting away with murder" in the short run. Even if evil is used against us personally, we know that God will work it for our good in the long run, so we need not be the judge or the avenger. God is quite capable of handling those roles.

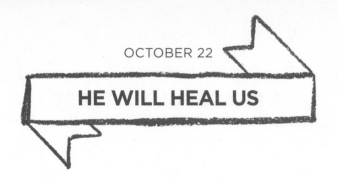

HE WILL HEAL US

Come, let us return to the LORD. He has torn us to pieces; now he will heal us. He has injured us; now he will bandage our wounds.

HOSEA 6:1

AT TIMES GOD allows his people to suffer deeply. Sometimes it's a result of their own sins. But sometimes it's because they've been faithful and the world hates them and persecutes them. Either way, how we bear suffering can lead others to the one who suffered for them.

Some years ago, Gracia Burnham and her husband were kidnapped by Islamists in the Philippines. They were missionaries at the time, laboring in a foreign land, faithful to their calling. Yet they were taken captive, and in the end, Gracia's husband, Martin, was killed in the firefight in which she ultimately gained her freedom.

Gracia now travels the world telling the story of her capture and loss. She also speaks about how God blessed her and her husband's ministry through the pain they suffered. Many people have heard her testimony in churches in every corner of the globe, and many have become Christians as a result—many Christians have been moved to deepen their commitment to God as well. Gracia tells her audiences that though she lost her dearest friend in the kidnapping, God remains close and has blessed her in numerous ways. She has experienced comfort and renewal, and she looks forward to seeing her husband in heaven.

In this verse, God promises that even the deepest pain and suffering are only temporary. In time, he will repair all the damage done and re-create something even more beautiful than before.

A PEACEFUL HARVEST

No discipline is enjoyable while it is happening—it's painful!
But afterward there will be a peaceful harvest of right
living for those who are trained in this way.

HEBREWS 12:11

IT'S A SCENE that's been played out for generations. A young girl runs to find her mom, tears streaming down her face, crying that her brother hit her after some silly argument. The mom confronts her son, but the boy denies any wrongdoing. "I didn't do anything. I never hit her."

The mom has witnessed all this before, however, and she sees the boy's lowered eyes. She sees his shuffling feet, and she demands the truth. She remains firm until the boy says, "It was an accident" or "I didn't mean to hit that hard" or "She started it."

Then she nods. A wrong has been done. Rules have been broken, which means a punishment must be assigned. She sends the boy to his room and encourages him to think about what's been done and what should have been done. The boy is angry, however, and he shouts bitter words as he leaves. The mom has heard such words before, and she says nothing. She waits.

Later, the mom again speaks with her son, offering gentle words. The boy listens. His anger is gone, replaced by guilt and regret. He apologizes to his mom and his sister. He learns not to react in anger. His relationship with his mom and sister is restored.

Most of us have experienced discipline from our earthly parents. And as Christians, we will also receive discipline from our heavenly Father. He has promised there will be negative consequences for us when we sin. Thankfully, he's also promised that such discipline will not be in vain. And like the son in the story above, we will learn the lessons we need for future right living. God's discipline will always lead to a harvest, to peace, if we're willing to submit and accept what's offered.

LOST AND FOUND

His father said to him, "Look, dear son, you have always
stayed by me, and everything I have is yours. We had to
celebrate this happy day. For your brother was dead and has
come back to life! He was lost, but now he is found!"

LUKE 15:31-32

THE PARABLE OF the Prodigal Son in Luke 15 is a story most Christians know and greatly treasure. But there are also many stories of prodigal children in families today—even families in our churches.

One such prodigal, a girl of eighteen, stormed out of her family's house one night and refused to return. She went to live with a boyfriend and quickly forgot all her vows of purity from earlier days. She didn't get pregnant, but she did spend many nights with different guys who wanted little more than her body.

Meanwhile, her family prayed repeatedly for her to turn around. They prayed every day and every night—until the night she came to the front door, broken and fearful. When her father answered, she said, "I know you probably hate me. I've really messed up. Can I stay here tonight? I have nowhere else to go."

Her father swept her up in his arms, kissed her, and assured her she could stay for as many nights as she wanted. She stayed for a while, began going to church again, and met a young man who had been through some bad things like she had. Their hearts resonated, and soon they were in love. But they both decided to obey the Lord and remain pure until their marriage. Today, they have a happy home with two small children they love.

The parable of the Prodigal Son is, in effect, a promise that God will welcome his prodigal children back home. No matter how far they have wandered, God will always celebrate over prodigals who realize the futility of their wanderings and return to the Father's unconditional love.

WISDOM

My child, pay attention to what I say. Listen carefully to my words.
Don't lose sight of them. Let them penetrate deep into your heart, for
they bring life to those who find them, and healing to their whole body.
PROVERBS 4:20-22

SOME TIME AGO, a long article was published in a significant liberal magazine about the search for wisdom in today's world. It spoke of a certain professor's journey as she sought to find what real wisdom is. She studied religious texts, interviewed people young and old, and read the works of philosophers galore. She even gave Solomon's proverbs a scan.

The crazy thing is how even a definition of wisdom eluded her. No one seemed to know precisely what it is. Knowledge? The ability to think through a situation or problem? Intelligence? Something only the elite could fathom? Then why are so many people considered wise who have little education and have read very few books?

One has to look only a few pages into the book of Proverbs to find some ideas about what wisdom does. As Solomon says above, it brings life to those who listen to wise people. Wisdom heals the whole body. A seminary professor used to define wisdom as "skill for living." The wise person, like a master craftsman, has a tremendous skill for living well and solving problems, rising above them to reach success, influence, and accomplishment.

The world doesn't get it, but the Christian does. Do you want skill for living? Do you want to know how to live well? Then study the words of people like Solomon as well as those of Jesus, Paul, Moses, Malachi, and many others. You will find life and healing in them. Guaranteed.

DIRECT YOUR CHILDREN

*Direct your children onto the right path, and when
they are older, they will not leave it.*

PROVERBS 22:6

WHEN ALAYNA WAS eighteen and still in high school, she moved out of her house and began making some really bad choices.

"What did we do wrong?" her parents cried. "After all, the Bible promises that if we raise our kids right, they'll not walk away from the Lord. It must be our fault."

So many parents consider this Scripture verse a reason to go on a guilt trip when their kids go astray. But actually it's not. Once they're in or beyond their teens, our kids start making their own life decisions. They begin to choose between right and wrong, just as we did when we were younger. And sometimes they choose wrong, no matter how well they've been raised and how godly their homes were. Sometimes, discovering who they are and what kinds of choices they want to make in life leads children on a path that looks as if it's far from our faith, but we don't need to despair. No matter what choices our kids make, God is with them.

And the promise in this verse does hold true. No matter what choices our kids might be making now, they know what the right path is. And most kids who walk away from their faith eventually return.

So know that when you teach your kids how to walk with the Lord, you're teaching them a lifestyle that will stay with them the rest of their lives—whether they take a side road for a while or not.

WAIT QUIETLY

It is good to wait quietly for salvation from the LORD.
LAMENTATIONS 3:26

AN OLD PASTOR suffered several major setbacks. He lost his retirement fund because the managers of it had made some bad investments. His wife died unexpectedly. And his son and daughter were simply too busy and too far away to come visit regularly. He could have spent many hours depressed and feeling sorry for himself. But instead, when people asked him what he would do now, he said, "I'm waiting."

If they asked for more explanation, he referred to the verse above and spoke of how he waited "quietly for salvation from the LORD."

Sometimes circumstances become so bad that you simply can't do much to change them. It might be a sickness that has struck you down. It could be the loss of something you can never get back. It could be a fire that has burned down your house and destroyed all your possessions.

This is a not a time to do nothing. What you can do in such times is "wait quietly" for the Lord to do his part. His promise is that he will do it. All we have to do is trust and quietly look to him. One way or another, he'll use your life for his glory.

THE DEAD WILL RISE

Don't be so surprised! Indeed, the time is coming when all the dead in their graves will hear the voice of God's Son, and they will rise again. Those who have done good will rise to experience eternal life, and those who have continued in evil will rise to experience judgment.

JOHN 5:28-29

THE DAY IS coming. Even during the time of his earthly ministry, Jesus warned people that the voice (or trumpet of the archangel) will sound and suddenly multitudes of Christians will be carried off to heaven, joy, bliss, and perfect love forever.

It will be an incredible moment. Why is it important, though? Why should we look forward to it?

Because it's the ultimate fulfillment of God's promise. This world is not the end. No matter what we've suffered here, something far better and greater awaits us in heaven. Christianity is the only religion that promises a returning Leader and Savior, the one who conquered death and paid for the sins of the world.

Paul, in 2 Timothy 4:8, speaks of how those who have longed for Jesus' appearing will receive a crown of righteousness. Do you long for that event to happen? Or are you so settled into this world that you actually dread it? He promises that no matter how placid things appear now, he will come eventually to reward and to judge. And he also promises that those who have awaited that coming with good deeds will receive even greater treasures.

IN GOD'S HOUSE

Surely your goodness and unfailing love will pursue me all the
days of my life, and I will live in the house of the LORD forever.

PSALM 23:6

WHAT A TREMENDOUS thing to look forward to: living in God's house forever! Can you imagine it?

What will happen in that house? What might we expect to go on there throughout eternity? The Bible reveals many things, but let's think of a few. Worship? Yes, we will worship God on a level we haven't even touched here on earth. Ever felt carried up in a special service, or some personal time of worship? Ever sensed the august presence and approval of God? For many, such times are rare. But they will be the daily experience of those living in God's house.

Other things we'll surely do are celebrate, hear great music, participate in grand feasts, and just have fun. We don't know what God has planned, but clearly heaven won't be boring. We'll undoubtedly have responsibilities in building the new society that will be vast and endless. Most of all, we'll get to know God more and more in his fullness.

Something else we'll all go through will be literally walking with Jesus, up close, side by side, perhaps hand in hand. He will be present to all of us without any of us ever feeling neglected, forgotten, or overlooked. He will be there at all times and in all places.

Do you look forward to heaven? There's a promise waiting for you to claim if you know God personally. He will get you there. Just trust him, and remember no matter how tough it gets in this world, this isn't the end.

OCTOBER 30

GOD'S PROMISES

Your promise revives me; it comforts me in all my troubles.

PSALM 119:50

WHEN SARAH FACED difficult times—a husband who left her for another woman, financial problems, loss of her house, and a battle to keep her kids—she turned to the Bible's promises to sustain her. She read the Psalms over and over, selecting specific promises of God's love and deliverance and comfort to memorize and pray about.

For a while it looked as if all was lost. But after the divorce, her husband ended up leaving the woman he'd left Sarah for. She won custody of her kids when he simply said, "Forget it." And she started a small catering business, using her ability to cook excellent gourmet meals to great effect. As her business grew, she added other hurting women to her organization, and in time she could look back and say, "God kept every promise."

Look to God in whatever troubles you face. Remember his promises. Consult the Bible, and memorize the passages that speak directly to your situation.

Promises from Scripture are not offered as empty platitudes. Bible promises are set in gold, as sure as God's own character. Though there may be times when it seems God has not heard your pleas or forgotten about your needs, his promise is that he hears all your prayers, and he will act on your behalf in his own time.

HE WILL BEAR OUR SINS

When he sees all that is accomplished by his anguish, he will be satisfied.
And because of his experience, my righteous servant will make it possible
for many to be counted righteous, for he will bear all their sins.

ISAIAH 53:11

IF YOU HAVE experience traveling long distances on foot, you know that any extra weight you carry becomes cumbersome after a while. The more miles you walk, the more you feel the pack pulling down against your back—the more your boots grow heavy with acquired dirt and clinging dust. Even essential items such as food and canteens of water can start to seem heavier than they're worth.

The same is true for all of us as we walk the long journey called life. The more months and years we travel, the more we feel the weight of our sins, and the more breathless and worn out we are. What used to bring temporary pleasure and a fleeting sense of life instead begins to drag us down. The lure of sin brings diminishing returns. We're slowed by the pull of shame and guilt, and we're crushed by the consequences of our actions.

The wonderful promise of this verse, however, is that we don't have to carry the burden of those past mistakes. We don't have to feel the weight of our transgressions, because Jesus—the "righteous servant" prophesied by Isaiah—has taken on the crushing weight of all our sins. And don't miss that key word: *all* our sins. Every single one.

This is the same Jesus who declared, "Take my yoke upon you. Let me teach you, because I am humble and gentle at heart, and you will find rest for your souls. For my yoke is easy to bear, and the burden I give you is light" (Matthew 11:29-30). If we're willing to accept the gift Jesus offers—the gift he suffered and died to bring us—we, too, can be counted righteous and thus be lighthearted and carefree, experiencing the freedom our Burden Bearer desires for us.

NOVEMBER

SEEK GOD NOW

Seek the LORD while you can find him. Call on him now while he is near. Let the wicked change their ways and banish the very thought of doing wrong. Let them turn to the LORD that he may have mercy on them. Yes, turn to our God, for he will forgive generously.

ISAIAH 55:6-7

ONE NIGHT WHILE Robin was serving in Iraq, she found this passage in a Bible someone had given her. When she came to these verses, she wept. She had joined the army to spite her parents. She wanted to fight because of the anger in her soul. But God melted her heart that night. She cried out to him and, as the verses promised, she found that God forgave her and helped her find new hope in a whole new life without hatred.

Some claim that the God of the Old Testament is angry, harsh, malevolent, bent on making our lives miserable.

But God's heart is right in the middle of a verse like this. He longs for us to seek him, to look at sin and admit it has hurt us and others, and to acknowledge that it was wrong. If we do that, he says he will have mercy on us and will forgive.

What a portrait! God's heart is a compassionate, gracious, and caring heart, so much so that he sent Jesus to make our salvation possible.

Are you having trouble in your relationship with God right now? Seek his heart. His promise is to have mercy. He doesn't just forgive, he forgives generously.

BEING THERE

*[God said,] "I will be your God throughout your lifetime—
until your hair is white with age. I made you, and I will
care for you. I will carry you along and save you."*

ISAIAH 46:4

BABY BOOMERS ARE hitting retirement age and drawing social security. Now they get to learn whether our country's social services are stable enough to support this vast portion of the population.

Retirement is a scary stage for most people. Very often, company retirement plans have been downsized through the years to save companies money. Investments are often disappointing. And cost of living continues to climb.

Some surveys report that 45 percent of working adults plan to work to seventy years of age or beyond. With people commonly living well into their eighties and above, the savings they tucked away for retirement have to cover many years of basic needs and medical costs, which increase through the years.

So when we look at the whole picture, we find living to old age may be even scarier than those middle years, when we often have other mouths to feed or are climbing in our careers.

This Scripture verse gives us the glorious promise that God will be with us all *throughout* our lifetimes. He's there for us during those early years when we're trying to find out who we are emotionally and spiritually. He's with us through career building and raising a family. And when our nests are empty and we're facing retirement, maybe even without a spouse or family, God is with us. He made us. He'll take care of us.

Don't fear the future; God is already there, waiting for you.

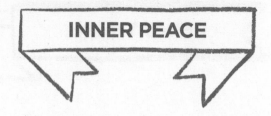

INNER PEACE

*[Jesus said,] "I am leaving you with a gift—peace of
mind and heart. And the peace I give is a gift the world
cannot give. So don't be troubled or afraid."*

JOHN 14:27

INNER PEACE IS something many people seek desperately. Every now
and then we read about Hollywood stars or other famous people who
struggle with a lack of inner peace. Some commit suicide; others lead
lives of terrible sin and debauchery. Many think they will find peace in
pleasure, fame, or money. They never find it there, though, and there's
a reason: peace can't be found in the things of this world. Only God has
the power to give us real peace.

Christopher, a reporter for a large newspaper, found this out when
he accepted Christ in his thirties. His coworkers ridiculed him. His
bosses sometimes slashed his stories for not following the "party line."
But Christopher wasn't troubled or afraid. He hung in there, reporting
the truth as he saw it, for himself and for the Lord.

The Lord never withholds peace from anyone who cries out to him.
Is it peace you need at this time in your life? Are you struggling with
anxiety, anger, hatred, or fear? God's antidote is his supernatural peace,
and his promise is to give it to any and all who ask. Like Christopher, you
will find God ever faithful.

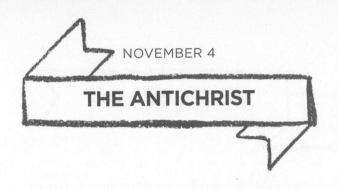

THE ANTICHRIST

*The beast was captured, and with him the false prophet who
did mighty miracles on behalf of the beast—miracles that
deceived all who had accepted the mark of the beast and who
worshiped his statue. Both the beast and his false prophet
were thrown alive into the fiery lake of burning sulfur.*

REVELATION 19:20

DO YOU EVER long for real justice in this world? Reading the news,
Jon often marveled at the injustice he saw: a police officer sentenced to
prison because a man struck him and he defended himself. A Christian
in a Muslim country convicted and sentenced to death for "insulting the
prophet" when it was merely a trumped-up charge against her because
of her faith.

How many times injustice reigns in our world. Many probably wonder why Stalin, Hitler, serial killers, and so many others seemingly "get
away with" their crimes and avoid answering to earthly courts. But such
people aren't listening to the truths of Scripture.

From the above passage, we see that God will call two of the worst
criminals of all time—the Antichrist and the false prophet—to account
for their deeds. And so he will with all other criminals.

You may not receive justice in this world. There are simply too many
corrupt police officers, judges, politicians, and others. But one day, God
promises to deliver final and perfect justice for everyone who rejected
him and committed indecent acts. Count on it. In fact, you'll be there
to see it happen if you believe in Jesus.

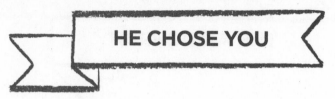

HE CHOSE YOU

[Jesus said,] "You didn't choose me. I chose you. I appointed you to go and produce lasting fruit, so that the Father will give you whatever you ask for, using my name."

JOHN 15:16

THIS VERSE POINTS to an issue many Christians wonder about. We all know that when we accepted Christ we chose him and gained salvation. But could we "unchoose" Jesus too?

This verse is a great truth and a greater promise. It says Jesus *chose us*. Jesus drew us to himself, opened our minds and hearts to his love, and influenced us to the point that we trusted him. This means that our salvation did not depend on our making the right choice. God was involved in bringing us to him from start to finish, and that makes our salvation all the more secure. We know that he will also see us through to the end.

Obedience is important. Faith is paramount. But never forget that God came and called you. Never forget that he loved you enough to make sure you heard the message and had the chance to believe. Never forget that somehow, even before you believed, he made sure you would make the right choice, too. It's a mystery that we don't understand, but let's be thankful he's chosen us and will hold us secure forever.

CHANGE YOUR WAYS

Turn to our God, for he will forgive generously.

ISAIAH 55:7

DAN JUST COULDN'T believe that God might care about him. "I've done bad things," he told the pastor. "I've done really bad things. I just don't see any hope for me."

The pastor, a man steeped in the Bible, turned to this passage and read it to Dan. The man was astonished. "God will have mercy on me? God will forgive me? All I have to do is turn to God in faith and change my ways?"

"That's all," the pastor said with a smile.

Dan went on to believe, to leave his bad ways, and to become a strong member of his church. He had discovered the heart of the living God. He does not want to judge us, to condemn us, or anything of the sort. Instead, he longs for us to seek him, to look at sin and admit it has hurt us and others and that it's wrong. If we do that, he says he will have mercy on us and will forgive.

What a portrait! God's heart is a compassionate, gracious, and caring heart, so much so that he sent Jesus to make our salvation possible.

Are you having trouble in your relationship with God right now? Seek his heart. His promise is to forgive you and give you whatever you need to get back on track.

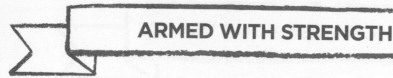

ARMED WITH STRENGTH

*You have armed me with strength for the battle; you
have subdued my enemies under my feet.*

PSALM 18:39

MOST BATTLES DON'T take place on physical battlefields. Far more take place every day between individuals or within ourselves, and they don't involve physical combat. Though they don't necessarily end in physical death, they can have deadly consequences. Business partnerships explode, marriages terminate, teenagers abuse drugs, and the elderly are neglected. Sometimes others unfairly malign us, sometimes we are our own worst enemies. And we get battle weary because these battles pop up everywhere and never seem to end.

The good news is that we may lose some of those battles temporarily, but we win the war because of Christ's victory. Not only that, but as we trust in God and take up his armor, he is victorious through us. Our enemies—spiritual, human, or internal—can never prevail against us in the long run. Study Scripture and learn of the tools God has given us to outwit and conquer our enemies, building ourselves up in him to grow ever stronger to withstand the evil days that may come our way.

For Christians, live or die, whatever battles we may face today—whether they're in the home, the office, or on an actual military battlefield—we can be sure we are never alone. God gives his word that he will be there, to stand at our side, to give us the power we need to succeed.

THE LORD KEEPS WATCH

The LORD himself watches over you! The LORD
stands beside you as your protective shade.

PSALM 121:5

THERE'S NO DOUBT about it: fear is a universal phenomenon that affects all people in all cultures throughout all time. It's something every human being can relate to because it's something every human being has experienced.

Sometimes we fear the fantastical—monsters or boogeymen or weird manifestations of our own imaginations. Other times we fear the unknown; we cringe at the immensity of everything that could go wrong just as a sailor cringes at the thought of a storm brewing on the open sea. Still other times our fears are eminently practical. We fear the loss of our jobs, for example. We fear the tension in our marriages and families. We fear beginning a task we know will be difficult.

So how do we deal with these kinds of fears? This psalm is a good starting place. It speaks of how God watches over each of us. He is our covering, our invisible shade to keep us from being scorched by spiritual forces and being destroyed by life's trials. If the sun were closer to the earth, we would be burned to a crisp. If it were farther away, we would freeze. God protects us from unseen dangers, both gigantic and minute. He watches over all these awesome forces just for our benefit. Nothing can touch us unless God allows it for purposes he approves.

When fear strikes, think of this psalm. God promises that he is watching and protecting, always.

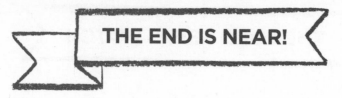

THE END IS NEAR!

*[God said,] "Only I can tell you the future before it even happens.
Everything I plan will come to pass, for I do whatever I wish."*
ISAIAH 46:10

IT SEEMS AS though every year a handful of people gain momentary notoriety because they claim to know the future. Often they claim to know something about an upcoming cataclysm—a terrible earthquake, a major storm, or even the end of the world. Other times these people make bold declarations about extreme changes in politics, the stock market, or future wars.

We typically react to these prophetic claims with a combination of amusement and scorn. We roll our eyes. We point to reason and the status quo. And yet, if we're honest, isn't there a ticklish spot in the back of our minds that says, *But what if he's right? What if she really can tell the future?* In our secret thoughts we long to find someone who can legitimately predict the future so we can prepare, because we're desperately afraid of the uncertainty that the future brings. We want to be able to control what threatens to take us by surprise and overwhelm us.

Isaiah 46:10 helps us get rid of that lingering question by making things crystal clear: only God can predict the future and control it. Only God has insider information about what's going to happen tomorrow or the next day, because God wrote out his plans for the universe before he created it.

Now here's the encouraging part, according to verse 10: everything God plans *will* come to pass. What God wants to accomplish will be accomplished. Nothing can stop it—which is wonderful news if we're willing to face the uncertainty of the future without fear by trusting in him and obeying his commands.

FEAR AND TIMIDITY

God has not given us a spirit of fear and timidity,
but of power, love, and self-discipline.
2 TIMOTHY 1:7

THERE ARE SUPERHEROES all over the world today—all over the entertainment world, that is. You can find them in movies, books, comics, graphic novels, and more. Sometimes it seems as if we have more do-gooders and crime fighters than we could possibly use!

Power is one of the traits we admire most in modern superheroes. Characters such as Superman, Wonder Woman, Spider Man, and the X-Men all have special abilities and areas of prowess that make them especially formidable. They can "save the day" when we are impotent. They can accomplish goals we can't even imagine and overcome obstacles we would be terrified to face—which certainly comes in handy when they have to face supervillains that seek to harm the innocent.

But it takes more than power to become a superhero. It takes a special character of heart defined by traits like love and self-discipline. Superheroes constantly place the needs of others above their own. They understand the consequences of right and wrong actions, and they use those moral boundaries and consequences to curtail and channel their power for the benefit of others.

There are no promises from God in Scripture that he will make us superheroes. We will have no mutant abilities or special powers to get us through—not in this life, anyway. But in 2 Timothy 1:7 we see that God has promised the character traits that truly matter. When we believe him and trust him with our limited abilities, he will grant us power, love, and self-discipline to overcome the powers of evil. That's a promise.

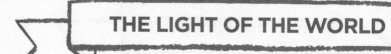

THE LIGHT OF THE WORLD

*Jesus . . . said, "I am the light of the world. If you
follow me, you won't have to walk in darkness, because
you will have the light that leads to life."*

JOHN 8:12

WERE YOU AFRAID of the dark as a child? Many children are. And whether we choose to admit it or not, even most adults are less comfortable in the dark than we are in the light of day. That's natural—darkness is mysterious and shrouds our ability to understand our surroundings. It keeps us from being totally aware of what's around us, which means we aren't sure what threats or possible harm may be lurking nearby.

That's physical darkness, of course, but there are other kinds of darkness as well. Many people today struggle with emotional darkness, for example—a phenomenon we commonly label as depression. There are times when the world seems to press down on us and squeeze us until every drop of happiness is gone.

We may also suffer from spiritual darkness. Even for followers of Jesus, there are times when we feel overwhelmed by doubt and despair—times when we can't seem to connect with God on any level. The spiritual dimension may seem nonexistent. These periods are particularly frightening because they bring into question the trustworthiness of the one who promises to appear beyond the grave. These times can lead us to doubt our salvation or even doubt the existence of God.

When Jesus promised his followers they wouldn't have to "walk in darkness," he wasn't implying they wouldn't encounter periods of emotional or spiritual distress in their lives. He wasn't saying everything would be smooth sailing. Rather, he promised to provide the "light that leads to life." Meaning, even in the darkest circumstances of life, we will always have his presence and his promises to illuminate our path and warm our hearts.

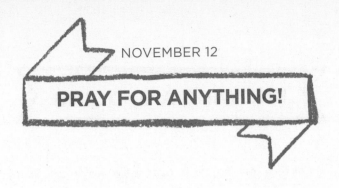

NOVEMBER 12

PRAY FOR ANYTHING!

*[Jesus said,] "I tell you, you can pray for anything, and if
you believe that you've received it, it will be yours."*

MARK 11:24

THIS IS A verse that often confuses those who read it. When new Christians come across Jesus' promise to "pray for anything, and . . . it will be yours," they may get excited and begin sending all kinds of requests and petitions toward heaven—new cars, new jobs, new houses, new gizmos, and maybe even a new spouse or new children.

Mature Christians have learned (often by trial and error) that such prayers don't work, but they can still feel perplexed whenever they encounter this verse. What did Jesus mean? How can he so clearly state that we can acquire "anything" when it's so obvious from personal experience that such prayers almost never come to fruition?

As with most promises in the Bible, this verse needs to be understood in relation to its context in Scripture. Jesus and his disciples were walking the road from Bethany to Jerusalem when they encountered a fig tree that Jesus had cursed the day before (because it wasn't bearing any fruit). The fig tree was withered and dead—a sight that amazed the disciples. The plant had shriveled and died simply in response to Jesus' words!

Jesus used the disciples' amazement as an opportunity to teach them about faith. When we make requests of God, we must do so with a genuine belief that God is capable of accomplishing what we ask—that's faith. We may not get the car we're hoping for, but we can confidently approach God with our needs and believe that he can provide.

KNOWING AND DOING

Now that you know these things, God will bless you for doing them.
JOHN 13:17

THIS STATEMENT OF Jesus comes just after he washed the disciples' feet in John 13. In that passage, Jesus advises the disciples to follow his example of servanthood and submission to the needs of the moment. On that evening, the disciples marched into the upper room to share the Passover. No slave or servant greeted them to wash their feet. Thus, one of the first things Jesus did as they all seated themselves was to shed his robe and go about washing their feet.

It was an example for these proud men to follow. They all knew that they should not sit to dine with dirty feet. Nasty odors, dust, and other bits and pieces of refuse stuck to those feet. Yet after three years together, learning from Jesus about their mission to serve, meet needs, and offer help to anyone and everyone, the disciples still didn't get it.

Do you?

God honors those who serve, even in the most menial tasks. In his world, a janitor is as respected and as important as the president of our country. God's promise to those who serve others is that they will be blessed by him in special ways they wouldn't want to miss.

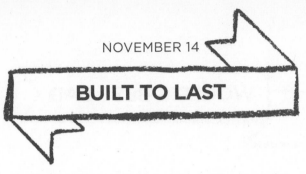

BUILT TO LAST

This world is fading away, along with everything that people
crave. But anyone who does what pleases God will live forever.

1 JOHN 2:17

THE WORD *PERMANENT* is a term used less and less in today's vernacular. Finances, families, moral values, religions—in recent times, these areas have seemingly lost the ability to remain stable.

In reality, nothing on this earth is really permanent in the true meaning of the word, and it never was, even in past centuries. That's because "this world is fading away" and will one day come to an end. Obviously this applies to our physical possessions. Televisions and cars aren't permanent. Phones and computers need to be replaced every few years just to stay up-to-date with technology. Even our houses and government buildings will eventually crumble and fall as the years give way to centuries.

The same is true for our greatest accomplishments on earth. Graduate degrees don't open the same doors they used to. Job promotions certainly don't last forever (nor do the jobs themselves, come to think of it). Even many of the memories we hold on to will be forgotten in the fog of years.

Don't let these realities depress you, however, because the wonderful promise of 1 John 2:17 is that people are different. Human beings are created with souls, and those souls will exist long after our physical deaths. Our souls are permanent, and so is the Kingdom that God is preparing. Therefore the primary message of this verse is that our lives—what we do and who we become when we follow God closely, when we please him—are the only things that will last for eternity.

WORLD'S BEST DAD

*I will be your Father, and you will be my sons
and daughters, says the LORD Almighty.*
2 CORINTHIANS 6:18

IN ONE SENSE it's true that every person alive today has a father. Excluding Jesus, every human being ever born came into this world because of genetic material contributed by a male parent—a father. Yet it's also true that a huge (and growing) segment of today's population has experienced life without the influence of a dad.

This epidemic of fatherlessness is often caused by men who are physically absent from their families. Sadly, there are a number of men who refuse to take responsibility for their actions. And, just as sad, there are a number of men who view "responsibility" as a financial term and use a monthly check to justify physical separation.

There are also many people living in families that are functionally fatherless. In these situations, men remain present in body but are absent in mind and heart. They've dedicated themselves to their careers or their hobbies, and they have little time and energy left over for those who need them.

The promise of 2 Corinthians 6:18 is that no person has to settle for a fatherless life. If you love and respect your earthly father, then you can take comfort in knowing that his best characteristics are infinitely magnified by your Father in heaven. And if you don't know your earthly father—worse, if you know him but wish you *didn't* know him—you can find comfort in the promise that the Creator of the universe himself will proudly name you as his son or daughter and love you as his own.

YOU HAVE ETERNAL LIFE

[Jesus said,] "I tell you the truth, those who listen to my message and believe in God who sent me have eternal life. They will never be condemned for their sins, but they have already passed from death into life."

JOHN 5:24

TRADITIONALLY WHEN WE think about the concept of eternal life, we picture a future reality that exists in complete separation from our life on earth. For most Christians, eternal life is directly connected with the concept of heaven—it's a state of being that starts after we experience physical death and continues forever.

According to Jesus' words in this verse, however, that understanding of eternal life misses the mark; it's not completely correct. Jesus started with a conditional statement. He spoke to those who listen to his message and "believe in God"—meaning, he was talking to Christians. But then notice what he says next: such people "have eternal life."

As Christians, we have eternal life. It's not something we're waiting to experience; rather, it's in our grasp right now. We have it inside of us! Jesus reiterates this idea at the end of the verse: we as Christians will "never be condemned for [our] sins" (which is great news), and we "have already passed from death into life."

Think about that word *already*. Eternal life is something that's already happened. As a follower of Jesus, it's something that you're already experiencing. That's a promise directly from Jesus' lips: as someone saved by grace through faith in Jesus Christ, you are already experiencing eternal life. Will things get even better once we enter into heaven? Of course. But God's promise to you is that your eternal relationship with him is already in full swing. So rejoice!

INVITE THEM ALL

Invite the poor, the crippled, the lame, and the blind.
Then at the resurrection of the righteous, God will reward
you for inviting those who could not repay you.
LUKE 14:13-14

HOW EASY IT was for Bonnie to simply ignore those people who didn't dress well, who didn't have the best grooming, who were usually homeless. She often thought badly of them too. Her nose wrinkled in disgust when they walked by, and her mind muttered harsh words about their lack of concern for cleanliness and for simply being presentable.

Nonetheless, God has always had a great heart for the poor, the hurting, the crippled, and all those who cannot fend for themselves in a high-paced, high-priced society. It's those who help such people, especially those who can never repay the favor in this world, whom God promises to bless.

Do you contribute to Christian organizations that reach out to the poor? Do you give money to your church's benevolence fund? If you do, God will reward you.

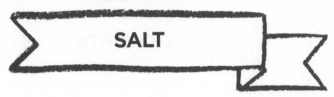

SALT

*You are the salt of the earth. But what good is salt if it has
lost its flavor? Can you make it salty again? It will be thrown
out and trampled underfoot as worthless. You are the light of
the world—like a city on a hilltop that cannot be hidden.*

MATTHEW 5:13-14

SALT IS GOOD for many things. For one thing, it simply makes food taste better. Meat, vegetables, and even some drinks are bland without salt. Salt spices things up.

It also can be used in healing. Soldiers often packed salt into a battle wound to enable the body to heal itself more quickly.

The expression "He's worth his salt" came from Roman times, when soldiers were actually paid in bags of salt.

Another thing salt does is preserve meats and vegetables for later use. Beef jerky, salt pork, and numerous other items can be saved for months and years with a little salt because it's such a great preservative.

Being salt, then, means several things: giving the world a good taste of God and his Kingdom, providing healing and help to the needy, and acting as a preservative against the power and progress of evil.

Does that describe you? Jesus tells us he wants us to be like salt. Those who are gain help from God in furthering his Kingdom and preserving the good that is in the world.

GOOD GIFTS

*If you sinful people know how to give good gifts to
your children, how much more will your heavenly
Father give good gifts to those who ask him.*
MATTHEW 7:11

IF YOU'VE EVER seen a video of parents giving a special gift to their child,
you'll notice the camera often stays focused on the child. We usually concentrate on the joy of the child receiving the gift, because it seems that
he or she is the one who's benefiting the most in the whole transaction.

But if you could pan the camera back and focus on the parents' faces
as their child opens something precious, you'd start to see a broader
picture. You'd notice the parents' secret smiles as they watch their child
erupt with squeals of happiness. You'd notice the satisfied glances and
sparkling eyes as the parents quietly receive their child's thanks—and you
might change your mind about who benefited the most after all.

Parents love having the opportunity to give good things to their children. They love being able to provide for needs and solve problems,
yes—but there's something special about a chance to bless a person you
love with a gift.

According to Matthew 7:11, that's how God feels about us. God
delights in giving us good things. He's the source of every blessing we've
ever received, and he's promised in his Word to respond when we come
before him with open hearts and speak of our needs *and* our wants. He
doesn't give us everything we ask for, of course. That would be a disaster
for us! But God has promised to give good gifts to his children.

FAITH REWARDED

It is impossible to please God without faith. Anyone who
wants to come to him must believe that God exists and
that he rewards those who sincerely seek him.

HEBREWS 11:6

ALTHOUGH FAITH IS one of the main foundations of Christian doctrine, we often think of it as something "out there." We tend to treat faith as if it's merely a theological term that has little practical application to our everyday lives. We keep it on the same shelf as other church terms, such as "justification" and "Trinity."

The truth, however, is that we actually practice faith many times each day. Every time you drive through an intersection when the light is green, you're demonstrating faith that other drivers will obey the red light in front of them and stop. Whenever you eat a meal at a restaurant, you're demonstrating faith that the food was prepared correctly and under sanitary conditions. You even demonstrate faith by doing something as simple as sitting down and believing the chair won't fall apart and dump you on the floor.

So when we read that "it is impossible to please God without faith," we don't need to be worried. We practice faith every day! The trick is simply to intentionally believe what God says in his Word. We obey him and serve him even though we can't see him. That's faith.

All of us want others to have faith and trust in our reputations and reliability. God is no different. Here's the best news: God always knows when we demonstrate faith in him, and it causes him to feel pleasure. In fact, our faith pleases God so much that he's promised to reward us when we sincerely believe and sincerely seek him.

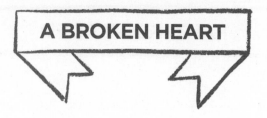

A BROKEN HEART

The sacrifice you desire is a broken spirit. You will not
reject a broken and repentant heart, O God.

PSALM 51:17

SACRIFICES WERE IMPORTANT to the Jews in Old Testament times. They learned from Moses a whole system of sacrifices necessary to deal with sin, show thanks, and give God praise. The book of Leviticus outlines all these special "gifts" to God.

Some Jews followed the laws precisely. Undoubtedly, many obeyed them in faith, believing God would bless them through their obedience. But other Jews focused only on performing the rituals, and they thought this somehow gave God pleasure. Without a broken heart and repentance, though, what was the significance of a sacrifice? Nothing. The sacrifice itself was meant to symbolize the internal spiritual death we all experience when we sin, not be merely a simplistic ritual.

You can sacrifice every possession you have. Yet if it's not accompanied by a submissive, repentant heart, it does no good. However, with brokenness comes great blessing, God says. To those who come to him broken and repentant, he offers everything. Is that a sacrifice you are willing to make?

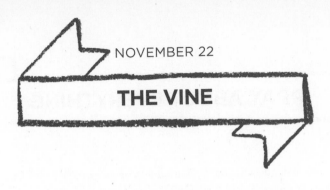

THE VINE

[Jesus said,] "I am the vine; you are the branches. Those who remain in me, and I in them, will produce much fruit. For apart from me you can do nothing."
JOHN 15:5

JESUS USED THIS illustration to help us understand our relationship with him. The vine in his picture was the part of the plant rooted in the soil, rising up into the air, and supporting all the outer parts and branches. The branches, on the other hand, are the parts people notice and enjoy, because they produce the fruit. But cut off a branch from the vine and it soon withers and dies, never bearing a single grape.

Similarly, Jesus shows us that by abiding in him and depending on him, we will stay connected and produce an abundance of fruit. That fruit can be any of the many spiritual realities the Bible speaks of—the Spirit's fruit: love, joy, peace, and so on; good works to others; and sharing the faith so that others come to believe in him. God wants us to produce all those kinds of fruit in abundance.

But there is one thing we need to remember in the midst of this: without Jesus, without being connected to the source of nourishment, we can "do nothing." Jesus is the key to everything. We can't go it alone. His promise, though, is that when we live in him, we will go out there and bear luscious, beautiful, and abundant fruit.

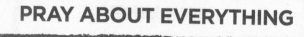

PRAY ABOUT EVERYTHING

Don't worry about anything; instead, pray about everything. Tell God what you need, and thank him for all he has done. Then you will experience God's peace, which exceeds anything we can understand. His peace will guard your hearts and minds as you live in Christ Jesus.

PHILIPPIANS 4:6-7

"I DON'T WANT to alarm you, but we need to send your son to the ER—*now*," the pediatrician told Darlene after he'd found her ten-day-old infant's heart racing at twice the normal rate.

At the hospital, Darlene comforted her tiny baby while the ER doctors unsuccessfully tried to get an IV line into his tiny hands and arms and then into his bald head. She stayed with him through every invasive attempt.

"Are you okay with this?" several nurses asked. "You seem very calm for a first-time mom. . . ."

"Amazingly, I was calm," Darlene recalls, realizing that any new mom could have understandably been freaking out. "I had a peace that even I couldn't understand. Probably because with every needle jab and electrode attachment, I was praying."

Perhaps you can relate to that unexplainable peace. Maybe you've gone through a family illness and felt unexpectedly buoyed. Perhaps you've gone through a heartbreaking situation and survived better than you thought you would.

What a precious invitation and promise in these verses! First God invites us to take all our concerns to him—whether minor or major. Then he promises to give us that peace that's so deep, so unexpected, and so unexplainable!

Want peace? Tell the Lord all your concerns.

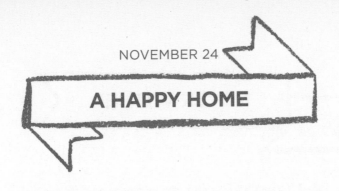

A HAPPY HOME

How joyful are those who fear the LORD—all who follow his ways!
. . . Your wife will be like a fruitful grapevine, flourishing within your
home. Your children will be like vigorous young olive trees as they sit
around your table. That is the LORD's blessing for those who fear him.

PSALM 128:1, 3-4

FOR THE AVERAGE Israelite, the dream was not a house on the beach or an estate in Scotland but a plot of land that grew grapes and olives. Wine and olive oil were two of the staples of life, and the person who had a measure of each was truly blessed.

But the psalmist took it a step further. "You want to see God's greatest blessing? The first blessing is a good, loving, and healthy wife. The second is children full of life and spunk." In other words, the blessing for those who followed the Lord included a happy, joyous, and fulfilled family—a spouse, kids, grandkids. The whole shebang.

If you ever question whether God cares about you, don't look at the bank accounts, the number of rooms in your house, or the backyard in-ground pool. God's care can be found in other ways. For example, look at the faces around your table. If they're smiling and laughing and just enjoying a great meal together, you will know God's face is shining on you.

NEVER WITHER

*They delight in the law of the LORD, meditating on it day and night.
They are like trees planted along the riverbank, bearing fruit each
season. Their leaves never wither, and they prosper in all they do.*

PSALM 1:2-3

PSALM 1 TALKS very explicitly about how delighting in God's Word makes us like trees planted by a riverbank. But what does that mean?

A tree planted by a river will always have the nourishment it needs to grow and thrive. Anyone who has gone to elementary school knows how crops planted near a water source always grow better than those in a desert.

Another thing those trees have is security. They won't wither, even in a tough time. They get the support they need to stand through droughts and storms. That's the essence of the person "delighting" in God's Word. He or she will be secure, safe, and sure.

One more thing about this type of tree: because it's near the source of nourishment, it flourishes and becomes beautiful in the eyes of those who look on it.

Do you want to have God's blessings of help and support, security, and real beauty? Let his Word be your primary source of sustenance. He gives his word that, if you drink in his nourishment, you will be like that tree planted by a river.

WE REALLY DON'T KNOW UNTIL . . .

Dear friends, we are already God's children, but he has not yet shown us what we will be like when Christ appears. But we do know that we will be like him, for we will see him as he really is.

1 JOHN 3:2

THE WORLD OFTEN looks at Christians and calls us hypocrites. While all of us will sometimes do stupid things and make mistakes that some people will use to claim we're fakes, the truth is that God promises in his Word that we are his children.

The world won't always believe this. We may apologize for our mistakes, but they will claim it's all just a ruse. We may dust off some strong arguments to give them a reason for why we believe what we believe, but many will still think we're believing in a God who doesn't exist.

One day, though, Christ will return. In an instant, we'll all be like him in beauty, in character, in perfection. The whole world will see us then, and they'll realize what a grave mistake they made in thinking we were the fools and they the wise ones. God's claim is that though the world may not see the truth now, one day everyone will when Christ appears.

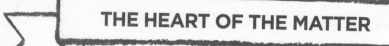

THE HEART OF THE MATTER

People judge by outward appearance, but the LORD looks at the heart.
1 SAMUEL 16:7

TODAY'S MEDIA-DRIVEN CULTURE is steered by image as opposed to reality. What is appealing on the surface is what is of value, so we all feel like failures in at least some areas. We probably don't have the perfect hair, teeth, weight, skin, and so forth, of the models in magazines and commentators on television. Maybe we can't afford to drive the sleekest automobile, and we may not have the huge retirement portfolios of the investment ads.

However, the important question is, What is the state of our hearts? We are not failures based on the physical and material things mentioned above, which will eventually perish. Although in our unregenerate state our hearts are desperately wicked, God has given us new hearts by his grace to desire the things that are above, the things that have eternal worth.

The good news is that the Lord looks at the heart and not at our outward performance or appearance. Life's circumstances may hinder us from doing great things for God. But God will reward us for actions big and small, as long as the desire of our hearts is to serve him. Blessed, indeed, are the pure in heart, for they shall see God and will benefit accordingly.

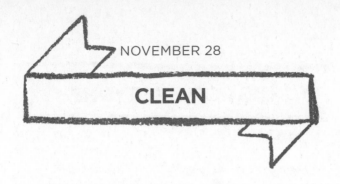

CLEAN

[The Lord said,] "I will sprinkle clean water on you, and you will be clean. Your filth will be washed away, and you will no longer worship idols. And I will give you a new heart, and I will put a new spirit in you. I will take out your stony, stubborn heart and give you a tender, responsive heart."

EZEKIEL 36:25-26

FOR CENTURIES, THE people of Israel struggled with all kinds of sins: idolatry, rebellion, hatred, violence, stealing, lying, and everything else. Of course, many of them didn't really care what they did, and God often had to carry out judgments against them that punished many.

But the faithful always remained, and many of those people felt guilt, pain, and remorse over their sins, no matter how small. They must have longed for some change internally that would make them pure, clean, and whole.

It's in this passage that God promises through Ezekiel what he will do for those who repent. First, he will sprinkle clean spiritual water that will wash away all the filth of sin. Second, he will give them new hearts to replace the stony, stubborn hearts they were born with. Tenderness toward others and responsiveness to God will follow.

Do you long for such a heart? That's what Jesus came to do: to make us new on the inside. That's what being "born again" is all about. If you have trusted him, God promises that you have a new heart inside you that will give you that tenderness and responsiveness you seek. Let him remove the stones of unbelief and lack of compassion for others.

IT'S FOR EVERYONE

*Together, we are his house, built on the foundation of the
apostles and the prophets. And the cornerstone is Christ Jesus
himself. We are carefully joined together in him, becoming a holy
temple for the Lord. Through him you Gentiles are also being
made part of this dwelling where God lives by his Spirit.*

EPHESIANS 2:20-22

ONE OF THE greatest truths about the gospel is that it's for everyone.
Many of the first Christians, who were all Jews, had a difficult time
understanding this. Even Peter and some of the other disciples had a
difficult time getting it. Paul seemed to be one of the few apostles who
not only accepted that Gentiles could be saved but also applied that truth
and preached God's gospel to them so they could find salvation in Christ.

In this passage, Paul speaks of the "house" God is building. Jesus was
the cornerstone, the piece that held it all together. Through the apostles
and prophets, God laid the foundation on that cornerstone, building a
spiritual house and temple that was holy to God, utterly given over for his
use and love. This is the place where Jews and Gentiles come together,
with all of us in that house.

God has made it possible for everyone everywhere to become part of
his family. No matter who your ancestors were, no matter what your family of origin, you are a candidate for living in God's house. He promises
that if we come to him and accept his Son as our Savior, we're in the
family!

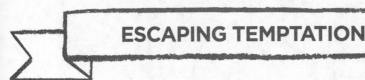

ESCAPING TEMPTATION

The temptations in your life are no different from what others experience. And God is faithful. He will not allow the temptation to be more than you can stand. When you are tempted, he will show you a way out so that you can endure.

1 CORINTHIANS 10:13

IF YOU WANT an adrenaline-pumping two hours, watch an action movie! You'll probably see the hero dodging bullets, narrowly escaping being pulverized by part of a building or something else practically falling on him or her, barely missing being crunched in a car chase, and running away from an explosion. Although he or she will eventually be captured by the bad guys and possibly beaten around a bit, the good guy will somehow escape—sometimes several times. No matter what the predicament, the good guys always escape.

This Scripture verse promises us that those who love God can always escape too. We can escape the temptation that comes our way. Just as we can trust those screenwriters to keep a movie from becoming so intense that the hero doesn't get out, we can trust God to keep the temptation from becoming so strong that we have to give in. We can trust him to provide an out, even if it's at the last minute.

It's not always easy to escape temptation, but it is always possible. So remember that the next time you feel as if the bad guys are closing in!

DECEMBER

GOD GIVES YOU TIME

The Lord isn't really being slow about his promise, as some people think. No, he is being patient for your sake. He does not want anyone to be destroyed, but wants everyone to repent.

2 PETER 3:9

MANY TIMES PEOPLE ask why the world is the way it is. Why is there so much evil? Why do so many things go wrong? They claim that if God is all-powerful, he must not be loving, because he hasn't removed evil from the world. Or, if he is perfectly loving, he can't be all-powerful, too, or he would have cleaned up this mess.

Both propositions are wrong, though. God is both perfectly loving and all-powerful. The Bible offers several reasons why he has not fixed the earth and all of us permanently. One of the answers is found in today's verse: he is giving everyone a chance to repent and express faith in Christ, and thus find salvation.

What would happen if God did clean up this mess on earth? Everyone who hasn't trusted him would be banished to hell. Anyone who didn't believe in Christ would not survive. But the truth is, God is patient, waiting for the right moment when everyone has had an opportunity to believe. His promise is that he loves us too much to exclude anyone.

THE POWER OF FOREVER

*You have been born again, but not to a life that will
quickly end. Your new life will last forever because it
comes from the eternal, living word of God.*

1 PETER 1:23

THERE ARE LOTS of frightening things in the world today. War is frightening, for example. So are the many types of unknown and uncurable diseases that seem to spring up every year. Whether we admit it or not, monsters (both real and imaginary) can alarm children and adults alike.

But when you think about fears, is there anything more frightening than death? Is there anything else that sets your pulse beating faster than the inevitable truth that someday you will die—that your heart will stop and your breath will cease and your muscles will stiffen? In truth, death is the veiled threat that serves as the foundation for almost all other fears.

That doesn't have to be true in your life, however. As a follower of Jesus, you can stand against the fear of death by holding on to something even more awesome and even more unfathomable: the power of forever.

The word *forever* is common, but it carries tremendous weight. God has promised that if you are a Christian, you will live forever. You will not end. Long after the stars have all burned out and the universe has come apart at the seams, you will still be going strong. You won't even be halfway toward the end of your existence at that point because *there will be no end!*

You will exist for eternity, which is an amazing gift, because you will spend that eternity basking in the presence of the living God, your heavenly Father.

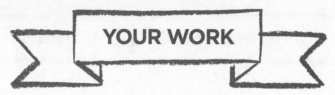

YOUR WORK

Work with enthusiasm, as though you were working for the Lord rather than for people. Remember that the Lord will reward each one of us for the good we do, whether we are slaves or free.

EPHESIANS 6:7-8

MANY CHRISTIANS TODAY must work, keep jobs, and obey bosses they neither like nor respect. Although in the United States many of us really do have the opportunity to live out our dreams, much of the rest of the world has no such right or chance. What does God say to all of us who must work for a living, whether we enjoy our jobs or not?

Do your work with enthusiasm. How can you do this? Remember, you're not working for a "big boss" here in this world; you're working for Jesus, even if it doesn't always seem like it. Be honest. Do what's right, even when it hurts. Keep performing, even if you're not reaping the benefits. Why? Because your paycheck in this world is small, but the one you get for faithfully serving Jesus is huge—beyond anything you could earn in this world.

The Bible says much about work. You may have the most fulfilling job possible. But ultimately, you serve the Lord first. Remember his promise: your reward for doing well is still coming!

CAPTURE THOSE THOUGHTS

*We use God's mighty weapons, not worldly weapons, to knock down
the strongholds of human reasoning and to destroy false arguments.
We destroy every proud obstacle that keeps people from knowing God.
We capture their rebellious thoughts and teach them to obey Christ.*

2 CORINTHIANS 10:4-5

ONE AFTERNOON AS Jane puttered around among the shelves of the store she worked in, straightening and restocking products, she overheard one of her coworkers talking to their boss about Christ. It seemed for every word the coworker offered, the boss batted it down with wit and scorn.

After listening for a moment, Jane walked over. "What's the problem?" she asked. The coworker said, "Samantha thinks the Bible is just another book written by men. She thinks most of it was made up." Jane thought a moment, then pulled out a pocket Bible and read from 2 Timothy 3:16, about how all Scripture is inspired by God. When she was done, she looked up at Samantha. Instead of her usual sarcastic remark, Samantha just shrugged and said, "Fine, you believe it. Fine. I don't." She walked away.

That story illustrates the above passage from Paul. Human arguments often fail, but God's weapons—his Word, his Spirit, his wisdom—knock down even the most scornful. His promise is that if you use such weapons, you will eventually see success in telling the world the truth.

THE WITNESSES

*Since we are surrounded by such a huge crowd of witnesses
to the life of faith, let us strip off every weight that slows us
down, especially the sin that so easily trips us up. And let
us run with endurance the race God has set before us.*

HEBREWS 12:1

HAVE YOU EVER realized that a "huge crowd of witnesses" watches and cheers you on as you work in the fields of the Lord? Although we can't hear them, this passage assures us that we are not out there alone. Like the crowd cheering on the miler who struggles to the tape in a track meet, this crowd encourages us, and some even pray for our success.

Knowing such things, how much more determined should we be running our race? The passage tells us to strip down, get rid of all our excess baggage, so we can run with freedom and real hope. What should we get rid of? Sin, basically. What is holding you back these days? An addiction? A bad habit? Perhaps there is something you need to start doing in your life but aren't doing, such as reading the Bible regularly, praying for your coworkers, working with others at church to reach the lost. God calls on us to get out there and run with endurance. But if you have a knapsack full of junk on your back, you won't run well.

Get rid of the bad things, the useless weights that drag you down, the sin that trips you up. God's promise is that when you do, you will run a race that pleases him.

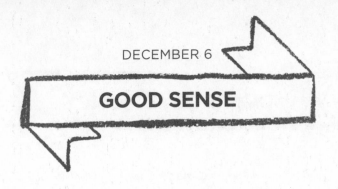

GOOD SENSE

*A house is built by wisdom and becomes strong through
good sense. Through knowledge its rooms are filled
with all sorts of precious riches and valuables.*

PROVERBS 24:3-4

AT A TIME when families are besieged on all sides by our secular culture, many want to know, How do I preserve my family? How do I keep us together? How do I protect everyone from the assaults of the world?

These verses provide a powerful answer: through wisdom, good sense, and knowledge. What are these abilities? Wisdom is the capacity to solve problems skillfully. Thus, a wise father will understand how to help a son learn to cope with taunts from classmates. A wise mother knows when to stoop down and give her little one a hug instead of a lecture.

Similarly, good sense might be better termed *common sense*, the ability to apply experience and the wisdom God gives us all for difficult situations. As a result, parents will see when lax discipline would lead to further trouble, while a firm and steady hand would get everyone back on course.

Finally, knowledge is that reservoir of simple truth gleaned from the ages. Good families spend time in God's Word to gain that precious knowledge that will keep everyone safe through a storm. God clearly communicates the fact that if we cultivate and nurture such qualities in our home, God will fill it with every good thing.

DON'T LOVE MONEY

Don't love money; be satisfied with what you have. For God has said, "I will never fail you. I will never abandon you."
HEBREWS 13:5

HALLOWEEN ISN'T EVEN over before Christmas decorations are hitting the shelves. And instead of waiting until "Black Friday," the day after Thanksgiving and the traditional beginning of the holiday shopping season, the deep holiday discounts begin much earlier.

Why the push for sales? The sales-powers-that-be like to use the time to drive up consumer lust and promote consumer spending so they can make more money before the end of the year.

Perhaps today's Scripture verse should be our motto to help us rein in temptation during the holidays. Granted, it doesn't sound like the best Christmas verse, but it gives us two very powerful reminders for the season.

First of all, the verse reminds us to keep money in its place and not lust after all the new "toys" the world constantly dangles before our eyes—the desire for more, more, more. The longing for things takes our time and distracts us from focusing on God.

Second, the Scripture tells us to be happy with what we have *because* God has promised never to fail us or abandon us.

And isn't that what Christmas is all about? Instead of abandoning humans when they sinned, God went to the other extreme—he gave the gift of his Son to live among us and make sure we would never have to be separated from God.

During this holiday month, practice satisfaction. You'll be rewarded with the true gift that only God can give us—himself.

KEEP WITH IT

He will give eternal life to those who keep on doing good, seeking
after the glory and honor and immortality that God offers.

ROMANS 2:7

WHILE FAITH ALONE saves us, doing good confirms that faith and assures us of a reward in heaven. Many Christians argue that simply accepting Christ, walking an aisle, or praying a prayer makes us fit for heaven. But the Bible adamantly shows us that although faith is the starting place, it's not the end point. God wants to change us, make us vehicles of his grace and good works, and use us to transform the world.

What do you seek in this world? Riches? Honor? Position? Power? Fame? Many people get sucked in to such pursuits, but most soon find them empty. It is only through the pursuit of true glory and honor by serving and worshiping God that anyone ever achieves great things in God's eyes.

Take a brief assessment. Do you seek the things that last, that God alone can give? That's a sign you are a true believer, with a faith that will make your life a blessing. God promises to give you the things that last too. You can be sure he will not hold back any good thing from those who call on him to use them in his Kingdom and service.

GOD IS UPON US

*The Spirit of the Sovereign LORD is upon me, for the LORD
has anointed me to bring good news to the poor. He has
sent me to comfort the brokenhearted and to proclaim that
captives will be released and prisoners will be freed.*

ISAIAH 61:1

WHEN JESUS CAME to our planet, he had an important and clear mission:

1. To bring good news to the poor.

How often do poor people get bad news? Sometimes every day. But for them Jesus brought tremendous hope. This world is not the end. Those who are poor will not always live in poverty. He will take them to a place where all their needs will be met.

2. To comfort the brokenhearted.

This world is full of disappointment and heartache, but Jesus came to comfort those who weep, whether because of unmet expectations or the loss of a loved one through divorce or death.

3. Finally, to proclaim release to the captives.

Many things in life can make a person a spiritual prisoner. Sin. Addiction. Hatred. Depression. Disease. Abuse. Hurt. Jesus came to fix all such problems.

What is your problem? Jesus' promise is that he can help you with it now and ultimately get you to a place where such things will never affect you again.

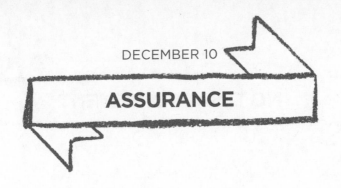

ASSURANCE

*May our Lord Jesus Christ himself and God our Father, who loved
us and by his grace gave us eternal comfort and a wonderful hope,
comfort you and strengthen you in every good thing you do and say.*

2 THESSALONIANS 2:16-17

THE THESSALONIANS FACED some steep problems in their day. Persecution. Fear. Misunderstanding of God's truth. Paul wrote to them to correct some of those problems. But here in today's verses he speaks of something that goes beyond all of those things.

Here we find Paul's words of assurance that although he will do what he can to help the people of God, the ultimate truth is that God himself will take up all the slack and help far beyond anything Paul could do. Think about it. Though you probably have a kind pastor who can offer you counsel and friendship, though you have good Christian friends who can help, and though you even have God's Word to bolster you in times of trouble, the greatest truth of all is Jesus himself.

It's the person and presence of Jesus that ultimately meet our greatest needs. With him inside us, we can face anyone and anything.

Are you depending on him for all your needs of comfort and power? He gives his word that he will give you all you need, and then some.

NO DISAPPOINTMENT

*This hope will not lead to disappointment. For we
know how dearly God loves us, because he has given us
the Holy Spirit to fill our hearts with his love.*

ROMANS 5:5

CHRISTIANS FACE MANY disappointments in life, even as believers and followers of Christ. The Lord sometimes does not answer prayers we may consider the most important of our lives with a yes. While God tells us over and over that he has a plan for our lives, we may not always like the plan that unfolds. Tragedies and setbacks can seem to set us up for greater failures. The Christian life in the here and now can be difficult, painful, and frustrating.

Yet in the long run the Christian life is not a disappointment. Edward Smith, a nineteenth-century Wesleyan pastor, used to say he wanted "Satisfied in Jesus" written on his tombstone. He faced hard times and losses, as we all do in life. But Edward Smith saw things from the long view, and in that respect he could honestly say that God was good.

Refuse to look at the setbacks of the day as the final word from Jesus. Many times God plans to do things down the road that will thrill and fulfill you. His promise is that you will never be disappointed in him if you have faith.

DEFEATING EVIL

Every child of God defeats this evil world, and we achieve this victory through our faith. And who can win this battle against the world? Only those who believe that Jesus is the Son of God.

1 JOHN 5:4-5

THERE'S NO DOUBT that evil exists in the world today. More than a concept or an intellectual point of argument, evil impacts us all in a myriad of ways. We can see the presence of evil in historical events, for example. Wars have been fought because of evil men with evil ambitions. Entire cultures have been threatened through the evil of prejudice, discrimination, and hate. Even the natural world has lashed out with outbreaks of evil in the form of natural disasters and disease.

Today we can see evil on a large scale through practices such as sex trafficking, where millions of young people are abducted and sold into a life of slavery. We see evil when illegal drugs are distributed to children or when people rise up to oppress others because of greed or ambition or the love of power.

Evil doesn't exist exclusively on a large scale, however. We are all intimately associated with evil in our own hearts. If we're honest under the scrutiny of the Holy Spirit, we know we all think evil thoughts. We all take evil actions in our own self-interest. We all sin against God and against our neighbors.

How comforting, then, to know we aren't forced to succumb to the evil of this world—to the evil in our hearts. We can fight back! The promise of 1 John 5:4-5 is that our choice to follow Jesus will strike a blow against evil. We are engaged in a battle against the evil of this world, and God has already promised victory for us even as we follow him and lean on his strength.

HOW TO FIND SUCCESS

Commit your actions to the LORD, and your plans will succeed.
PROVERBS 16:3

SUCCESS IS A popular topic in the world today. Whole shelves of books have been written about how to achieve success in business, success in your marriage, success in raising children, success in losing weight, and so on. People attend huge seminars in multiple disciplines to learn how to be known as "successful." They think that if they follow a strict formula used by a successful person, they will find the key to their dreams and attain the happiness they deserve.

But these recipes for success have limited success in themselves, and they often leave us disappointed and disillusioned. As it turns out, we have to read only a single verse in God's Word to attain the secret: "Commit your actions to the LORD, and your plans will succeed."

So here's the question: Are you willing to commit your actions to the Lord? Are you willing to behave in a way that's obedient to his Word? Are you willing to do the things he asks you to do—and *not* do the things he's asked you not to do? That's the price you'll need to pay if you want your plans to succeed as promised.

Committing our actions to the Lord isn't easy—it requires sacrifice even to the point of killing our own will and desires (see Galatians 2:20). When we do, God brings success by blessing both us and others. And the great news is that committing to follow God's plan will lead to much greater rewards than earthly success alone; it will lead to eternal life in heaven with our Creator. What could be more successful than that?

CELEBRATION

*Every time you eat this bread and drink this cup, you are
announcing the Lord's death until he comes again.*

1 CORINTHIANS 11:26

THE ORGAN PLAYED softly as ushers walked down the aisle. The church
lighting was dimmed, and the sober atmosphere was somewhat like a
funeral. Everyone looked down as he or she took a tiny wafer and quietly
passed the plate to the next person. The pastor led the congregants to
focus on their sin. They pictured the horrible, painful death of Christ
on the cross before partaking of the bread and wine.

In another church, it was also Communion Sunday, only this church
referred to the act as the "Celebration of the Lord's Supper." Tables were
filled with laughing people in the bright, cheery fellowship hall. They
passed around fresh-baked focaccia bread topped with some of their
favorite ingredients. The church members rejoiced as they talked about
how much Jesus loved them and how they could celebrate because he had
risen from the dead.

Two churches practicing the same sacrament, each with a different
tone and focus. Which was more biblical?

Neither! When we celebrate the Lord's Supper, it is appropriate to
take time to reflect. It's fitting to think about the pain and agony Christ
suffered. We should think about our lives and measure to see if we're
living in a way that is worthy of Christ's death.

And we should also celebrate that Christ is no longer in the grave. He
not only died for our sins but also rose, proving he's victorious over sin.
And someday he'll return to us, freeing us from the payment of eternal
death, to lead us to an eternal celebration with him.

Next time you take Communion, remember to reflect and to rejoice!

CLEANSED

I will cleanse you of your filthy behavior.
EZEKIEL 36:29

TODAY'S VERSE IS one of God's great promises to help each of us "clean up our act," as people in the seventies used to say. Christianity is not a religion of trying and failing and being miserable. Though the Christian life is sometimes a struggle and we go through bad times, God is in the business of making life better for us—on the inside, if not on the outside.

God wants to clean you up. He will take you where you are and begin chipping away at all the junk in your life. In time, you will be a resplendent example of his grace. You won't be perfect. But you will be far different from what you were. While we come to Jesus "just as I am," as the song says, God has no intention of leaving you "just as you are."

He especially doesn't want you to experience spiritual famine in your life as a result of not partaking of fellowship, the Word, and prayer. If you are not already practicing these spiritual disciplines, get back into them so that as you sow in the Spirit, you will reap a deeper, richer spiritual life. God will transform you into the image of Christ day by day. His promise is not to leave you where you were, but to get you to where he wants you to be.

WAITING ON GOD'S HELP

I waited patiently for the LORD to help me, and he turned to me and heard my cry. He lifted me out of the pit of despair, out of the mud and the mire. He set my feet on solid ground and steadied me as I walked along.

PSALM 40:1-2

A GIRL NAMED Stormie found herself in the middle of a "storm" herself. Her car ran out of gas in a dangerous part of town. She had to get help, but how?

"God, help," she murmured. She didn't know whether to get out and walk to a gas station or stay put and hope that someone kind would stop and help.

Fifteen minutes later, when she saw a man approach, Stormie locked her car doors. But the man called out to her, "I'm a local pastor, ma'am. Can I help you?"

David, the author of this psalm, could relate. Many times in David's life, he cried out to God to rescue him, and God heard his cries and saved him, whether it was from his enemies or from depression.

What situations in your life require a "Lord, help!" kind of prayer? Call out to the Lord. He has promised to hear your cry, and he will set your feet on solid ground and steady you as you walk along.

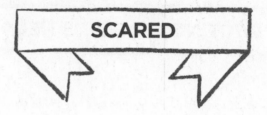

SCARED

The LORD himself watches over you! The LORD stands beside you as your
protective shade. The sun will not harm you by day, nor the moon at
night. The LORD keeps you from all harm and watches over your life. The
LORD keeps watch over you as you come and go, both now and forever.

PSALM 121:5-8

HAVE YOU EVER felt scared lying in bed at night, as if something horrible
hung over your head or the knell of doom had sounded on your life?

All of us have been paralyzed by fear at one time or other. Fear of losing our jobs. Fear of troubles in our marriage. Fear of never meeting the
right person to marry. Fear for our children or fear that we'll never be
able to have children. Fear of being robbed or hurt or killed in a crime
gone wrong. Fear of losing a loved one. How does one deal with that
kind of crippling fear?

Meditating on this psalm is a good starting place. It speaks of how God
watches over each of us. Even in the dark of night, when fear and worry
seem to surround and overwhelm you, the Lord keeps watch over you.
Earlier in the psalm, we are told that the Lord "never slumbers or sleeps"
(verse 4). That means, whether you are scared in the middle of the day
or in the dark of night, God will always be standing guard to protect you.

The next time fear strikes, think of this psalm. God is there watching. He never sleeps. He never grows weary. His promise is that he is
always there.

STRIVING FOR HUMILITY

*Those who exalt themselves will be humbled, and
those who humble themselves will be exalted.*

LUKE 14:11

HUMILITY IS A tricky trait for us to wrap our minds around. That's because as soon as we think we've achieved humility—we've lost it. After all, truly humble people don't have any idea that they're humble, right? They don't concentrate on themselves enough to even form that conclusion.

Even so, it's important that we strive for humility as followers of Christ. Or, to say it another way, it's important that we avoid exalting ourselves at all costs. It's important that we do everything in our power to prevent tooting our own horns and promoting our own interests over the interests of others (and the interests of God). Because if we exalt ourselves, God has promised to teach us true humility in a way we probably won't enjoy.

On the other hand, if we choose to live humbly and avoid self-exaltation, God has promised to lift us up. Why? Because humility allows God to trust us with his blessings. When we're humble, we don't allow success to go to our heads and result in the kind of pride that can derail God's work in our lives (and in the lives of others). Humble people are eminently usable in the Kingdom of God.

So humble yourself before God. Give him the complete freedom to work in and change your life for the better, even if it hurts your pride. His promise is that you'll be blessed—even exalted—as a result. And being exalted by God is much better than exalting yourself.

ON RECORD

LORD, if you kept a record of our sins, who, O Lord, could ever survive? But you offer forgiveness that we might learn to fear you.

PSALM 130:3-4

HAVE YOU EVER worried that God might be keeping a record of your sins? You may believe that one day when you stand before him, he'll pull out these giant books, and an angel will read off every bad thing you ever did.

If you're a Christian, have no fear. God keeps no records of his children's sins. When he forgives us through faith in Christ, every bad thing we ever did is wiped away. As this psalm says, God does not keep a record of our wrongs.

By the same token, God does keep records—of all the good things we've done. He promises to one day reward us for those things in heaven. And his rewards are better than any Oscar or Pulitzer or Nobel Prize this world could give.

Look to God. If you worry about sin, make sure you have trusted Christ about your past, present, and future. If you have, remember there is nothing to fear from a God who loves you as much as our God does. If you haven't trusted him already, trust him now.

DECEMBER 20

STARS FOREVER

Those who are wise will shine as bright as the sky, and those who
lead many to righteousness will shine like the stars forever.

DANIEL 12:3

JASON KNEW, AS one who had experienced salvation through Jesus, that he needed to share this message with those who are lost. And in his heart he truly wanted to do that. But he was a shy and sensitive person at work and "hid his light under a bushel" for fear of criticism and rejection.

When Jason read this passage from Daniel, however, he had renewed determination. He realized what great glory awaited those who faithfully pointed others to the Savior. He may not be a "star" in this world, but he had a chance to be a bright one in the next.

We know we'll be rewarded by God for any good deed, however small. But God has a special place in his heart for those who share the good news of what Jesus has done for us. He doesn't desire judgment; rather, he's delighted when someone repents and comes to the knowledge of the truth. Though not everyone will respond enthusiastically, we may be surprised—some will accept our invitation to know God. And one day, they will rejoice with us, thankful that we led them into the presence of the one who is the source of the light of all believers.

So, become like the wise people Daniel speaks of, and boldly but prudently share your joy in what God has done for you. God promises that you'll end up shining brightly in heaven above.

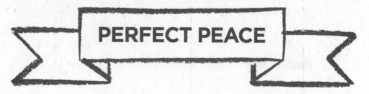

PERFECT PEACE

*You will keep in perfect peace all who trust in you, all
whose thoughts are fixed on you! Trust in the LORD
always, for the LORD GOD is the eternal Rock.*

ISAIAH 26:3-4

PEACE ON EARTH. We see those words a lot during this season. But is this peace really possible? Can we truly find peace while sin rules in this world?

Whether or not the earth can truly find peace, we Christians can enjoy peace in our lives. How do we enjoy this calm, peaceful certainty in our hearts, spirits, and emotions?

These verses tell us: by trusting in God and keeping our thoughts focused on him.

Anytime we feel the turmoil of worry, fear, uncertainty, or anger, we can turn to him. As we begin to focus on the Lord—instead of on the temptations and troubles surrounding us—he fills our lives with a peace that is truly unexplainable. He gives us a calm certainty that he is in charge and that we can trust him to guide us no matter what.

Though our world will never truly see peace until Christ reigns, we can have a taste of that peace in our hearts every day. The antidote for the wars or discomfort raging within us is to keep our thoughts on the Lord.

WICKED PEOPLE

The strength of the wicked will be shattered,
but the LORD takes care of the godly.

PSALM 37:17

CAROL WAS THE woman all the other women in town were jealous of. Her still-youthful face, thanks to plastic surgery, was all over the society pages. She and her husband took vacations to exotic locations multiple times a year. She drove her children around town in a luxury SUV. Housework wasn't a chore for her because her family employed a live-in maid to take care of their mansion.

One day, though, Carol and her husband were arrested for embezzling money. The extravagant lifestyle they had led was the result of criminal activity, not hard work. Suddenly, the wealthy kingdom they had built for themselves came crashing down. The other women in town had nothing to be envious of after all.

God promises to deal justly with wicked people in the long run. Never envy them. Never even wish you could have what they have. Those who trust God are taken care of in a multitude of ways people like Carol can only dream about.

Satan will try to suck the life out of you through such envy. But God promises that when you trust in him, he will give you the real blessings that not only build up but also last.

Though we might not receive all the material things we've ever wanted, we have the assurance of eternal life through faith in God, as well as the righteousness, peace, and joy promised through the Holy Spirit.

HIS NEVER-ENDING PRESENCE

[Jesus said,] "I am with you always, even to the end of the age."
MATTHEW 28:20

DURING ADVENT, AS we get closer to Christmas Day, we are made fully aware of the miracle of the Incarnation—Immanuel, God with us, God in human form. We're joyful and excited that God would meet us face-to-face and become like us in every way except our sinfulness. But when the festivities are over and the Christmas decorations are taken down, we seem to return to the mundane grayness of our everyday problems. The disciples faced that possibility as Jesus prepared to rejoin his Father, and that's why he gave them the promise that they would not be orphans.

Sometimes we may feel as if Jesus has taken a vacation until the Second Coming. He's way up in heaven somewhere, busy on the throne of God while we are left in our loneliness, trying to wade through some tough situations on the earth. But Jesus came to earth as a man and was born, died, and then rose again for a purpose—to be able to be with us here, right now, always, never forsaking us. This is perhaps one of the greatest promises in the Bible. Jesus doesn't just hear our prayers from the far reaches of heaven; he lives in us and is active in the midst of every situation we are in.

He's not just the Baby in a manger, the Intercessor on his throne, or the victorious King coming back for us. He's also an alive, spiritual Person in our midst, sharing all our daily trials and joys and working through them all to bring about good on our behalf.

A GIFT FOR ALL FAMILIES

[The Lord said,] "I will make you into a great nation. I will bless you and make you famous, and you will be a blessing to others. I will bless those who bless you and curse those who treat you with contempt. All the families on earth will be blessed through you."

GENESIS 12:2-3

DO YOU KNOW where you can find the Christmas story in the Bible? Most of the time we look to the Gospels—specifically Matthew 1 and Luke 2. But do you realize the Christmas story actually extends back to Genesis, the first book of the Bible?

When God promised that his servant Abraham would have a son, he also promised that Abraham's family would grow into a great nation—the nation of Israel. God also promised that this nation would somehow, some way, bring about a blessing for "all the families on earth." That's quite a prophecy! That's quite a promise, given the billions of people that have lived and died on this planet over the years.

So how would one man produce a legacy that would bless the entire world? The answer is Jesus. Jesus' entrance into the world as a descendant of Abraham signaled a blessing for all people. The angel declared this to the shepherds on the night of Jesus' birth, saying, "I bring you good news that will bring great joy to all people" (Luke 2:10). The angel clarified things a bit for Joseph when he said, "Jesus . . . will save his people from their sins" (Matthew 1:21).

As you celebrate the miracle of Christmas this year, remember also the miracle of Genesis 12. Thousands of years ago—thousands of years even before Mary and Joseph—God promised to bless all the families of the earth through the birth of his Son. That includes your family; that includes you. And just like Abraham, step out in faith with all of God's promises, going wherever he asks, and watch as the blessings follow!

THE GRAND BIRTH

A child is born to us, a son is given to us. The government will rest on his shoulders. And he will be called: Wonderful Counselor, Mighty God, Everlasting Father, Prince of Peace.

ISAIAH 9:6

TODAY, CHRISTMAS, IS for all Christians one of the great times to remember who Jesus is and why he came into the world. Look at the following titles for Jesus, and think of the ways he has ministered to you through those roles.

Wonderful Counselor. How many times has God's counsel—from his Word, from others, from the still, small voice in your heart—kept you out of danger or from making bad decisions? Perhaps now is a good time to thank him for his wonderful guidance and presence.

Mighty God. Yes, Jesus was God in human flesh, and he is mighty. Back then he did miracles. He still does them today. He protects you. He has written your name on his hands. He has defeated and will defeat all your personal enemies. He loves you always.

Everlasting Father. Your relationship with Jesus is eternal. It won't end; it cannot end. And undoubtedly, it will only get better and better with time.

Prince of Peace. Has he brought peace to your heart? Think of the many times you might have fallen apart, except that he was there, through the church, through friends, through the internal Comforter.

All these pictures of Jesus are great promises of his love and commitment to you. Why not worship him now as you remember the many great things he has done in your life this year? Relax and be at peace in the knowledge that the governing of every detail of your life is on his shoulders—so your burden is indeed light!

GOD LIVES AMONG YOU

On that day the announcement to Jerusalem will be, "Cheer up, Zion!
Don't be afraid! For the LORD your God is living among you. He is a
mighty savior. He will take delight in you with gladness. With his love,
he will calm all your fears. He will rejoice over you with joyful songs."

ZEPHANIAH 3:16-17

MANY TIMES IN Israel's history the people lost faith, committed sin, and ended up in serious trouble. God, ever merciful, ever loving, rescued them again and again. When they repented, they found him welcoming them all back with extended arms. The God of Israel couldn't wait to put aside his judgment, because his desire is mercy that then leads to his own rejoicing in us. After all, he created us for his own pleasure. He doesn't want to leave all the joy and gladness to us!

Perhaps you have committed some sin, or sins, that have left you feeling God has deserted you. Or maybe he simply seems distant, for reasons you don't know. What is the right response to such circumstances? Call out to him. Cry out for help, strength, and new joy. When you do, the presence of his love will minimize your fears and give you a holy calm.

His promise is not only that he will rescue and restore you but also that he will literally rejoice over you "with joyful songs." Imagine God himself embracing you with a song on his lips like those of Tevye in *Fiddler on the Roof* or Harold Hill in *The Music Man* or Captain Von Trapp in *The Sound of Music*. God is a singer, and his promise is not only to send help but also to send it with style.

GOD'S EYES ON THE EARTH

The eyes of the LORD search the whole earth in order to
strengthen those whose hearts are fully committed to him.
2 CHRONICLES 16:9

ONE OF THE most difficult things about enduring trials and suffering is the sense that we have to bear them on our own. When we go through difficult situations, we long to know that someone out there cares about our pain and notices when we need help—especially if that someone is willing and able to aid us in our distress.

That's why the promise in this verse is so comforting. God's eyes constantly roam throughout the earth looking for people whose hearts yearn for him and seek him. God is longing to help us. And when he finds such people, he immediately supports them in their work, their families, and the struggles and challenges they face, both big and small.

So imagine you're one of those people within God's range of vision even now. Where's your heart these days? Is it "fully committed" to God, as the verse says, or are you on the fence, loving or trusting in other things as well? Do you doubt God's goodness? Do you keep him at arm's length because of bad things that have happened in your life or because of choices you want to make that are counter to his will?

Take some time even now to intentionally focus on God. Submit to him. Listen for him. Tell him that you're not "fully committed" to him and his Kingdom but you want to be. He longs to bless you. He knows everything involved with your situation, and he will strengthen you in every challenge you face.

WATCH YOUR TONGUE

Watch your tongue and keep your mouth shut,
and you will stay out of trouble.

PROVERBS 21:23

OVER THE PAST few years, different parts of the world have seen fresh outbreaks of an old disease: foot-and-mouth disease, sometimes called hoof-and-mouth disease. This is a viral disease that primarily affects cattle and pigs. It can also afflict deer, goats, sheep, and other animals with cloven hoofs, as well as elephants, rats, and hedgehogs.

This disease rarely affects humans. However, we face a similar-sounding disease all the time: foot-*in*-mouth disease.

Maybe you've experienced this one. You're in the middle of a conversation and realize you've said the wrong thing. Or you make a snide comment about someone and learn the person you're talking to is that person's relative. Or when you're upset, you make the mistake of opening your mouth, and—oh my!—the words that come out!

Don't you love the Bible's honesty about humans? Christians aren't portrayed as superior beings that never mess up. Instead, the Bible deals with the problems we realistically face—like getting in trouble because of something we say. And it gives us realistic advice.

If you are sometimes afflicted with foot-in-mouth disease, follow the Bible's advice. Ask God to help you practice keeping your mouth shut! If you can't find anything good to say, there may not be anything that is worth saying. But if our minds and hearts are set on him, he will eventually give us words that build up and heal.

GIVING UP TO SERVE

Everyone who has given up houses or brothers or sisters or father or mother or children or property, for my sake, will receive a hundred times as much in return and will inherit eternal life.

MATTHEW 19:29

MISSIONARIES SEEM TO get one of two responses in our world. On the one hand are those who think such commitment is foolish, a waste. On the other hand are those who revere them as the great saints of our time, people who have given everything, sacrificed all for their Lord. Think of people such as John Wesley, Adoniram Judson, Hudson Taylor, Mother Teresa, and more recently, the Burnhams, who were kidnapped by militant Muslims in the Philippines.

But there are many ways to "give up" something for God that don't call for a lifelong journey to Africa or Indonesia. The woman who, in the name of Christ, gives up her time to watch a single mother's son so she can work is as worthy of a reward as any missionary. The CEO who refuses to compromise the principles of integrity to gain more money, the NFL player who responds to a call to the ministry, the young woman who gives up a dream of becoming a doctor to help the love of her life through medical school by working as he studies—all these kinds of sacrifices done for Christ are noticed and will be rewarded by God.

Over and over the Bible assures us that anything we give up for Christ— whether it's Monday Night Football to help the kids with their homework, going out with friends so we can give the money to support a missionary, or traveling to a disaster area to help rebuild homes and lives instead of taking a vacation to the beach—will never be forgotten or overlooked on that great day when God opens his big basket of rewards.

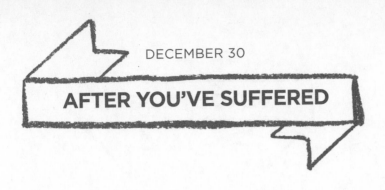

AFTER YOU'VE SUFFERED

In his kindness God called you to share in his eternal glory by means of Christ Jesus. So after you have suffered a little while, he will restore, support, and strengthen you, and he will place you on a firm foundation.

1 PETER 5:10

CARLY FOUND THE truth of this verse one night after suffering through a terrible divorce and custody trial. Her husband did everything but snatch her children and go into hiding. But God protected her, and she won the case. Then she realized how great her legal expenses were.

She took an extra job, worked hard, and began slowly paying the bills. One day her boss called her into his office and told her what a great job she was doing. He then asked if she would like a promotion. Her new job doubled her salary. Today she says, "You know, I thought my life was over. But God came through. I went through the valley of the shadow and came out the other end onto a beach!"

Every Christian, when he or she has faced suffering, has asked, "Why me? What did I do wrong? When will this end? Why is God letting this happen to me?"

It's natural to ask such questions. Often, God does not answer until you actually emerge from the trial, perhaps years later, free and whole.

Notice what Peter said: "after you have suffered a little while."

Going through cancer treatments, depression counseling, or seemingly endless persecution can seem like forever. But God promises it is indeed only "a little while." You can trust that the end will come, and then God will restore you and put you back on that foundation that will never allow you to slip.

HAVE YOU FOUGHT?

I have fought the good fight, I have finished the race, and I have remained faithful. And now the prize awaits me—the crown of righteousness, which the Lord, the righteous Judge, will give me on the day of his return. And the prize is not just for me but for all who eagerly look forward to his appearing.

2 TIMOTHY 4:7-8

PAUL WROTE THESE words to Timothy as the apostle awaited possible execution by the Romans for preaching the gospel and turning the world upside down. Paul was perhaps the greatest missionary ever. And yet he never considered himself great. He only tried to run his race day by day and remain faithful.

Look back on the past year. How have you been running? In what ways have you been faithful? God has noticed. He knows when you've faltered and failed and when you've surged forward for him with great courage and determination. He knows about everyone you've influenced, every person you've tried to steer in his direction, every good word you've spoken, every prayer you've uttered for others. Scripture tells us he has written it all down.

Paul's coming death didn't worry him or make him feel sorry about his failures or lost opportunities. Nor did he take credit or pride in all the great things accomplished through him. He saw it all as part of God's plan based on God's power. He also looked forward to a crown in heaven. God's promise is for those who run consistently—slow, fast, or otherwise. If they remain faithful, they will receive a great crown in heaven. It's something to look forward to, isn't it?

ACKNOWLEDGMENTS

SPECIAL THANKS to the acquiring editor and longtime friend, Jon Farrar, for adding this volume to the One Year series, along with *The One Year Men of the Bible*. I am also immensely grateful for the excellent editorial input of Jeanette Littleton, Dave Lindstedt, Erin Gwynne, and Susan Taylor.

ABOUT THE AUTHOR

JAMES STUART BELL is the owner of Whitestone Communications, a literary development agency. He consults with numerous publishers, represents various authors, and provides writing and editing services. He has previously served as executive editor at Moody Press, director of religious publishing at Doubleday, and publisher at Bridge Publishing. He also has more than one hundred books with cover credit. He coauthored the bestselling *Complete Idiot's Guide to the Bible* (more than 300,000 sold) and numerous other Christian guides in that series for the Penguin Group. He has also contributed numerous Christian volumes to the bestselling Cup of Comfort series by Adams Media.

THE ONE YEAR® WAY

Do-able. Daily. Devotions.

START ANY DAY THE ONE YEAR WAY.

For Women

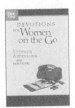

The One Year®
Devotions for
Women on
the Go

The One Year®
Devotions for
Women

The One Year®
Devotions for
Moms

The One Year®
Women of the
Bible

The One Year®
Coffee with God

The One Year®
Devotional of Joy
and Laughter

The One Year®
Women's
Friendship
Devotional

The One Year®
Wisdom
for Women
Devotional

The One Year®
Book of Amish
Peace

The One Year®
Women in
Christian History
Devotional

For Men

The One Year®
Devotions for
Men on the Go

The One Year®
Devotions for Men

The One Year®
Father-Daughter
Devotions

For Families

The One Year®
Family
Devotions, Vol. 1

The One Year®
Dinner Table
Devotions

For Couples

The One Year®
Devotions for
Couples

The One Year® Love
Language Minute
Devotional

The One Year® Love
Talk Devotional

For Teens

The One Year®
Devos for Teens

The One Year®
Be-Tween You
and God

For Personal Growth

The One Year®
at His Feet
Devotional

The One Year®
Uncommon Life
Daily Challenge

The One Year®
Recovery Prayer
Devotional

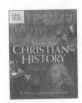

The One Year®
Christian History

The One Year®
Experiencing God's
Presence Devotional

For Bible Study

The One Year®
Praying through
the Bible

The One Year®
Praying the
Promises of God

The One Year®
Through the
Bible Devotional

The One Year®
Book of Bible
Promises

The One Year®
Unlocking the
Bible Devotional

CP0145